Secrets of Shangri-La

An Enquiry into the Lore,
Legend and Culture of Nepal

Nagendra Sharma

Nirala Series - 18

With a Foreword by
John Frederick

Nirala Publications
Jaipur   New Delhi

Nirala Publications
G.P.O. Box 394
Nawab Ka Chauraha, Ghat Gate
Jaipur-302 001 (India)

2595 Kucha Challan
Dariyaganj, New Delhi-110 002

First published 1992

© Nagendra Sharma

Cover Photo : Arjun Rai

Other Photos: Laxman Shrestha, Yeti Photos, and Gyanendra Das, Das Colour Lab

Cover Design : Vinod Bhardwaj

Typesetting at
Computer Port
2 Noor Chambers
M.I. Road
Jaipur-302 001

Printed at
Nazia Printers
Lal Kuan, Delhi-6
and
Shalimar Offset Printers
Daryaganj, New Delhi

Nirala Series

A Series of Contemporary Writing

1. *The British and the Brave*
   Kamal Raj Singh Rathaur
2. *The Khasa Kingdom*
   Surya Mani Adhikary
3. *Sources of Inflation in Asia*
   Raghab D. Pant
4. *Fire of Himal: The Sherpas*
   Ramesh Raj Kunwar
5. *Nepalese Plan Performance*
   Gunanidhi Sharma
6. *Folk Culture of Nepal*
   Ram Dayal Rakesh
7. *Fundamentals of Library and Information Science*
   Madhusudan Sharma Subedi
8. *Transit of Land-locked Countries and Nepal*
   Gajendra Mani Pradhan
9. *The Gurungs: Thunder of Himal*
   Murari P. Regmi
10. *Folk Tales of Sherpa and Yeti*
    Shiva Dhakal
11. *Gods and Mountains: The Folk Culture of a Himalayan Kingdom: Nepal*
    Kesar Lall

12. *Art and Culture of Nepal*
    Saphalya Amatya
13. *The Dhimals: Miraculous Migrants of Himal*
    Rishikeshab Raj Regmi
14. *Sales Promotion in Nepal: Policies and Practices*
    Parashar Prasad Koirala
15. *Glimpses of Tourism, Airlines and Management in Nepal*
    B.R. Singh
16. *The Taming of Tibet*
    Tirtha Prasad Mishra
17. *Dolpo: The Hidden Paradise*
    Karna Sakya
18. *Secrets of Shangri-la*
    Nagendra Sharma
19. *Transportation Systems in Nepal*
    Mukund R. Satyal
20. *Indo-Nepal Trade Relations*
    Shri Ram Upadhyaya
21. *Politics and Development in Nepal*
    Narayan Khadka
22. *The Gorkha Connection*
    Purushotam Baskota
23. *Lore and Legend of the Kathmandu Valley*
    Shiva Dhakal
24. *Recent Nepal: The Analysis of Recent Democratic Upsurge and its Aftermath*
    Laxman Bahadur K.C.
25. *Popular Emblems and Images of Nepal*
    Dhrub K. Deep
26. *The Cultural Heritage of Nepal Terai*
    Ram Dayal Rakesh

Nagendra Sharma (b.1934-) is Nepal's foremost folklorist, culture critic and journalist. He made his debut into journalism with an article "Nepalese Literature Today" published in 1953 in *The Illustrated Weekly of India* followed by occasional contributions in the *Far Eastern Economic Review*, Hongkong. Meanwhile he did quite a few "commisioned" write-ups on Nepal, Sikkim and Bhutan for a Calcutta-based English daily, *The Hindustan Standard* in capacity of a Special Correspondent for a few years. From Calcutta, he moved into Nepal on an assignment with the then *Near & Far East News (Asia) Ltd,* London (NAFEN for short) and its sister organisation, *Afro-Asian News service* (A-Ans). He also worked for a while with *World Feature Services Ltd.*,(London) and the daily, *Himalchuli* (Siliguri).

After his Master's Degree in Literature from the Tribhuvan University (1962), he served the Nepal Industrial Development Corporation and Royal Nepal Airlines for about ten years, prior to his appointment as Director of Information, His Majesty's Govt. of Nepal, a position he resigned after two years. Then followed other appointments such as Member, Communication Task Force, HMG; Co-ordinator, Television Project Cell HMG; Member, Board of Directors, Nepal Telecommunication Corporation; Executive Chairman, Industrial Districts Management till 1991.

Awards and decorations received by him include a Royal Victoria Order conferred by Queen Elizabeth II, an International Honorary Citizenship conferred by the Mayor of New Orleans (USA) and the Manila Grammy Award on T.V. Film Production (1984) among others.

Mr. Sharma has published about a dozen books, most notable being, *This is Nepal* (Sajha Prakashan, 1974), *Nepal A to Z* (1978), *Nepali Literature in a Nutshell* (1984), and *Folk tales of Nepal* (Sterling Publishers, Delhi), the book which has now been republished by Macmillan & Co. Ltd., London.

Currently he lives in Kathmandu and is working on a manuscript of Selected Nepali Short-Stories.

Acknowledgments

Secrets of Shangrila, although slightly pumpously, if not inappropriately, titled comes as the fourth in the series of my English publications on Nepalese legends, literature, history, culture and lores.

As Shangri-la, in its usual connotation, stands for a fictional and exotic land somewhere in the Himalayas, readers might question its appropriateness as an epithet for the Kingdom of Nepal. However, countries like Nepal and Bhutan — even Sikkim for that matter — have commonly figured in many a recent travel literature as modern-day Shangri-las; hence this adaptation. Forming as it does a supplement to such earlier titles as *This Is Nepal* (1974), *Nepal: Some Tales, Some Truths* (1987) and *Nepal A To Z* (1978), the contents incorporated herein can claim little originality in the sense that many of the earlier stories re-appear here in nothing more than a new garb.

Only that, this time, an enthusiast on Nepal like Mr. Yuyutsu R.D. Sharma has come forward to re-assemble them into a new format along with necessary additions and deletions, while another friend, John Frederick (Editor, *The*

Nepal Traveller), has thought it fit to write an eulogy in the shape of a Foreword. To both of them, therefore, I owe a deep debt of gratitude.

Kathmandu,
October 1, 1991 —Nagendra Sharma

Foreword

When I was a child I would spend idle, rainy days in my grandfather's library. Most of the titles that filled the shelves of his house were a century or two older than I, and their convoluted syntax and esoteric subjects made them seem as if they were written in a foreign language. On one shelf was a slender, old volume called *Gleanings for the Curious*. I've long since forgotten the author's name, but I remember the book well. It sat on a shelf near the crockery pantry, third shelf up and maybe eight volumes to the right — each book in that house had its place and after being read each was always returned there. The gentleman who wrote the book, I fancied, was like the man I thought I would be some day: he had spent his life poking through volumes and extracting fragments which piqued his interest, the quirks and divergences of all those old, mysterious authors. He had a singular feature, exemplified in the title — he had curiosity.

And he performed for me an essential function in that library whose old-style writing was almost a different language — he allowed me to follow the tracks of a scholar's interest while neither playing down to my youthful ignorance nor requiring me to be as learned as he.

Mr. Sharma's book is cast from the same mold. Comfortable access to volumes of Nepalese history and custom are closed to speakers of a foreign tongue, unless they be scholars. Years of gleaning from that rich literature are also closed to a middleaged man — we can only live so long. Mr. Sharma has provided us an invaluable service. A scholar and a journalist, he has spent his years in the stacks armed with the most powerful weapon of both those professions: curiosity. And he has gone outside the library into the world of the Nepalese with the same keen eye, talking with people, watching dances and festivals, and collecting, like an entomologist, strange new species of information.

This book, gathered in part from essays Mr. Sharma has written over the years, tells us as much about the author's mind as it does about Nepal: relentlessly curious, digging beneath the hardened complexities of history and scripture, rooting out the philosophical and hilarious from the bland simplicities of village tales. One feels, having read this book , that one has engulfed countless volumes of Nepali literature and history, heard countless folktales, watched countless religious performances and then, through a beneficial selective amnesia, forgotten all but the most piquant and interesting.

It might be said that what distinguishes a scholar from a pedant is the former's recognition that "fact", historical or scientific, is ever subject to revision. No conclusion can, or should , stand inviolable; new information will always, if the culture is open, arise to test the old. The challenging of accepted fact is one of the signatures of this book, no doubt much a product of Mr. Sharma's journalistic background. Jung

Bahadur, whose life every Nepali pedant will insist, is writ in stone, is revealed in new, and psychologically realistic, complexities. The *Ramayana*, which the same pedants will assure the foreigner he is too white to truly comprehend, is revealed as mutable and fantastic, changing its form as it moved over the Himalaya into the very non-Hindu land of Tibet. Slavery, whose spectre still walks (albeit under softer names), is revealed not as a tolerable social condition among passive, self-interested rulers of the past, but as an evil to be battled, by no less than premier Chandra Shumsher, of the family whom many Nepali historians like to decry as socially indifferent.

Tipping over the historical applecart is one of Mr. Sharma's greatest pleasures, and another is digging beneath the tired "significances" of Nepali customs, festivals and ritual practices. The visitor to Nepal, astounded by this wealth of color and event, and consumed by curiosity, is usually treated to a few myths and the attitude "You wouldn't understand. You're not one of us." Mr. Sharma reveals himself as being far greater than a "local scholar" in his delight in carrying the reader, outcaste and ignorant, into the fascinating byways of local custom. He is a humorous and intelligent guide into the subtleties of divorce, the beckoning songs of the villagers, and the mysteries of *tika,* clay and cowdung. One feels as if one has received a small initiation; one can see deeper into Nepal and, most important, one is inculcated with a strong respect for the depth and sophistication of the culture — denied the foreigner by the usual exclusionary tourist pabulum.

This is a little curious book — the kind too often destined to the shelf below pompous tomes of "true history and religion" and below the sorry, simplified pure local worthies think the only suitable information for the outsider. But like the tiny volume, *The Elements of Style,* it is one that deserves to be a classic, a read-this-first work. For the Nepalese, it is potent medicine for the disease of pedantry. For the foreigner, it is a gracious and respectful sharing of a rich, elaborate culture. For me, it is more. It is also a paean to that rarest and most stimulating human trait: curiosity.

October 1, 1991. — **John Frederick**

Contents

Acknowledgments	IX-X
Foreword	XI-XIV
Chapter One ORIGINS	21-30
Chapter Two FESTIVALS AND FUN	31-48
Chapter Three FOLK SONGS AND DANCES	49-67
Chapter Four HISTORY	68-98
Chapter Five LIFESTYLES	99-134
Chapter Six LANGUAGE AND LITERATURE	135-155
Chapter Seven RELIGIONS	156-183
Chapter Eight CONTROVERSIES	184-210

Chapter Nine
FOLK TALES AND FABLES　　　211-227

Chapter Ten
LEGENDS　　　228-254

Chapter Eleven
PROVERBS, IDIOMS AND
RIDDLES　　　255-288

Photo by *Gyanendra Das, Das Colour Lab*

Photo by *Laxman Shrestha*

Photo by Laxman Shrestha

Photo by **Laxman Shrestha**

SECRETS OF SHANGRI-LA

Origins

CHAPTER ONE

'Nepal'

The term Nepal has lent itself to many interpretations at the hands of scholars.

Historically, one of the first references to Nepal as an independent kingdom is said to have been made in the Prayag (Allahabad) Inscription of king Samudra Gupta (4th century A.D.). But even prior to that, the well-known historian and astrologer, Kautilya, is said to have mentioned Nepal by name in his famous treatise, *Arthasashtra*, thus pushing this country's antiquity back another 6 or 7 centuries.

A legend associated with the composition of the *Ramayan* epic by sage Valmiki also has it that he had referred to Nepal, possibly by name, in the course of his discourse with another sage, Narad. Asked about the inspiration he got in composing his *magnum opus*, Valmiki is said to have replied that to Nepal goes the credit of inspiring poets. Though it is not possible to assign an exact date or time when the first *Ramayan* was written, one could assume that it antidates the birth of Christ by about 9 or 10 centuries. Also, Nepal is said to have figured as a country during the age of the *Puranas*, a long drawn out time-frame that spanned about a 1000 years both before and after Christ. Among the *Puranas* that give a description of Nepal are included, mainly, the *Skanda* and the *Deva*.

The *Nepal Mahatmya*, which forms a part of the Himavat Khanda portion of the *Skanda Purana*, for instance, con tains eulogies of Nepal as a 'divine' land. Ancient Buddhistic treatises which contain similar references to this country also include the *Barahi Tantra* and the *Mula Sarvastibad Vinaya*.

Now, to come to the etymological interpretation of the term, 'Nepal'. Noted Indian scholars like Satyaketu Vidyalankar and Dr. Rangeya Raghav, in their works such as the "Ancient History of the Agarwals" and "Mahayatra" respectively, are said to have suggested that Nepal was named after its founder, Nemi Nath. The story runs thus :

Agrasen, an ancient king of the Agravas (Agrawals?), was descendant of Dhanapal; of the eight sons of Dhanapal, the eldest was named Shiva, who, in his turn, sired seven kings, namely, Vishnuraj, Sudarshan, Dhurandhar, Samadhi, Mohandas and Nemi Nath. This last-named king founded the kingdom of Nepal and named it after himself, says the story.

Another version, better-known and more popular than the one outlined above, also runs along similar lines, and credits one ancient sage, Nemi, with the founding of this kingdom. 'Ne', according to this version, is an abbreviation of Nemi and the land protected and nurtured by him came to be known as Nepal. The origin of the Nemi story can be traced back to the *Nepal Mahatmya*, a portion of the *Skanda Purana* above-referred. And if cre dence can be lent to it, it seems this sage was a contemporary of lord Krishna.

For, the Krishna legend associated with this version has it that two demon-kings, namely, Mahendra Daman and Kachhapasur, were great oppressors of the people in the vicinity of the Kathmandu valley. Pradyumna, lord Krishna's son, is believed to have come here all the way from Dwarika (in western India) along with his father and vanquished both the demons. Another local king, Sat yaketu, had a beautiful daughter, Chandravati, whom Pradyumna married. But before the father-and-son team returned to Dwarika, they paid obeisance to lord Pasupatinath and, in the large assembly of sages and saints gathered there on the occasion, one was Nemi. It is said that lord Pasupati himself chose Nemi as the leader of the sages and entrusted him with the governance of this Himalayan tract of land which, consequently, came to be known as 'Nepal', meaning a land protected by Nemi.

Another school of thought believes that the word Nepal also lends itself to Tibetan interpretation thus : *Ne* (Central) *Pa* (Country), thereby indicating its 'central' location as a 'Middle Country'. Yet another version of the same interpretation would have us believe that *Ne* and *Pa* in Tibet an mean 'house' and 'wool' respectively, thus referring to Nepal as the "House of Wool". The expression 'Ne', still others suggest, stands for caves or pilgrimage centres, and the 'Home of Gods' that the valley of Kathmandu is referred to in the present times could have been a famous pilgrimage centre even in the ancient times and hence referred to as Nepal.

Some Buddhist scholars suggest, however, that the term Nepal is of a much recent vintage and, originally, Kathmandu was known as Manjupattan after the Chinese or Sankhu savant, Manjushree, who is credited with having drained out the waters of the legendary lake called *Nag Hrada* followed by the establishment of civilisation. Among the other names that was given to this region in different *Yugas* (aeons) included "Satyavati" in the *Satyayuga*, "Tapovana" in the *Treta Yuga*, "Mukti-Sopan" in the *Dwaparyuga* and "Nepal" in the *Kaliyuga*.

We also have scholars who would treat the terms Newar and Nepal as synonymous. They suggest that the original inhabitants of this area were initially known as *Neparas* and the 'ra' in Nepara subsequently changed into a 'la', thus giving birth to the term Nepala. This interpretation, however, has found few adherents mainly on the grounds that the term 'Newar' appears for the first time in a 17th century Kathmandu inscription only, whereas the term 'Nepal' is of doubtlessly much greater antiquity as is evidenced in the Prayag (Allahabad) inscription (335-376 A.D.) referred to above, as also in the Tristung inscription ascribed to Lichhavi kings like Basanta Deva and Amsuverma, dated 512 A.D. The latter inscription is said to contain the expression "Swasti Nepalevya", possibly inviting divine benediction for the welfare of Nepal's residents.

Lastly, some others would also have us believe that inhabitants of this land were originally referred to as 'Gne-Wa' or 'Gni-Wa' which transformed itself into 'Ne-Pa' or 'Ni-Pa' in subsequent centuries. The basis of this contention seems to be that some old chronologies contain the expression 'Gni-Pa' while referring to the inhabitants of Kathmandu valley. The Gopal Vamshavali, like wise, is believed to have referred to an ancient king by the name of "Nepa", possibly the first builder of the Pasupatinath temple, after whom the kingdom came to be known as Nepal. Whether the term 'Nepa' or 'Nipa' denoted just one person or an entire community is still a bone of contention among some leading interpreters, however. Whatever may have been the origin of the term 'Nepal', there is hardly any doubt that the term has come down to us from a very, very ancient era indeed.

The Khasas

The Khasas, possibly the forbears of many a Nepalese race, were almost as ancient as the Kiratas. While the Kiraatas-- the earliest historical rulers of Nepal known to --date -- figure even in the Vedic literature dating back to some 2500 years before Christ, the Khasas find mention in epics like the *Mahabharata* and some *Puranas*. And that means nothing less than some two thousand years ago.

Interestingly enough, no two scholars seem to agree as to where the Khasas originally hailed from. While many of them are often at pains to prove that they came from as remote an area as the Caucasus mountains, the Khasgar valley in Iran or Khasmir (present-day Kashmir), there is no doubt that the major Khas concentrations today are limited to the geographical area between Kumaon and Garhwal in the west and Nepal in the east.

Likewise, there is no agreement among scholars as to who the Khasas originally were. While the term 'Kirata', even in its narrower sense, encompasses almost the entire Tibeto-Burman races in Nepal such as the Newars, Tamangs, Magars, Gurungs, Rais, Limbus, etc. (even the Lichhavis, according to some), it is difficult to pin-point which races go to fit into the general description of the Khasas, despite the fact that 'Khas-Baahun' is a common enough expression in Nepal.

Balkrishna Pokhrel, a Nepalese scholar, has something to this effect to say: "Even those people who are in fact Khasas often try to disclaim being one... For example, almost all the Brahmans amongst hillmen deny that they are Khasas. So do the Thakuris".

Dr. Lakshmidatta Joshi, in his treatise "Khasa Family Law", makes an interesting reference to the various customs and practices of the Khasa people in general, including the following:

(i) that a Khasa woman may have more than one husband at a time without incurring social stigma;

(ii) that an elder brother's widow may be "inherited" by the younger one;

(iii) that bride-price is common among them;

(iv) that little or no religious rituals are called for in solem nising a Khasa wedding;

(v) that divorce is a matter of right for their womenfolk;

(vi) that wearing of the *Janai* (holy-thread) is not com pulsory; and

(vii) that the dead ones are buried rather than cremated.

What appears interesting, however, is the fact that many of these customs and traditions will only help us bracket the Khasas together with either one or the other of the many tribes and races whom we have referred to as the 'Kiraatas' earlier. Frater nal polyandry, for instance, is nothing uncommon among the Sher pas, Dolpaalis and the like; burial of the dead is the rule rather than exception amongst the Rais and Limbus; divorce, again, is as much a prerogative of many a non-Brahmin and non-Chhetri woman--like the Newar, Tamang, etc., as it is of the Khasas; and, likewise, few other Nepalese, apart from Baahuns and Chhetris, wear the holy thread.

Thus, by the above reckoning, there is hardly any particular tribe or community in Nepal that can fit into the description of the Khasas. What's more, even famous scholars like Atkinson make confusing statements like: "Some of the Khasas are Muslims, some others (are) Buddhists,...(and the rest) Hindus". Another well- known book, the 'Holy Himalayas', likewise adds that the Khasas have a "Scythian blood running in their veins", and that "in Nepal and Assam, (the Khasas) are Buddhists".

If either of the above two versions is to be given credence, we can at least be certain that the term Khasa does not embrace the "Khas-Baahuns" alone, as we traditionally understand the term. Who, then, are the Khasas proper?--the question remains unan swered, as ever !

Not, therefore, venturing to hazard any guess on the subject, a cursory glance on the Khasa antiquity and the possible routes of migration to Nepal (and the adjoining areas) in particular may be in order.

The first reliable evidence of a Khasa ruler having invaded Kathmandu is contained in the oldest extant chronological ac count, *Gopal Vamshaavali*. It mentions the *Sapaadalak sha* (present-day Jumla) king, Jitarimalla, as having laid seige over Kathmandu three times in succession, notably in *Newar Samvat* 408, 409 and 410 (A.D.1287, 88 and 89 respec tively.) Other Khasa kings like Ripumalla and Adityamalla are also said to have repeatedly invaded the valley in A.D. 1292, 1311, 1319, 1327 and 1334. The Karnali kingdom of the Khasas is said to have been very extensive--incorporating Kumaon and Garh wal in the west, Guge and the Mansarovar lake in Tibet, the river Trisuli in the east and the north Indian plains up to Bodh Gaya in the south. The eulogical references to the Khasas contained in, among others, the Ashoka Pillar inscription at Lumbini, the adjacent Nigalihawa inscription and a Gaya inscription are said to corroborate this claim.

According to the *Harivansha Puraana*, the Khasas were none but Kshatriyas who had fled India in the wake of 'sage' Parasu ram's threat to exterminate them. Atkinson, on the other hand, holds that the Aryan invasion into India drove the Khasas into the laps of the mountains, implying thereby that they were not even Aryans, not to speak of being Kshatriyas!

Were the Khasas then a pre-Aryan- even possibly a non-Aryan--people akin to the Kiraatas? The *Shrimad Bhaaga wat* is perhaps right in bracketing the Khasas together with the Huns, Kiraatas, Yavanas, etc. and in suggesting that they were "devoid of (or lacking in) religion", which implies, of course, that they did not subscribe to the Hindu religion proper, but to some 'non-Hindu' cults.

Lake and a Lotus

This is a tale of ancient days, of bygone times. Of a time when a lotus floated on a legendary lake.

A huge lake it was, so they say. Water, water everywhere, engulfing all of today's Kathmandu valley and more, stretching miles and miles around it. Homes and habitations were non-existent and the only humans around were some curious and occasional visitors from distant lands and strange climes, who came to admire the near- celestial beauty of the mythical waters.

One such personage was Vipaswi Buddha. He threw a lovely lotus bud into this vast, sprawling lake. As it went circling over, he chanted hymns and prophesied: "This bud will blossom one fine morning to reveal *Swayambhu*, the Self-Born, in the form of a flame."

Aeons passed by, and when Sikhi Buddha paid a visit to this lake, it had seemingly started drying up, for he exclaimed with pleasure : "A delightful valley this will soon be". By the time the third Buddha, Vishwambhuva, was here, a Bodhisatva had already "caused" land to appear at places above the waters.

The Buddhists would have us believe that Manjushree, a Chinese savant, split the engulfing hillside at Chobhar with strokes of his sword until the waters of the lotus lake were released.

Others would have the credit for the outlet go to Vishwakarma, the Hindu designer of the universe, and a re-incarnation of lord Vishnu. To watch in admiration the Chobhar gorge today, with the combined Bagmati, Vishnumati and other rivers gushing out of the valley and cascading countless feet down the rocks through a narrow, gurgling hill chasm, is to be convinced of this pre- historic, if not legendary, human effort.

Also stands amidst us today, in all its majestic architectural splendour and with all its halo of a romantic heritage, the towering stupa of Swayambhunath, atop the fabled "Hill of The Lotus Lake", in Kathmandu's vicinity. This stupa, many accounts agree, was constructed by the disciples of Manjushree who cherished in their memories this momentuous event of a millenium. The sanctified spot of the legendary lotus and the *Swayambhu* (Selfborn) flame is where the shrine is believed to stand today.

The first human to hold the reins of regal authority over Kathmandu valley's human habitation following the draining of its waters was the *Puranic* Dharmakara, himself a reputed disciple of Manjushree. Then came, from far away Bengal, king Prachanda Deva to pay obeisance to the Guhyeswari shrine that he himself possibly built. It was followed by the Pasupatinath temple built under the patronage of Dharmadutta, a king of distant Kunjeeveram in south India. Another famous landmark, the Bodhnath stupa, is the legacy left to posterity by Manadeva, the Lichhavi king, it is said.

If Suprabha, where Yalambar, the first Kirat king of Nepal, held his royal court, was the first human habitation that sprung up after the lake dried up, Jitedasi, seventh in line of his succession and an ally of the Pandavas in their internecine war against the Kauravas, seemingly did likewise. Indications are that the present Thankot, an entry point to Kathmandu valley from the south, was the site of the ancient Suprabha.

But what particular charm did this legendary lake and the settlements that sprang up later in the relatively inaccessible Himalayan fastnesses hold for visitors and even rulers from far away Bengal and Madras, besides savants from China and India, must always remain a guess. Why, one would like to surmise, was Manjushree, who found it a lake, bent upon leaving his marks here in monuments of marble, with all his life's toils ? What must have the waves of the lotus lake whispered into the ears of so many Buddhas with voiceless woe ?

No kindred of the original flame is here to guide us in our surmises. And no flower to reflect the blush of the Self-born at Swayambhu.

We only ruminate, and reminisce, but hardly go beyond a void, a vision, almost a waking dream; of the past that is no more, of the glory bygone, but which, nevertheless, gave Kathmandu, nay Nepal herself, a habitation and a name.

Festivals and Fun

CHAPTER TWO

Know Thyself

When egocentric man worships one, or more, perhaps all, of the 33,00,00,000 gods and goddesses on this side of and beyond the Milky Way, he is in a terribly tiring process and liable to forget the most important element in the whole creation-- Himself, the Alpha and Omega of his own world.

For centuries, if not millennias, *Vedantis* have been dinning into the ears of the spiritually-inclined: *Tat Tuam Asi,* "You are That" (meaning you are all that exists) !

Yet man, his own star, and the "roof and crown of things", has failed to worship Himself, the world over.

Except among the Newars of Kathmandu.

They have set apart a day in the year for *Mha Puja* (Self-worship) during Diwali, which, incidentally, marks the Newar New Year, also known as Nepal Samvat. On that day the Newar does full justice to himself, his personal cravings and desires, both in respect of feeding the body and purifying the spirit, with none other than Himself as the deity, the benefactor as well as the beneficiary.

Not to be outdone, however, the Nepalese male in general would also have himself made the object of worship and veneration at the hands of his sisters, elder or younger, the very day. Known to Nepalese the world over as *Bhai Tika,* or the Brother's Day, the Nepalese girls on this day virtually vie against one another in this business of ceremonially adoring their brothers. Not entirely out of an altruistic motive, however, for immediate ly as they complete offering *puja* to their brothers, the latter, rather in an expansive mood after having been thus propi tiated, shower cash and gifts on their fair devotees.

Not only this. The Nepalese have set apart one day each in their annual ceremonial calendar for the ritualistic expression of gratitude to their mothers, their fathers, their preceptors, their husbands, and even to such humble animals and birds as the cow, the bull, the dog and the crow.

The *Mata Tirtha Aunsi,* for example, is their ceremonial Mother's Day. Celebrated on the moonless fifteenth day in April, the Nepalese sons and daughters, if living separately, make a bee-line for their parental abodes with gifts in the shape of delicacies and presents in cash and kind, in a bid to repay the debt of gratitude they owe their mothers.

Those who do not have their mothers any more make ritual offerings to Brahman priests in the fond hope that whatever is given to the Brahmans will ultimately reach the departed souls in the other world. Others visit a pond, near Kathmandu, named after this day as the *Mata Tirtha Pond*, to participate in the ceremonial annual bath in the name of their mothers.

How this particular pond attained celebrity as an abode of all lost mothers has an interesting legend behind it. A shepherd, it is said, one day sat by its edge and was about to have his midday meal, when, to his amazement, he noticed reflected in the placid waters of the pond a clear profile of his mother, who had been dead for years.

Evidently the poor thing was hungry, thought the shepherd, otherwise why shadow him like that at lunch time ? In reverential pity, he left his food there untouched and went his way. When, back from work, he passed the pond again, the food had disappeared, and so too the reflected image.

As the news spread, the otherwise peaceful pond came to be re garded as the repository of the spirits of all departed mothers in the community.

Well may this institution be reminiscent of a matriarchal antiquity of the Nepalese people, or at least of some indigenous communities, as some hold. But how does this explain the preva lence of a parallel Fathers' Day celebrated by Kathmanduites with equal gusto on another moonless night in August known as the *Gokarna Aunsi* ?

On this day, all Kathmandu roads lead to the Gokarna forest, beside which flows the holy Bagmati. There, in a shrine, sons make oblations and offerings in the name of their departed fathers. Those that have their fathers living repeat rituals reminiscent of the Mothers' Day, but this time at the houses of their fathers, for whose benefit the rituals are organised.

The teachers and preceptors, in the traditional sense of these terms, have their annual day too, or rather two days. The *Jhaankris* and *Dhaamis,* the Nepalese shamans, cele brate the full moon day in July (otherwise known as *Rakhsha Bandhan)* as their *Gurus'* (Teachers') Day, and dance demented to the tune of jingling bells and raucuous cymbals night-long, either in some improvised shrine at home or in a temple nearby.

For the rest of the preceptor-worshippers, there is another day known as the*Rishi Tarpani,* or literally, the day of obla tions to rishis, the sages and preceptors of old.

Nepalese married women, especially those among the hill tribes, also observe an annual Husbands' Day known as *Teej* in August, while, for the unmarried ones, this day of fasting in honour of Lord Shiva is believed to land a husband in their laps in the course of the year !

During the five-day affair that is known as *Panchak* or *Tihar* (Divali), the innately humane outlook of the Himalayan people towards their domesticated pets as also other animals and birds, finds a formal and ritual expression, in order of priority, thus: first the Crow's Day; second, the Dog's Day; third, the Cow's Day; fourth, the Bull's Day; and fifth, the day of the Cowdung !

The worship of the crow, one would imagine, is in return for the unique and virtually irredeemable debt of gratitude that the Nepalese owe this feathered tribe for their incessant and voluntary service to humanity as universal scavengers and also as healers. The dog is, in its turn, the perennial sentinel of every threshold, while the bull is the right arm of the farmer in a predominantly agricultural Nepal. The cow, of course, is the universal mother, a feeder of milk, and the cow-dung is both a manure for the farmer's land and a fuel for the household.

Of all things, even the pariahdogs that all along remain an irksome and lice-infested eyesore to the community emerge overnight as rare objects of reverence during the *Panchak*. Their pup-faces tidied up by human "devotees", their fore-heads plastered with *Tika* paste and colourful marigold garlands dangling down their necks, the dogs, as they are lovingly fed with sumptuous dishes of meat and rice by their fellow humans, present a touching sight indeed.

Every Dog has his Day

A Nepalese house may have come to associate the *Jaanto* (grinding stone) with *sati* or the Goddess of Destiny and the husking paddle with Lord Vishwakarma (God of Industry and Work); in like manner, the tools of the ironsmith, the mechanic, or the wood-cutter, have been featuring all along as objects of worship at least once a year. But to add motor-cars, trucks, buses, bikes and even aeroplanes to the list of divinities would certainly appear rather far-fetched. These objects nevertheless, assume sudden religious overtones almost overnight during the annual *Dasai* festival and must receive a holy sacrifice each, be it a goat, a fowl or a duck ! Totem-worship at its best ?

Extremely religious-minded Nepalese parents would even have their children learn to live with rats or snakes and not to kill them, for the former commands esteem as the mythological conveyance of Lord Ganesha, the God of Success, and the latter as constant companions of Lord Shiva, whose arms and neck they perennially coil around. In fact, one day in the Nepalese religious calendar is also set apart for the worship of the *Nagas* or mythological snakes. Though actual snakes do not form the object of popular veneration on this day, Nepalese people do litter their doors and gates with pictures displaying snakes and comprising of hymns in praise of the "holy" reptiles. Monkeys that throng holy shrines like Kathmandu's famous Pashupati temple seem to enjoy immunity against the instinctive wrath of a Nepalese devotee visiting that religious landmark, even when these mischievous animals snatch flowers and fruits right off his or her hands, for the scriptures have taught him or her to regard the monkey as a progeny of Hanuman, the Monkey God !

In the world of vegetation, the Banyan tree and the Peepul tree are objects of special veneration. While, to the Hindus, these trees symbolise Lord Vishnu and his consort, Laxmi (goddess of wealth), to the Buddhists the Peepul tree has had associations with Lord Buddha, as he, according to legends, attained Enlightenment under the Bodhi tree. Another holy plant that features familiarly in a clay flower-pot placed atop an especially erected mud-and-brick pedestal in one corner of the Nepalese courtyard is the *Tulsi* or the basil plant. Elderly Nepalese men or women mostly do not partake of their food before watering these plants or burning little earthen lamps beside them.

Every dog has his day, so goes a popular saying in the West. And seeing the Nepalese worship and ceremonially feed the crow, the dog, the bull and the cow on the four consecutive days during *Tihar* or the Festival of Lights, this saying appears to have found a literal application in the religious life of the Nepalese people. The Newar peasents of Kathmandu go one ahead of the rest in their fetish for animal worship. A day is set apart for frog-worship. *Byan Janake* ("Day of the Frog") falls sometime during the month of *Shravan* when farmers proceed to their fields with offering of food meant for frogs, leave the stuff there and return home. If the food is not there the next morning, it is a good augury for a bountiful harvest!

What else, dear readers, would you like us to worship? You name it -- we are probably already worshiping it!

Curing an Erring Husband

Come August, and in the shadowy gloom of the monastic sanctuary of Rudra Varna Mahavihara, Patan, we see a row of female forms lying prostrate day in and day out, for a month; looking more dead than alive, they are the country wenches going through a month-long fast, *Goonla*. Seven handfuls of consecrated water given by the Buddhist priest out of the font is their only daily ration. If you visit the place on subsequent occasions, the increasingly pitiable sight of the great devotees is bound to prick your conscience and arouse in your mind a feeling of sympathy and reverence for them. Towards the end of the holy month they can hardly move, their voice has sunk into a feeble whisper and they are more bundles of bones and skin -- a ghost of their previous selves.

Photo by *Gyanendra Das, Das Colour Lab*

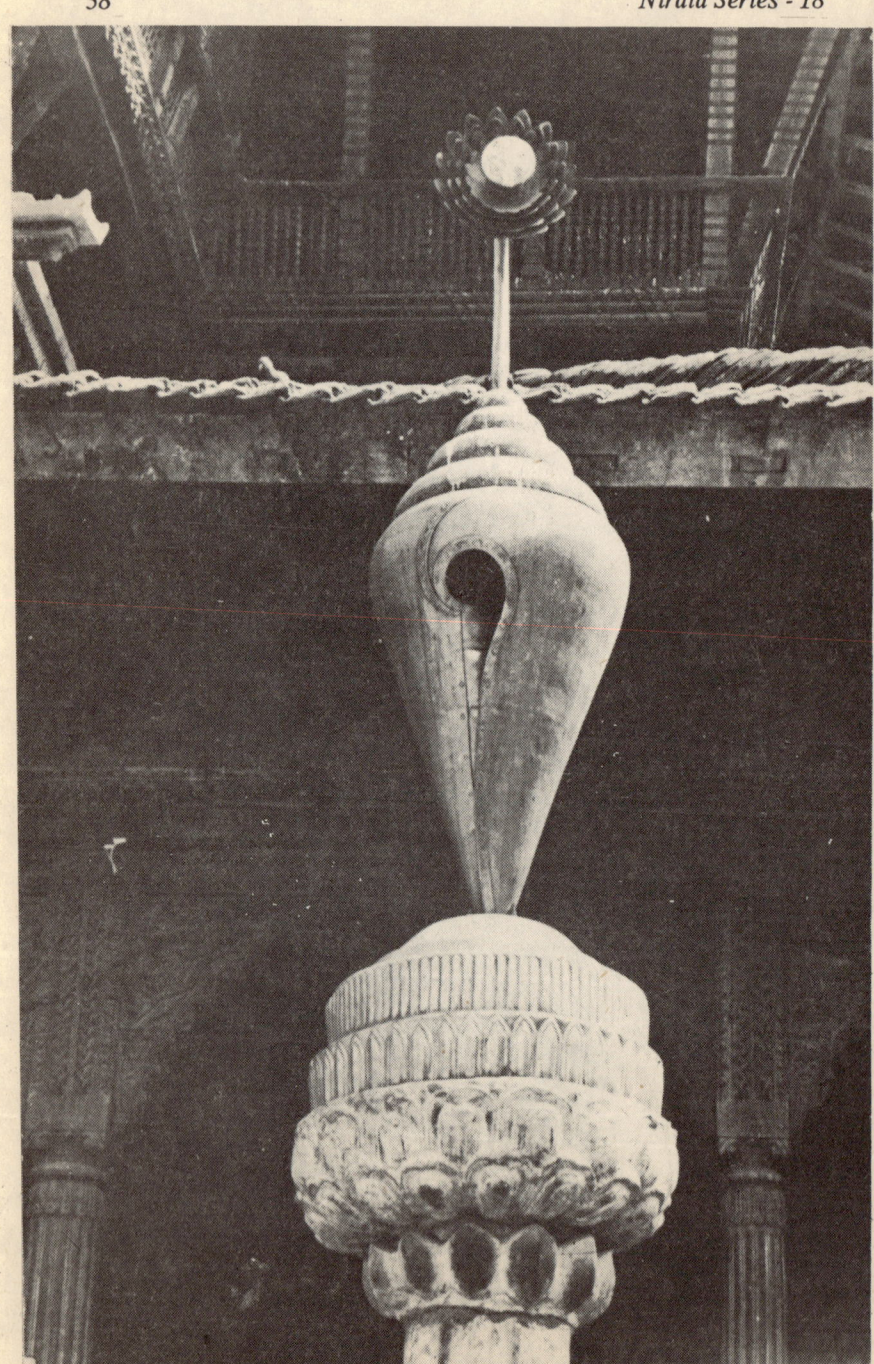

Photo by Yeti Photos Centre

Secrets of Shangri-la

Photo by *Laxman Shrestha*

Photo by *Laxman Shrestha*

But why are they subjecting themselves to such a horrible penance with so single-minded and exemplary a devotion ? The objective is just to win back the lost love of their husbands who have either deserted them or may be running after other girls.

But do the erring husbands oblige them ? Yes, if they are sensible enough. For one thing, the fear of scandal among neighbours and relatives who invariably visit the *Vihaara,* acts as a very potent goading factor. For another, he will be socially censured for murder, should his wife die in the process of fasting.

It is expected then of the 'penitent' hubby to come along with a local band and a palanquin to take his apparently sinking wife home, don her in a new suit of clothes and treat her to eggs, fish and other delicacies followed by a group feast in honour of her 'home-coming'.

The husbands' attitudinal change from one of cold negligence and apathy to a feeling of 'warm' love has also another edge to it; for it is believed that their wives' penance will bring Buddha's blessings and a lucky turn of the tide either in the shape of a son or acquisition of a big fortune.

Should, however, the husband prove himself so much of a wretch as not to turn up either during or after the penance, it means divorce with immediate effect and she is then free to seek other life-mates for her purposes. While this wifely penance is a month-long affair, the fourteenth day of the dark moon in Bhadra is the most important day of the *Goonla*. It is called *Panchdan*--the day of alms giving. On this occasion, Dipankara Buddha is said to have accepted the alms of a blacksmith in preference to that of a king. And, when asked, the saint it said to have replied that the foodstuff, offered by the artisan, was earned by the sweat of his brow, while the king's was not! So, on this day, the Buddhist priests, some with sacredotal robes and most without, go about seeking alms while housewives vie against each other to offer the best they can, for you never know when Dipankara Buddha himself may come to the door in the garb of a monk ! Charity and benevo lence is the order of the day.

The *Goonla* month concludes with the first day of the dark fortnight of *Bhadra* and calls for a family picnic *(Pato)* in Swayambhu hillock whose surrounding greenery is literally covered with colourful groups enjoying open-air dinner and a hearty drink.

This holy month of fast, penance and prayer is to the Nepalese Buddhists what Ramadan is to the Muslims. In Kathmandu it is particularly marked by daily pre-dawn religious processions, accompanied with thumping drums and clanging cymbals, that wind their way to the famous Shwayambhunath, the holiest of Buddhist holies. The object, it is said, is to entertain their Lord with early morning music !

Worshipping a new Buddha image each day is another *Goonla* feature; most houses preserve moulds that come in handy on this occasion in impromptu shaping of clay figures of the Lord, "brought to life" by thrusting a grain of unpolished rice into each. The clay images that have grown into a sizeable heap by the month-end are then taken in a ritual procession to the river for ceremonial immersion, followed by a sumptuous feast.

Kumari, Nepal's unique living goddess, also stirs out of her temple-residence for her only annual public appearance (besides the ceremonial chariot-procession during *Indra Jatra*) on this occasion. She is carried aloft in a wooden palanquin to the *tableaux vivant* displaying Buddhist temple treasures such as priceless ancient relics, tapestry paintings, rare masterpieces of the temple-sculptor's art, gold and silver-lettered parchment paper scriptures and mammoth "rice" grains supposedly dating back to antediluvian days.

Another Aspect of the Indra Jatra

The *Indra Jatra* as a Kathmandu tradition is popular to this day. But it has undergone quite some modifications with the passing of time.

During the Rana heyday, for instance, two prominent features of this festival included the dance of the *Bhadinis* at Hanuman Dhoka quadrangle and the *Bhakku* sacrifice within the Narayanhity palace premises. *Bhadinis* were professional dancing women and their rather erotic antics were a prominent attraction in the evenings. It is said that, once a young army officer was so enamoured of a comely *Bhadini* as to be "seduced" by the latter. That was the end of the *Bhadini* dance tradition too !

The *Indra Jatra* chariot procession, carrying the 'vestal virgin' used to be taken round down-town Kathmandu, including the Lagan, Brahma Tole and Bhimsenthan areas, jointly known as the *Tallo Tole* or *Desh*. The procession was joined, in person, by all the state dignitaries, including the ruling monarch or his representative and the prime minister as long as it lasted. This practice was also discontinued in 1950.

The other procession route passed through the *Maathillo* (or Upper) *Tole* comprising more or less the area through which it is taken around till this day.

The *Bhakku* sacrifice may be described as Bull-Fight, Nepali version. Only that, here it was a he-buffalo that took the place of the Spanish or the Mexican bull. There were two areas selected for holding this pageantry--one at the Hanuman Dhoka palace and the other inside the Narayanhity Royal Palace. The contestants included the *Lakhe* ritual dancers of Kathmandu and the youth of the *Duiyan* community hailing from areas adjacent to the Halchok Bhairav temple.

Making an offer of a he-buffallo to the *Bhukku* was a great spectacle, the greatest single attraction of the *Indra*

Jatra. Two persons, one known as the *Bhakku* and the other as the Bhairav, primarily featured in this pageantry *par excellence*. The role of the former was more akin to that of an animal-teaser or a 'diverter', while the latter was the man chosen for actually sacrificing (or rather slaughtering) the he-buffalo.

The arena was known as the Bombai Chowk--reached by outsiders after crossing two entrances, first the main south-gate entrance leading to the palace compound and, second, another eastern-gate entrance leading to the arena proper.

That many a gate-keeper closed his eyes on the townsfolk, particularly youngsters, seeking an entrance into the bamboo or woodfenced and expansive arena was not without purpose: a shouting, hooting and clapping crowd would not only add to the spectacle but would also help scare the chosen animal in the process. But the hawk-eyed guards were always on the look out for Brahmin youths--anyone suspected of being of Brahmin blood would find his entry doubly difficult. For the simple reason that, should the intoxicated and infuriated he-buffalo gore a Brahmin to death, the organisers of the pageantry would invite a 'heavenly wrath' for having committed the unthinkable sin of a *Brahma-Hatyaa* ("Brahmin-cide").

For many days in advance, a number of stout and selected he-buffaloes would be reared in darkened dungeons in preparation for their doomsday. Prior to their being led into the arena on the final day, the he-buffaloes were even said to be treated liberal ly, if forcibly, with alcohol so as to get them sufficiently intoxicated. Attendants entrusted for the purpose would usher the sturdy he-buffaloes in, and, among them, only those considered fighting-fit would be left in the arena, others being led back to their sheds. Then the bars would be closed against the selected animal, his destiny being to face, all alone, the *Bhakku* and the *Bhairav,* both of them armed with deadly scimitars, besides the jeering, teasing, and fence-sitting crowds.

The turn of the teasing crowds over, two persons, garbed in red and masked as *Bhakkus*, would enter the arena.

Their role it was to further scare the already perplexed animal at a closer range- twisting its tail and the like. Once the he- buffalo was sufficiently tired, the armed Bhairav would enter for dealing the *coup de grace* with his sharpened scimitar. It was a gory end for the animal, much as that of a bull in the present day bull-fights in either Spain or Mexico.

The last Bhakku Bhairav and Buffalo spectacle one witnessed in Kathmandu was in the early 'sixties. And the arena, for once, was the present Dasarath Rangashala (sports stadium). Then came the unfortunate total ban-- thereby denying not only the Kathmanduites but also the visiting tourists the opportunity, perhaps for good, of witnessing a spectacle, which, with certain civilised modifi cations and improvements, had in it the seeds of a major poten tial sport attraction in the shape of an Oriental Bull-Fight--and a unique one at that.

The Machhendra Jatra

The name of Johnny Gurkha, which has acquired some legendary overtones over the last ten decades or so, itself owes its habitation and name to a legend, the legend of Gorakhnath.

To the small principality of Gorkha in the mid-western Nepal hills goes the credit of cradling King Prithvi Narayan Shah, the founder both of modern Nepal as we know her today and of Nepalese nationhood. And when one recalls that Prithvi Narayan had em barked upon the great adventure of unifying the various warring kingdoms that dotted the Himalayan landscape after having ceremo nially enshrined Gorakhnath as his guardian deity, one can readi ly connect the adoption, by later Nepalese generations, of this savant as symbolic of their being. Little surprise that coins struck by Prithvi Narayan and his successors invariably bore the legend *Sri Sri Gorakhnath* on the obverse for hundred years or more, till as late as the turn of the present century.

This savant Gorakhnath, according to a story, hailed from legendary Gaud. But while the last word is yet to be said on whether Gaud refers to the present-day Gaur district in Nepal terai or to Gauda (ancient Bengal), there is no dearth of stories that would rather associate him with distant Assam on the one hand and Varanasi on the other.

A popular Nepalese anecdote is woven around this legendary par ticipant in a marathon boozing session in a *Bhatti*, or a liquor-bar, a typical and unfailing signpost of the Nepalese landscape. (Why then blame the poor Gorkha if he occasionally displays similar propensities as that of his savant, pray?) But if he could, in his single-minded devotion to Bacchus, gulp barrels of booze and be none the worse for it, (few Gorkhas are, for that matter !) he also had the tenacity to plunge into an unbroken spell of cross-legged meditation for twelve long years at a stretch ! The site he chose for that marathon meditation was Mrigasthali, a popular landmark extant till this day in the vicinity of Kathmandu's famous Pasupatinath shrine.

An unprecedented 12-year spell of draught followed in the wake of his penance beginning in the 3600th year of the *Kali* era, however, and starvation and pestilence stalked the countryside. His courtiers advised an alarmed King Narendra Deva that *Guru* Gorakhnath be persuaded to give up his penance if the country was to receive succour in the shape of rains. And the only person whom the savant would obey without question was his preceptor, Lord Machhendranath. At this, the king decided to personally act as his people's errand-boy and undertook the long and arduous trek to Kamrup in the company of, amongst others, his court scholar Bandhudatta and Lalit Jyapu, an affluent farmer.

If it took the team pretty long to reach the abode of Machhendranath, it took longer to coax the Lord to a trip to Nepal. When, however, he did ultimately come, Gorakhnath promptly rose from his seat in order to greet him, thus releasing the *Naagas*, the legendary serpent kings or harbingers of rain, from underneath his seat. And lo and behold, the long-awaited rains came in welcome torrents throughout the drought-scorched kingdom.

This event is commemorated to this day in the Nepalese capital in the form of a month-long *Rato* (Red) Machhendranath chariot festival every summer. A huge chariot, its 14 storeyed apex almost literally skyhigh, is dragged by devotees for days on end, till the month-long exercise reaches its climax in the display of an antique bejewelled tunic purported to have belonged to the great savant himself. A Newari language inscription at the temple of Machhendranath (local name: *Ta Bahal*) in Patan even enjoins that Nepalese kings must also make it a point to join the public display of the tunic, and kings have obliged their people to this day by observing this tradition in letter and spirit. Display of scabbards and ceremonial umbrellas belonging to the kings of yore also form a part of this festival, believed to be the harbinger of rains.

Some farming families of *Ibahal Tole* in Patan are said to claim their descent from *Lalit Jyapu* — the farmer who had accompanied king Narendra in his great mission to fetch Machhendranath.* Such is the undiluted devotion of the local people in Lord *Bunga-dyo* (Newari name for Machhendranath) that they expect to be guided by him

---

* Lalitpur, the old name for Patan, is also said to have been given after *Lalit Jyapu*, according to one version.

even in matters as mundane as the marriage of their children. Instead of consulting astrologers as is the practice with the majority of Nepalese, in deciding match es, the inhabitants of Ibahal are said to visit the temple of Karunamaya (another name given to Machhendranath) and come with the residual offerings to be put under the pillow at night. If the dreams that follow are adjudged auspicious, the proposed match is accepted; otherwise not!

Folk Songs and Dances

CHAPTER THREE

Nepal, a tiny independent country, the size of Iilinois and mainly mountainous, is situated in the southern slopes of the mighty Himalayan range. Majority of its twenty million odd inhabitants belong to the stocky, flat-nosed and slit-eyed Mongoloid strain, known the world over as the Gorkha warriors.

As General D.K. Palit, himself an erstwhile Indian army officer who served with the Gurkhas for some time, aptly put it in the course of an article titled "Song and Dance of Nepal" (1955) : "The music of the Nepalese, as indeed of most hill peoples of the world, plays a much more intimate and personal part in their lives than, say, in the lives of the more sophisticated communi ties of India." He adds: "The Nepalis of the hills sing in pray er; in love and in sorrow; in battle or at work; in praise or in regret. They yodel across their valleys; call to their cattle or woo their paramours in song. When in service in the Army, all they require is a *Madal* and a little encouragement, and wherever they are they will keep themselves and the company entertained for hours".

Like much of the hill music all over the world — whether Scottish, North Indian, Tibetan or American — the Nepalese hill people's folk music is also simple in style and almost entirely pentatonic in character, (i.e., giving only five differ ent notes to the octave), a scale which is almost a tune in itself, whatever scheme the notes follow. It is for this reason the Western ears, normally unaccustomed to the intricacies of microtonal Hindu music, can readily appreciate typical Nepalese songs whilst being entirely ignorant of and even hostile towards, the more complex forms of Indian classical music.

A typical example of a folk song in the pentatonic scale is the *Daang* Salyaan. This tuneful and lively village song, named after Daang and Salyaan districts of Western Nepal, repre sents the purely hill type of folk song, often accompanied by the beating of the *Thaali* (or metal plate). Its rhythm and steps might well be mistaken for a Highland fling and there is a marked similarity between this and certain types of Mongolian songs and even, as some experts hold, Negro folk music from America. The words and the accompanying notes are as follows:

"After a search of twelve long years, I have now found a clown- like husband, who resembles the green grass-hoppers of the *Ukaalo* (steep track) of Saribang village. *Shyam Bai*: *Shyam Bai*: no wonder even the *Bhoteni* (a Tibetan woman) has donned her festival bangles (for the occasion.)"

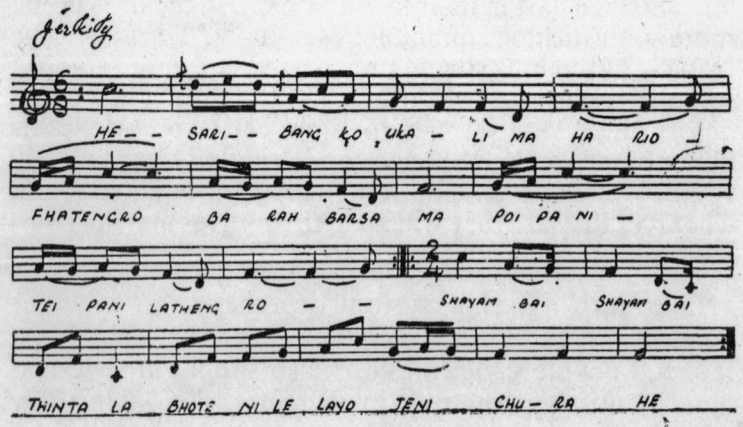

There are other types of folk songs, particularly in eastern Nepal foothills, which closely resemble the fascinating Bhatiali songs of Bengal on the other side of the Nepal-India border, adapted by the local Nepalese in the form of a semi-devotional folk music like the *Tungnaa*.

The *Tungnaa* is a small string instrument resembling a mini *Saarangi* and is popular among the Gurung goatherds of western (rarely also eastern) Nepal midhills. A devotional folk ballad is named after this instrument and built around the well-known *Ramayana* theme like the following adaptation which sings of the goat-herds' devotion to Lord Rama: "When Sita was kidnapped by Ravan, who was the person entrusted as her guardian ? With a *Tungna* made of wood stretched over with the skin of sheep, Rama's second brother (Lakshman) was the person guarding her." The notations are as follows :

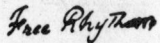

There has of course been no recorded or written music in Nepal. All its folk songs, religious strains and historical chants have been passed down from father to son for generations and most of them are yet to be put to recorded scores. Nepal's repertory of popular folk melodies include such catchy tunes as the "Naini Taala" and "Jham Jham Pareli", obviously Gorkha army favourites popularised by Regimental and club bands. They are not unoften sung in a chorus to the accompaniment of the *Madal*, the *Damfu* or the *Tungnaa* musical instruments.

Though in practice it is difficult to classify Nepalese music either by regions or by tribes except for songs like the Tamang or Bhotay *selo*, many of them are common to all tribes and castes. Then again, in many cases songs differ only according to the tune, the words being identical or *vice-versa*. Very often normal or standard songs in a whole region will have words improvised on the spot or for the particular occasion, as with West Indian Calypso singing, and if there is a good song-leader amongst them, they can go on for hours with the same tune and dance. These local

"Calypsos", often termed "Jhaaurays", usually take the form of couplets sung by the song-leader, with a chorus in between in which the whole gathering joins in.

The couplet consists of a first line, called the "phed" or base, which leaves the listener in a state of expectation; this line is then repeated, to add to the general suspense. Then comes the second line, the "tuppaa" or the climax or top, which relieves the pseudo tension with a joke or a pun and an epigrammatic sting. And then the chorus joins in with great gusto to signify their appreciation of the "tuppaa". Sometimes two or three song-leaders engage in contests of punning ability which have known to last as long as twenty-four hours or more.

The 'Jhyaaure' can be described as a cross between a Spanish clogdance, in which rhythm is kept by slight stamping of the foot (instead of the castanets), and the vigorous Cossak dances. As the chorus gets going and the gathering joins in, the dancer or dancers approach the centre of the circle, and the *Jhyaaure* begins. With circular and rhythmic hand movements each dancer proceeds alternatively forwards and backwards in a circle, in a one-two beat, dragging one foot behind the other and tapping the ground with the heel to match the rhythm. In the forward movement, this tapping is done with the rear foot; in the backward move, with the forward foot.

The direction of the movement changes at the end of each phase of the song, the indication for the change being given by a double thump on the *Madal*. After two or three such changes, or when the "tuppaa" is finished and the chorus started, the dancer quickens his steps, according to the dictates of the *Madal*, and crouches down on his haunches. He then again proceeds in a circle, dragging his legs forward, Cossack style.

It is an interesting and ancient dance, requiring great skill and body-control. Although there is no variation in the steps or the beat, somehow each performer introduces a new style into his dancing.

The Sherpas, known almost the world over as hardy mountaineers, are almost entirely Tibetan in outlook, food and dress. Also, they think nothing of merry-making with their womenfolk in the largest of gatherings. Much of the present Nepali folk dancing is increasingly influenced by their uninhibited approach to music and it is not uncommon these days to see men and women dancing together, in contrast to the more formal--and devotional-- dances like the *Maaruni*, about which mention will be made later.

A great favourite of the Rais and Lumbus of eastern Nepal hills is the *Juwari*, which can be described as a musical "question and answer" contest, especially between a boy and a girl who may be walking out together. They may sing to each other in a social gathering, at the bidding of their elders; or across the valleys whilst tending their cattle; or even as a serenade between groups of young boys and girls in a village fair or festival. A popular tune in the *Juwari* tradition of the Rais is the "Lai- Bari". It is sung in a haunting lilt, unaccompanied by any musical instruments, because it is really a sort of yodelling- with-words, passing from low to falsetto as a variation. The meaning of the words is: "Like a flitting bird of passage I come to this pasture which the cattle have grazed clean. Is there any young damsel here who can return my love?" The girl will then reply to her young man, and encourage him to make further advances in song. Sometimes a single valley will resound to the haunting notes of numerous *Juwaris* sung from village to village and from house-top to house-top. This style of group- duets is equally popular among the Gurungs of western Nepal hills, where the traditional *Rodi Ghars* or community singing houses dot the landscape and encourage free mixing.

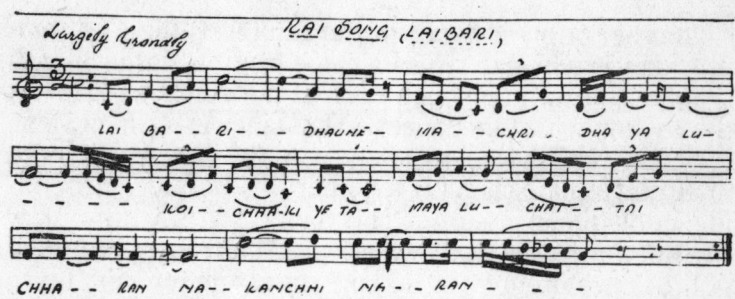

Another popular dance of eastern Nepal is the *Dhaan* (or Paddy) dance. Although originally a Lumbu dance, this is now popular with neighbouring peoples like the Rais, Magars and even the Lepchas of Sikkim across the Nepal-India border. The purpose of the *Dhaan Naach* is two-fold. Firstly, the dance may be held in the courtyard where the freshly cut paddy has been laid out on the ground, so that the collective foot-stamp of the dancers help separate the grain from the stalks; and, secondly, it is a celebration at the harvest season. Men and women both take part in these dances, linking and holding each other by the waist, European fashion.

The "*Paanchthare*" variety of this song and dance celebration, given in these pages, sings the Dhaan song slowly; but the high pitched "Ha Ha Ha" chorus at the end is shouted out by all in quick succession; the dancers also join in this chorus of Ha's.

Another popular dance of the Limbus is the *Chhyaab-rung* dance, which derives its name from the large *madal*-shaped tom-tom on which each of the dancers beats out the rhythm whilst he dances. The dance is normally performed to celebrate a marriage, and the dancers are both male and female, dancing together or separately, depending upon the occasion. The dance starts with a slow rhythm on the *Chhyaab-rungs*, which increases in tempo as the dance progresses, and may last from ten minutes to an hour non-stop. There are no songs to accompany the dancers and spectators bark out a series of high pitched notes indicating ecstatic appreciation, especially when the rhythm becomes really fast.

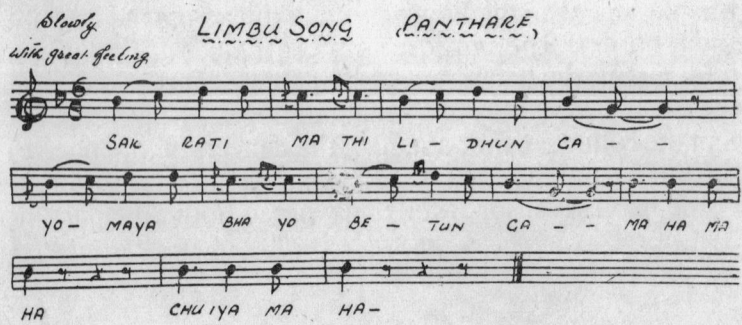

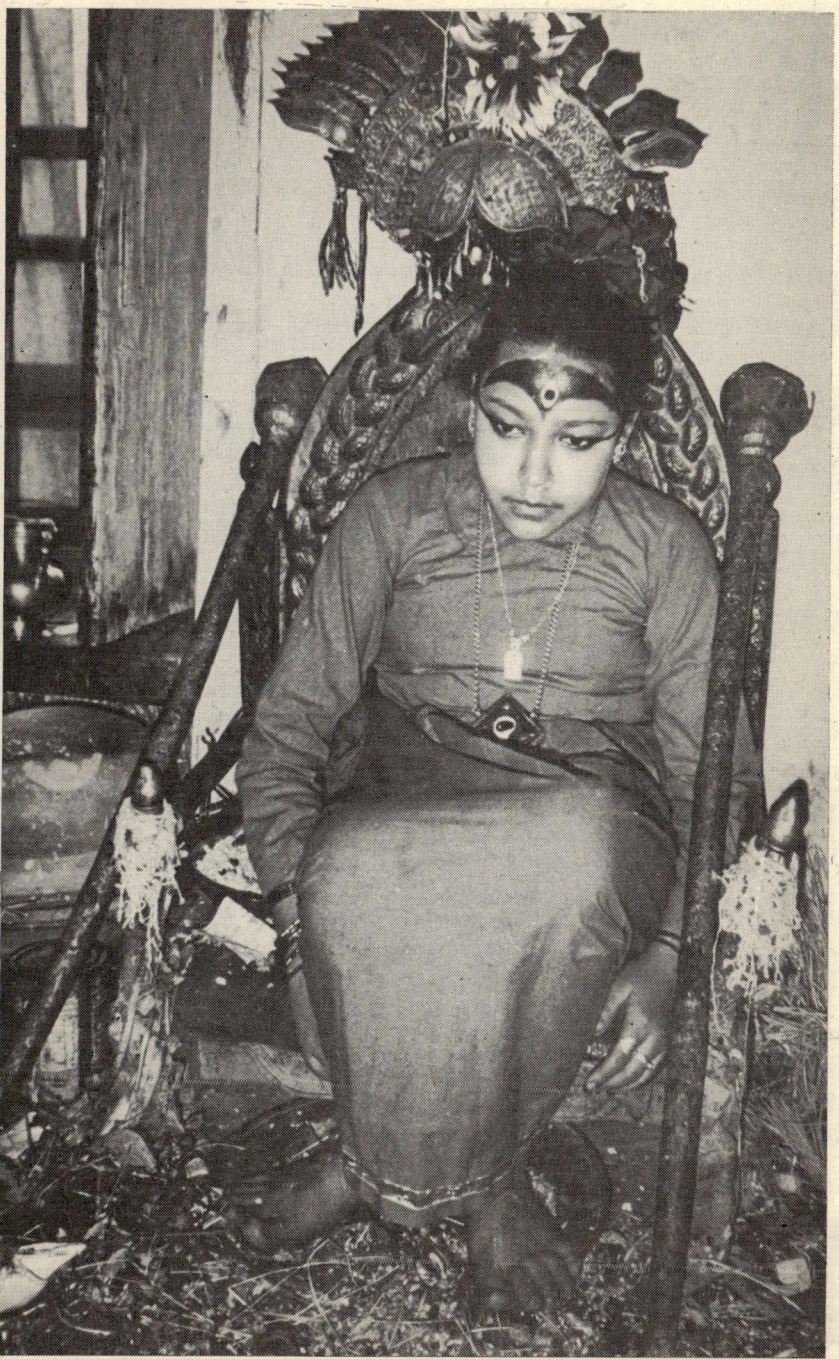

Photo by *Laxman Shrestha*

Photo by Yeti Photos Centre

Photo by Laxman Shrestha

The favourite dance of the Tamangs, another tribe hailing from eastern Nepal hills, is the Damphu Naach, also named after their one-sided tom-tom called Damphu, consisting of a round wooden frame about two feet in diameter, over which is stretched calf or goat skin. In appearance it is not unlike a crudely made tambourine. Certain damphus have a carved wooden bird with movable wings perched on top of a stick mounted on the wooden frame. Whilst playing on the instrument, the player manipulates the wings of the bird by pulling on a string, and the impression of a live bird keeping time to the beats on the Damphu can be very real.

This dance is mostly an all-male affair, but of late, some innovators have blended it into a *Juwaari*, (question-answer or cross-talk song of clever improvisation) with both women and men taking part. A typical *Juwaari* song for a Damphu dance is the "*Lekh - Lekh*" (*Lekh* means the lower Himalayas). The meaning of the words is: "Yonder, on the way to the Lekh, where stands the pious *deoraali* monument; I shall offer a virgin goat in sacrifice (so that) I may follow you to your parent's a *bode*; and there will bow my head in humble obeisance at the feet of your father and mother, taking them for my parents-in-law." (Notation of this song has been given earlier.)

Unlike the songs and dances prevalent in eastern Nepal, where the songs and dances of the various hill tribes can be more easily distinguished from each other, those of western Nepal hills is more intermixed. Certain Gurung, Magar and other songs do exist which are named after one particular sub-caste, but these are not large in number. To name the more popular ones here, we may begin with the 'Nautune', a song of the Nautunwa area of mid-West Nepal, its slow rhythm reminiscent of the foot-hills music. The next is the "Baaglunge", also popular in another mid-hill district of Nepal. Its tune, however, is too slow for any dancing, and is often sung as a lullaby. The Gulmi *Chandrakote* song from the Andhi Khola region, is a more lively song and improvised dances can accompany a good song leader. The meaning is: "Up beyond the zig-zag of Rakhu village and the rocks of the mountain, dwells *Sainloo* (beloved). There is no denying facts, and I am already tied to her by the bond of marriage, but peace of mind does not dwell in my heart".

The Lamjung district of Western Nepal, home of the Gorkha warriors called Gurungs, has always been well known for its songs, and was the home of the famous poet and singer Deo Bahadur Dura. It is said of this maestro that he so excelled every rival at the art of the *Juwari* duets that he had won himself seven wives in his singing contests, and was only saved from further obligations in this respect by being defeated by a *Sarkini* (a low caste woman): this defeat appears to have broken the spell. He made a gift of land to this worthy lady for having saved him from further matrimonial alliances !

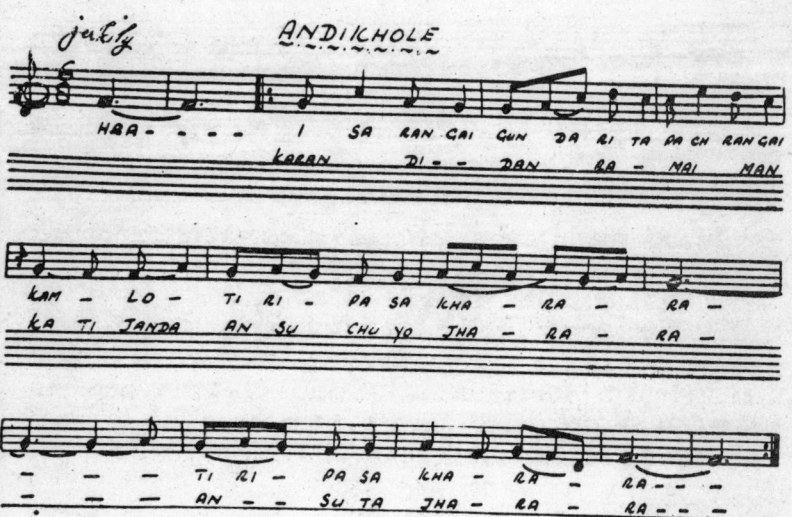

Three Lamjung songs are included in our repertoire, the first being a *Dura Geet*, or song improvised and made popular by the legendary Deo Bahadur. "The *ghungru* I have brought at great Dhunga Bazar to dance with the partner of my choice," goes the song", but so long as the one nearest my heart does not sing, I have little desire to dance". The next is a popular Jhamre or *Jhyaauray* from the same area which says: "Yonder at Kali Lekh Kailash, branches have broken under the heavy snow-fall; what have you to say to this poor soul, who has no further interest in life"? And lastly the *Phulbaasaa* or an autumn song, often sung without any instrumental accompaniment. The words of one run thus: "Down below the track there stands the *Amliso* tree (from which broomsticks are made) whose leaves have withered and fallen. My heart also has been torn to pieces, like a dirty rag."

In and around mid-west Nepal's Pokhara area, a popular tourist resort, a devotional folk song known as *Kaaski Bhajan,* is popular. It tells of an episode from the Ramayana epic! "The left-overs from the courtyard (feast) serve to feed the pigeons: the bees hover over the blossoms looking for nectar. In the court of Rama there is a window looking out to the east. It was the selfish desire of Queen Kaikeyi to banish Rama and Lakshman".

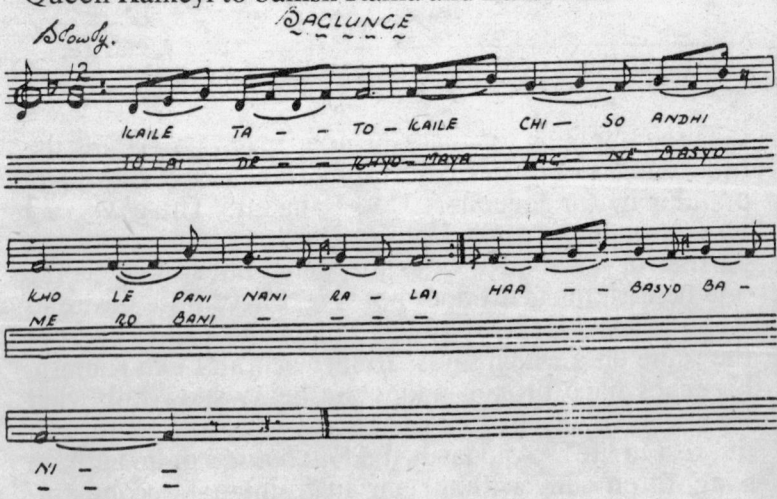

This in a way completes our cursory musical ramble through the Nepal hills, as far as folk music is concerned.

But mention must be made of yet another variety of Nepalese hill folk-songs and dances that is more or less popular almost everywhere, with, of course, some minor variations. Almost entirely derived from the formalised vocalism and intricate cadence of the Indian *ragas*, these basically devotional songs go by the name of *Maaruni* or a dancer. Many scholars consider the *Maaruni* to be a variety apart and, unlike anything else in Nepali folk dancing which are mostly marked by a vigour and the "fling" typical of the *Jhyaauray*, or the abandon of the Damphu, these are slow, more formal, long drawn-out and plaintive in character.

These dances are also symbolical of the divine love-play between the legendary Lord Krishna and Radha, or reminiscent of goddess Durgaa's exploits symbolising the victory of the good over the evil. If one were to follow past customs strictly, then the *Maaruni* dance should not be held except at a few occasions such as the *Dassain and Dewali festivals. The period of Maaruni* dancing lasts from the *Teej* festival (when the ladies of the house fast in the name of their husbands in early September) to the month of *Paush* (January). After that the *Maaruni* should normally layaside his dancing ensemble until the next *Teej* day.

If all the proper formalities are to be observed, the performance must start with an invocation to Saraswati, goddess of learning and the arts. After singing the praises of Saraswati, the *Maaruni* and the *Phursungay* (clown), both of whom are males with feminine garb, often go on to recite verses in praise of other patron deities, until the time approaches for the main performance to start.

The "*Nach Kholne Geet*" (literally, the "Opening Song") which opens the proceedings, is at once a prayer and a dance- song. When it is over, the *Phursunge* slowly makes his way through the crowd, leading the *Maaruni* to the centre of the courtyard.

The most popular song in this category, is known as Sorathi. This song is believed to have been named after Queen Sorathi, a legendary heroine of the Gorkhas. Sorathi songs sing of the tragic story of this famous queen, and the accompanying dance is a mostly monotonous swaying of the arms and slow beating with the heels, to the invariable accompaniment of the *Madal* drum- beats. Another popular theme for *Maaruni* singing and dancing is the *charitra*, meaning and episode in lord Krishna's life, often depicting the divine love-story of lord Krishna and Radha. The climax is reached as the time and tempo turn to what is known as the "khyaali" in which the rhythm quickens and the dance is more lively.

History

CHAPTER FOUR

Jung Bahadur

Kudos to *Ka. Dee* (Kamal Dixit), the well-known literary researcher, for coming out with yet one more jewel of a publication, listed as number sixty three in the Jagadamba publications series. Titled "Janga-Geeta", probably in keeping with the spirit of some earlier titles like "Rama-Geeta" and others, this well - researched yet tiny publication isn't, however, all eulogy of premier Jung Bahadur, as the term "Geeta" (meaning 'Song') might normally suggest.

Well, this is not purported to be a critique or a review of this illuminating publication. What is sought here is to share, with my readers, a couple of interesting insights on Jung Bahadur thrown by Mr. Dixit in his usual inimitable style. What's more, as each single anecdote, each single comment, bearing on the personality of the enigmatic historical hero comes right from primary and contemporary sources like his wives, 'courtiers', priests and the like, their authenticity can nowhere be in doubt. What, however, adds the right 'spice' to these stories is Ka. Dee's brilliant editorial notes without which much of the meanings and subtle nuances would have been lost, particularly to a lay reader. And I entirely agree with the erudite editor when he has something to this effect to say: "The many new facets of Jung Bahadur's life, the changing nuances presented by every successive account, lead us to presume that both the pictures of Jung, whether drawn by the English historians or by their Nepalese counterparts, aren't perhaps as authentic as we thought they were."

Particularly interesting are the accounts attributed to *purohit* Shivaraj, Jinarani, Babarjung's wife, an army officer Khadga Singh Gurung, and Rama Bhakta. Of these, Jinarani was one of Jung Bahadur's "numerous" wives, while *Mir Subba* Ram Bhakta could have been "an old and faithful court official", according to Mr. Dixit. As for Khadga Singh, it is said that the second edition of Ambika Prasad Upadhyay's "History of Nepal" has made a pointed reference to a namesake Gurung officer in these words: "There was an old man aged 86 years, in Kathmandu. He had been Jung Bahadur's security guard for a long time. His name was Major Khadga Singh Gurung." Upadhyaya, the author, was a lawyer from Patna (India) who had visited Kathmandu once or twice as a guest of premier Chandra Shumshere. Consequently, the second edition of his above referred book is stated to bear a greater stamp of authenticity in view of some "hitherto secret and unknown" information provided by the author's contact with erudite scholars like *Pandit* Kashinath and *Mir Subba* Ram Mani, adds Mr. Dixit.

Khadga Singh, likewise, was one of such invaluable sources and he has been quoted at one place as commenting that Jung Bahadur's major 'weaknesses' included "elephants, gambling, acrobatic bouts, and sex". Singh is also said to add that in his later life, Jung had shown increasing addiction to opium and his daily intake would rise to as many as 18 'tablets'. These intimate insights into Jung Bahadur's character had never been made public by anybody in the past and it is for this reason that posterity owes its debt of gratitude to persons like Khadga Singh, as quoted by Upadhyaya.

Jinarani is said to have been the daughter of a Budhathoki hailing from Baglung. *Purohit* Shivaraj, in his turn, was a priest belonging to the Satyal clan and was instrumental also in making much valuable information available to, among others, Percival Landon, the noted British historian. Shivaraj, for instance, alludes to Jung Bahadur's "fits of blind fury", in the course of which he would think of nothing to physically batter people to near death; but, once he had let off his steam thus, he was also quick to repent what he had done. One is led to suspect, adds Mr. Dixit, that such an increasingly intemperate behaviour of Jung could have been a direct sequel to his intake of opium in ever larger doses in later life. This aspect of his character is highlighted, for example, in an incident where he had once beaten up his wife, mother of Babarjung, black and blue, and driven her out of the house; but, on having realised his 'folly' later, Jung not only fetched her back home, but also sought to assuage her hurt feelings by way of a cash 'compensation' of Rupees 2600--quite a hefty and tidy sum in those days !

But, lest this ancedote of a "hefty compensation" give one the impression that Jung was very generous with his purse, Khadga Singh is said to correct us by painting a rather unflattering picture of Jung's munificence otherwise. A touch of "stinginess" in Jung's character, suggests Mr. Dixit, seems only natural if we were to consider his rather none-too-rich upbringing that had taught him the value of money rather too well. What's more, if any more evidence of Jung as a "money-saver" was needed, we have only to turn to his own wife, Jinarani, who is said to have gone on record saying that even his "earnings" from gambling were invested by him in purchasing some Terai lands for himself !

The fact that he used to invest his own savings in buying plots of land opens an entirely new vista in the character of Jung Bahadur, rightly asserts Dixit, and adds: "Well, had he only wanted it, he could easily have, in his capacity as a

Prime Minister, appropriated to himself any number of *Birtaa* lands. The mere fact that he didn't choose to do so is enough to underline his sterling quality as a man--as far as honesty in matters of finance and state affairs is concerned.".

Some other interesting sidelights on Jung Bahadur the man rather than Jung Bahadur the premier are also worth noting, according to Mr. Dixit. For one thing, he wasn't very devout person-- religion, in other words, wasn't one of his fortes. For another, he was not very fond of reading and writing either. "Used to read once in a long while", his wife and dauther-in-law have been quoted as saying !

Another sidelight thrown by this illuminating "Geeta" on Jung is also no less interesting. It is revealed, for instance, that Jung didn't pin much faith on doctors on the one hand, and on the other, was quite adept in "reading the pulse" (*Ayurvedic*-style) himself: besides, he also knew quite a bit of the traditional "jharphook" system of curing diseases. What's more, he had also sought to revive the *Ayurvedic* system of medicine by bringing its practitioners together in a sort of meeting of minds on some occasions.

The Swami Maharaj

Nepal is now in the later forties of the twenty-first century, *Vikrama Samvat*. (The term 'twentieth', as applied to the present century, is thus a misnomer in the Nepalese context). Besides, Nepal has left behind more than three decades of Panchayat experiments and exercise. Out-dated social institutions like the caste-system have, at least legally, been cast off with the advent of the Legal Code (Mulki Ain) amendment some twenty years ago. Yet, even today, the majority of Nepalese haven't been able to shake off the hang-over of a caste-ridden past.

Imagine, then, the unflinching and exemplary courage of a young man, a reigning *Hindu* monarch at that, who had the guts to break the barriers and bondage of caste by publicly marrying a *Brahmin* girl some two centuries ago from now (in early 1790s, to be exact)! And, what's more, he even had the scruples to sacrifice his throne in favour of the offspring born out of such a loveunion. This admirably revolutionary effort on his part should have egged subsequent Nepalese generations on to even more laudable efforts. But, to an unappreciative posterity, he has come down as one of the most misunderstood men in history and, instead of elevating him to the pedestal of a rightful fame as the first social revolutionary who sought to demolish casteism in Nepalese society, it simply revells in taunting and denigrating him. He has, in short, erred less than has been erred against.

Not only was king Rana Bahadur Shah (otherwise also known as 'Swami Maharaj') a great social revolutionary. Had it not been for the fierce battle of wits he waged against the British East India Company (which had already securely lodged itself in capital Kathmandu on the strength of the treaty of B.S. 1858 or 1801 A.D.), and ultimately succeeded in packing it off, bag and baggage, out of this country, Nepal wouldn't perhaps have been waxing eloquent today on her nationalism, tradition of political independence, unimpaired sovereignty and what have you !

Now, to list a few of the historical blasphemies levelled against him by many, but which have been proved baseless and prejudiced in the light of recent researches on king Rana Bahadur Shah.

Francis Hamilton, a contemporary historian who had been to Kathmandu along with Captain Knox, the first British Resident, says, for instance, that the Swami Maharaj, on his return from self-exile in Benares (India), had made himself the Regent. And, many subsequent chroniclers like Hunter, Oldfield, Balchandra Sharma, Surya Bikram Gewali, K.P. Srivastava and even the redoubtable Baburam Acharya apparently blindly copied Hamilton. Yet, if the truth is to be told, a royal edict issued by king Girvan Yuddha Bikram Shah in B.S. 1862 (1805 A.D.) conclusively proves that the Swami Maharaj had been appointed a *Mukhtiyar* (Prime Minister) and not a regent.

It can also be mentioned, on the strength of the said edict, that quite contrary to examples of prime ministers stepping ultimately into the shoes of their kings (history is full of them), here we find a unique instance where a king not only volunteered to step down from his throne but also gladly assumed the role of a prime minsiter when a national contingency demanded it of him. A nobler sense of sacrifice on the one hand and of shouldering responsibility on the other is rare to come by. For, it was during his brief stint as a *Mukhtiyar* (hardly two months?) that he swiftly and cleverly snapped relations between Nepal and the British East India Company-- thereby shattering the latter's dreams of establishing an imperialistic hegemony over Nepal. Does this not establish him as a great nationalist, and a statesman ?

Another glaring distortion of facts is seen in respect to the expenses Swami Maharaj incurred during his self-exile in Benares. Here again, most historians including Oldfield, Aitchison, Sharma and Acharya are almost one in giving credit to the British Indian authorities for meeting the expenses of his stay there. But a letter written by his wife, queen Rajeshwari Devi, on her return from Benares, and a promissory note written by king Rana Bahadur Shah in B.S. 1860 (1803 A.D.) against a loan of Rupees 60,001 taken by him from a businessman, Dwarikadass, go to suggest that the royal entourage did not depend on British doles to see it through the self-exile days.

Also, the long and almost endearing letter queen Rajeshwari Devi dutifully wrote to the Swami Maharaj in

Benares soon after her arrival at Kathmandu (for a copy of this letter as also that of the promissory note referred to above, readers are advised to refer to Chittaranjan Nepali's well-researched book, "Rana Bahadur Shah") gives the lie, once again, to historians like Landon, Hunter, Northy and Gewali who have roundly alleged that her husband's "misdeeds", like philandering in Benares, were primarily responsible for her ultimate and lonely return to Kathmandu. On the other hand, it was part of a grand and statesmanlike strategy, jointly wrought out by the Swami and his consort, in order to threw off the British yoke.

Other falsehoods fabricated to paint a noble king in adverse light include the following :

In the course of the famous episode known as *Baasatthi Haran* (Confiscation of B.S. 1962), it is true king Rana Bahadur Shah did confiscate the *birta*-lands belonging to Brahmins and the *guthi*-lands dedicated to temples. But it wasn't the act of "a demented king bent upon avenging the death of queen Kantimati", as Bal Chandra Sharma puts it. The very fact that seven long years intervened between the death of Kantimati (B.S. 1856) and this confiscation is enough to counter Sharma's assertion. On the other hand, it seems the confiscation was justified by the needs of statecraft; pressed with lack of resources required to prepare his country to wage a war of defence against the British, an eventuality not altogether unforeseen in the wake of the unceremonious-- and almost forcible-- closure of the British Residency and a virtual deportation of Captain Knox, what other alternative was left for the Swami Maharaj ?

Swami Nirbanananda (not Nirgunananda as some have put it) has also been accused of destroying many idols and images of deities, including that of goddess *Haratimai*, following the death of Kantimati. While the death of his beloved wife may have driven a grief-stricken king to embark upon such a "spree", this aspect of his seemingly iconoclastic and erratic behaviour was possibly the consequence of his conversion into the Josmani cult--a Hindu sect opposed to idol-worship.

It is also true that he had banished most children from the capital in the wake of the smallpox epidemic that had brought about his beloved Kantimati's premature death. This seemingly irrational act of his can also perhaps be justified on two grounds; one, that in the absence of any other way of immunising the capital's children from this scourge, removing them temporarily from Kathmandu, despite the immense suffering it brought about to all concerned, was probably the only way out; and, two, that a smallpox death had been forecast by an irate punditry as being in store for his very young (three years old) son, Girbaan Yuddha Vikram Shah, who had also been made the king, and since a similar forecast in respect of the queen had proved to be only too true earlier, Rana Bahadur Shah could have acted the way he did in order to protect his only progeny.

What we must not ignore, also, is the remarkable fact that, despite the blasphemy spread against him by the *Birta*-- dispossessed Brahmins on the one hand and the driven-- out Britishers on the other, the army and the majority of the people remained singularly and steadfastly loyal to the Swami Maharaj till the very end. The very soldiers led by Damodar Pandey to arrest the Swami on his return from Benares not only laid down their arms the moment they saw their king, but also turned around to give a chase to Pandey himself till he was killed at Bhadrakali. What other evidence is needed to prove the popular love and loyalty that Swami Maharaj commanded at the hands of his people, even after a long self-exile ? That this great leader of men succumbed to court treachery some two months later goes only to add yet another halo to his royal mantle--that of a martyr to the cause of Nepal's freedom and sovereignty, the two ideals that were so dear to him till the very end of his short, 31-year long, career.

From Bagmati to Borubodur ?

It is said that a king of Nepal, in the middle of the seventh century, had invited some Chinese builders to Kathmandu, and to these builders goes the credit for the conception of a style of architecture now well-known the world over as the "Pagoda" style.

On the other hand, the story of Arniko, particularly popular in Nepal, goes totally counter to the above account.

Leaving aside the story of Arniko, which, in any case, dates no earlier than the 13th century, we have other sources that go to support the Nepalese claim of having "invented" the pagoda style of architecture. The most interesting and perhaps the earliest such record is to be found in the account of a Chinese travel book dating back to the days of the T'ang dynasty. The book cannot, says Percival Landon, "be later than the earliest years of the tenth century AD, and is almost centainly earlier than the middle of the eighth". This narrative, he adds, is probably based upon the records left by Wang Huien Tse about the year 657 AD.

In subsequent periods too, we come across some Chinese travellers who were awed by such Nepalese palaces "of many roofs", a point which must have been made simply in order to emphasise the absence, in China, of the "pagodas", at least till then. "It cannot even be said that China improved upon the Nepalese model," writes Landon, and the following account from his well-- known book, "Nepal" (1882), is relevant:

"As I write I look down upon the yellow roofs of the Forbidden City of Peking. In number and size these naturally eclipse the similar structures of Nepal. But magnificent as they are, they offer no instance of more than a triple roof, and in all that historic expanse there is nothing which can for a moment compare in beauty and richness with Changu Narayan or with the royal square of Patan".

This much for China. Now to turn to Sri Lanka and India. General L. de Beylie, recalling the parallels offered by the Boonze Monastery of a Thousand Cells, which, in the second century A.D., was ornamented with precious stones by King Dutthagamani at Anuradhapura (near Colombo), finds that the influence of Nepalese structure and ornament can be traced far beyond the limits of the country. He discovers them in another eleventh century work -- in the great Ananda Monastery at Pagan, and he also considers that the concentric circles of the "hit" in Burma and Assam also are taken from Nepal as well as the square entablature at the top of the dome (*toran*).

Monsieur Francois Benoit, writing about medieval and modern oriental architecture in 1912, also finds the influence of Nepal in Burma, in China, and in India.

To quote Landon again: "Apart from the temples, the *viharas* or monastic settlements exhibit a style which is also peculiar to Nepal. In the centre of a square courtyard, two storeys in height, there will generally be found a closely slatted cage containing an image. This structure is presumably intended solely to protect the figure from defilement, like the stone lattice-work that shelters each of the upper images at Borubodur !"

The mere menton of the world-famous Borubodur in an essay on Nepalese art and architecture is significant in our context. And it may be added that there are at least two conceptual characteristics in the Borubodur *stupas* that somehow are reminiscent of the Nepalese architectural tradition. The first is the recognition of the value of an entire hill as plinth, of the Swayambhunath variety. And the second, the stone lattice-work "that shelters each of the upper images at Borubodur" (as Landon puts it) is so much akin "to the closely slatted cages containing Nepalese images". And, thirdly, the fact that the "Chandi Kalasan", the first of the Borubodur stupas built in 778 A.D., "is dedicated to the Buddhist goddess, Tara", as mentioned by Ann Kumar in the book "The Civilisation of Monsoon Asia". And "Tara" is a very popular goddess in Nepali's Buddhist pantheon.

To add, the Borubodur temple-complex in central Java was built in honour of Mahayana Buddhism (around 750-850 A.D.), according to the Encyclopedia Britannica. That is, around the same time that the first Chinese travel book, mentioned earlier, so much extols Nepalese architecture. "And in these 100 years", adds the Encyclopedia Americana, "it is reasonable to imagine that many artists and architects from Buddhist countries may have been imported or invited". Could these "Buddhist countries" have included Nepal, to many the home of both Mahayana and Vijrayana varieties of Buddhism ?

That also brings us to the point if Gunadharma was one of such persons so "imported or invited"? Also if Gunadharma was the man behind the construction of Borubodur and if he hailed from Nepal as held by the noted scholar, Late Swayambhu Lal Shrestha, does this not go contrary to the more general assertion that to Gunavarman, from India, goes such credit ?

Kathmandu's First Europeans

Avtomne Winter L'hiver

It is hard to believe that the words above-quoted, not commonly comprehensible even in the 21st century Nepal, should have formed part of a 330-year-old Kathmandu stone inscription. Yet, the fact is, they do !

Needless to add, the first and the third of these words, possibly French, respectively mean 'autumn' and 'winter', while the middle one is perhaps English.

A blackstone tablet, embedded into a wall next to the Hanumandhoka palace and attributed to king Pratap Malla, is unique in another respect too. For, besides the three words quoted above, it contains words from 13 other languages in addition to Nepali, many of them unfamiliar even in today's Nepal !

The element of surprise is further heightened by the fact that not a single European soul seems to have been in Nepal till 1761-2 but the aforesaid inscription dates back to 1635, at least 106 years earlier ! If so, how on earth could king Pratap Malla possibly have familiarised himself with English and French words so as to have them correctly inserted into his inscription ?

One of the earliest European visitors to Nepal, as far as it can be easily ascertained, was father Horatius Della Penha, a Capuchin missionary, who had been allowed to establish a hospice in Kathmandu in 1714. Emmanuel Frere, another European, arrived in Nepal two years later and was followed by Fr. Dessidery, who had stopped at Kathmandu enroute from Tibet to Nepal. Fathers Grueber and D'Orville followed suit in the early 1760's.

But even considering that the trickle that had started with Della Penha in 1714 turned into a 'minitide' by 1742--when the number of Capuchins in Kathmandu valley totalled 59 and was expected to rise further following king Ranjit Malla's personal letter to the Pope at Vatican dated May 2, 1742, it still does not explain the seeming enigma of the English and French words that had "infiltrated" into king Pratap Malla's inscription at Hanumandhoka.

In this context it is worthwhile quoting the late Mr. Swayambhulal Shrestha, who has this to say:

"On the 13th April, 1626, a group of missionaries were sent from Cochin, capital of the Malabar Province (in India), to Tibet. One of them was Joab Kyabarel (*sic*). They had entered into Tibet's Utsaang area *via* northwestern Bhutan... Joab arrived at Shighatse in January 1628, roughly 20 months after they had left Cochin. As their earlier experience, while passing through Bhutan, hadn't been an entirely happy one, they felt inclined to explore some alternative routes back home...

"Towards the end of January Kyabarel left Tibet. He was carrying with him a letter from a local ruler addressed to the king of Kathmandu, Lakḥsmi Narasimha Malla.

"(It appears thus) that he had arrived at Kathmandu some 30 years prior to Grueber and D'Orville. As such, it can be said with certainty that Kyabarel was the first European to enter into Nepal. And it must be he, and those that followed him, who taught kings Lakshmi Narasimha and Pratap Malla the ABCs of the English and French scripts.

"Kyabarel was born in Portugal in 1599 A.D....and he died in Goa on the 4th july, 1660."

Hoping that the above excerpt establishes how the words AVTOMNE, WINTER and L'HIVER found their way into the Hanuman Dhoka inscription, we may now briefly dwell on certain other European pioneers who visited Nepal in the subsequent decades.

Fr. Dessideri's account of the life and times of king Mahindra Singh or Bhaskar Malla is contained in a separate Chapter entitled *The Account of Tibet*, edited by Phillippe. It reads in part: "While I was in Tibet I returned via Nepal. The ruling king there has annexed many surrounding principalities (in the recent past). As the king of Patan died without any heir, all those areas were (also) inherited by him in the shape of paternal property."

A letter purported to have been written to the then Nepalese ruler by the Viceroy of Goa in February, 1667 reads somewhat along the following lines:

"Your liberalism and greatness have been so well-renowned that I felt myself inclined to seek your hands in friendship and cordial relations. Not only that I have also friendship and cordial relations. Not only that I have also been instructed by the emperor of Portugal who is a great and powerful ruler... I was given to understand that the missionaries, the bearers of this letter, were proceeding towards your court to stay in your kingdom... Any kindness and hospitality extended to them will be considered by me as a personel *(sic)* favour..."

This communication implies two things: first, that the Portugese missionaries were already on their way to *Cadmendu*, as they called it, and were not completely unfamiliar with its situation, terrain and people. Second, that they seem to have already been "invited" to Nepal. The second conjecture is further stregthened by another reference to Nepal made by Grueber and D'Orville on their way back from China and Tibet to Europe *via* Kathmandu, that says: "We were very warmly received by the King of Cadmendu".

As the king referred to in Grueber's writing couldn't have been any other than Pratap Malla, concludes Mr. Shrestha, it is not completely inconceivable that whatever earlier acquaintance he may have had with Europeans like Krebal had made king Pratap Malla favourably disposed towards the Europeans in general and the Portugese missionaries in particular. No wonder this association also helped him familiarise himself with quite a bit of the English and French languages, as is evidenced in his Hanuman Dhoka inscription.

Father John J. Dahlheimer,* SJ, of St.Xavier's School, Jawalak hel, has this to add, by way of a rejoinder to the above write-up:

"Father John Cabral, SJ, a Portuguese priest of the Malabar Province of the Society of Jesus, was indeed the first non-Asian, European if you will, to enter the territory which was to become the present Kingdom of Nepal and the city of Kathmandu in early 1628. He was coming from

Shigatse, Tibet via the kuti-Nylam Pass, returning to his base in Houghli in the Great Delta.

"Arriving Christmas Eve 1661, Fr. John Grueber, SJ, an Austrian from Linz, of the Manchu Imperial Observatory and Fr. Albert d'Orvelle, SJ, scion of a noble Belgian family, making the over land transit from Peking to Agra, via Lhasa, spent a short time in the capital city of the Kingdom of Kathmandu. King Pratap Malla did in fact invite the Jesuits to work in the Valley then, but they had to wait something short of three centuries before really implementing that first invitation.

"Pushing the estimated date of blackstone tablet attributed to this King up a quarter century or so to the time of this visit, the mystery begins to dissolve like the Kathmandu ground fog in mid-morning. "Winter" in the inscription, while it could be English, is more probably German. In which case the finger does point rather steadily at the Austrian (German-speaking) and Belgian (French-speaking) Jesuit duo...

"Turning to the Capuchins (the Order of Friars Minor, Capuchin), by and large and originally Italians of the Province of Piceno in the Marches of Ancona on the Adriatic coast, from 1704 to 1742, the total personnel roster of their Tibet-Nepalese mission never exceeded 49. The "minitide" was not even a microtide in 1742 or any other year.

"Fr. Francis Horace of Pennabilli was the giant of the Capuchin effort, working in Tibet and Nepal from 1714 to his death at Patan in 1745.

"Fr. Manuel Freyre, a Portuguese Jesuit, passed through Kathmandu in 1716 hotfooting it for the lowlands leaving his companion on their roundabout from Agra through Ladakh and down the Indus-Tsangpo valleys to Lhasa, Fr. Hippolytus Desideri, SJ, the "pistol" from Pistoia, Italy, happy as a pickle floating in a barrel of brine in the Tibetan capital.

"Father Desideri spent something like five very wonderful years in his private *Shangri-la* there, becoming one of the world's most versatile and memorable Tibetologists in the process. He, too, returning to base passed through the valley of Nepal *via* the Kuti-Nylam route in late 1721."

A Social Coup D'etat

This is the story of a single stroke of statemanship, masterminded by one individual which altered the entire social power structure in Nepal. And that too at a time when many other Asian and African countries hadn't even dreamt of such drastic steps in the field of social reforms.

The date was 24th of November, 1924 A.D., some sixty years ago. Advanced western countries like Britain and America had come out with legislations abolishing the social evil of slavery in 1838 and in 1862 respectively. The League of Nations, set up after the World War I (1914-18), was still crying hoarse urging its member-countries to do way with this evil system. Why, some middle-east countries like Muscat and Oman abolished slavery only as late as the other day, in 1970 -- a full forty-five years after Nepal had done it.

Going slightly back into history, we can trace the beginnings of Nepal's desire to do away with slavery back to 1773 A.D., more than sixty years before Great Britain abolished it. At the time, king Prithivi Narayan Shah had issued an edict banning this social evil. Similar efforts were made later by premier Bhimsen Thapa (in 1824) and by king Rajendra Bikram Shah (in 1839). But Nepal's well heeled conservative coteries had scuttled these moves before they could take any effective shape.

Then came premier Jung Bahadur. He also enacted legislation which declared, in effect, that the slaves who had escaped out of the clutches of their masters and had settled in areas of Morang and the 'New Territories' would be automatically treated as having been "emancipated". He also laid down that the purchase of Indians as slaves would be treated as illegal and persons so engaged in the slave-trade would be punished under the law. But his efforts came to a naught against the backdrop of the same social and political opposition. So did those of premier Deva Shumsher after him, though he did provide an example by releasing his own private slaves, besides enacting yet additional legislation banning the slave-trade.

Daniel Wright estimated the population of slaves in Nepal those days at about 30,000 persons. And the majority of them, it is said, belonged to the Bihar and U.P. areas in north India, particularly those that had migrated to Nepal in the wake of the great Indian famine of 1924. The market price of a slave varied from Rs. 390 to 500, the young and pretty-looking girls fetching the highest price !

Premier Chandra Shumsher, who ultimately succeeded in abolishing slavery, "spent money from his own pocket" in order to "buy off" the freedom of the slaves. As all the unspent state funds those days used to go to the pockets of the prime minister, "the sum of Rupees fourteen lakhs spent by Chandra Shumsher for the purpose could be said to have been his personal money," reads one account.

Other accounts, apparently more authentic, put the amount spent for the purpose at Rupees 36 lakhs. And this amount, if true, was quite a staggering figure, considering both the value of money and also the state of Nepal's economy at the time. For, computed at today's prices, the amount would multiply itself to mean no less than Rupees fifty crores (500,000,000) approximately ! What's more, even in these days it is rare indeed to see this much money being allotted to a single social service Budget-head in any one year.

Also, since Nepal's annual state revenue did barely exceed Rs. 200 crores at the time, spending nearly one-fourth of the State's entire annual earnings for the slavery-abolition programme of a "dubious benefit" (at least in the eyes of the premier's opponents) was not short of a "revolution" -- and must have been opposed tooth and nail. But Chandra Shumsher stood his ground, went through his grand scheme, and deserved posterity's plaudits for doing so.

No wonder, the public declaration of his historic and courageous step had to be buttressed with as many arguments as premier Chandra Shumsher could muster in its favour. No wonder, too, that these arguments ran into fifty-seven pages which were read out, both in Nepali and English versions, from the famous (but also non-existent anymore!) tree, *Khariko Bot*, at Kathmandu's Tundikhel. Interestingly enough, the English version was seemingly for the benefit of just three foreigners present on the occasion-- the British Resident, his physician and one Mr. Kilburn!

"*Shiva Bhaktas*" (devotees of Lord Shiva) or *Shivabhaktis* was the new name given to the 59,873 slaves thus emancipated by Chandra Shumshere on the Nepali New Year's Day in 1925. Some people hold that the amount of Rs. 14 lakhs mentioned above was "drawn" from the 'private' coffers of Pasupatinath temple-- hence this name. But few today are known as either "Shiva Bhaktas" or "Shiva Bhaktis" as most of the emancipated slaves have merged into the mainstream of the wider Nepalese society already.

Nepal-Bhutan: The Early Phase

One of the earliest instances of Nepal-Bhutan historical contacts is provided by two friendly missions, one from Gorkha and the other from Nepal (Kathmandu), sent to felicitate Ngawang Namgyal, the Bhutanese king, on his victory against invading "Druk-pa" Tibetans, led by Depa Tsangpa, in 1639.

That the Bhutanese people had even earlier contacts with areas of Nepal like Mustang can be inferred on the basis of a land- grant, made by the Ladakh king Sengge Namgyal (1590-1645), to the north of the Himalayas around mount Kailash and Mansarovar.(Incidentally, it may be mentioned that both the Ladakhis and Bhutanese belonged to the same religious sect, the *Drukpa Kagyu*). A Bhutanese monk officer, designated Druk Kangri Lama, administered those villages and may have thus come into contact with Mustang.

It was during the reign of Sonam Lhendhup, popularly known as Deb Shidar, that Bhutan, which already had its grip over the state of Cooch Behar (Koch Bihar or the "Habitat of the Koch People"), invaded Sikkim as also Vijayapur in today's eastern Nepal. The territory of Vijayapur (or Morang) extended between Purnea in Bihar and Sikkim. Shidar was joined by Raikat Ram Narayan, the Cooch Bihar ruler, in the expedition against Vijayapur, but they "were thwarted by Prithvi Narayan Shah (ca. 1769-75), who took Vijayapur for himself".

Both Nepal and Bhutan as emerging Himalayan kingdoms were threatened by an ever-expanding East India Company. They had to come to one another's rescue if they wanted to jointly survive against the Britishers. In fact, while Deb Shidar was confronted by Warren Hasting's troops who had come to the "rescue" of Koch Bihar from the hands of the Bhutanese, the former had already established some sort of an alliance with king Prithvi Narayan Shah. The latter, an intrepid foe of the British, sought the intervention of Panchen Lama II on Shidar's behalf. For Nepal foresaw in Shidar's defeat a bleak prospect for herself too, and, as such, did not want this conflict to end in a disaster for the Bhutan king.

It is said that this kind of connexion between Bhutan and Nepal and the holding of estates by Bhutan in Nepal had precedents even during the earlier Malla period, but not much is known about them. Also, Bhutan's privileges in Nepal, whatever they had been, were said to have increased particularly after the conflict between Nepal and Tibet in 1788, with Bhutan holding estates in lower Mustang, and in some Tamang and Yolmo areas. The Bhutan Gomba (monastery) in Mustang, extant to this day, is said to commemorate a Bhutanese princess married to a former Mustang king. Bhutan has also retained some kind of a mission in Kathmandu since those days according to some sources.

When a *coup d'etat* was pulled off in Bhutan by the rivals of Deb Shidar, king Prithvi Narayan Shah refused to recognise the new regime in Bhutan and is said to have sent 200 troops to help Shidar. But that was too late. Also too late was the intervention that came from the Panchen Lama III as a result of Nepal's persuasion, for, by the time the Panchen Lama's (1737-80) letter reached Calcutta (March 29, 1774), Hastings had already accepted the terms of a "peace offer" from the new Bhutanese rulers. Hastings was quick to make political capital out of this intervention, however, and made it appear that he was ceasing military operations against Bhutan on the Panchen Lama's request !

During the reign of Deb Jigme Sengge (1776-86), the Bhutanese agent in Nepal was Lama Tenzing Druggyal. It is even said that Nepal presented Kalari and Thongman "estates" to Bhutan in return for its neutrality during Nepal's invasion of Sikkim (1773). Also, following the rupture in Nepal's relations with Tibet, the Swayambhunath temple was brought under the protection of Bhutan's Shabdung Rimpoche.

The Bhutan-Swayambhunath connection was not an abrupt development, however. A story has it that king Narbhupal Shah of Gorkha, who had been issueless, had invited a Bhutanese Lama,...to invoke divine benediction in his favour so that a son could be born. When the king had, in fact, a son in the person of Prithvi Narayan Shah, a highly obliged Narbhupal Shah had asked the Lama what he could do for the latter in return. He would ask for a gift at the appropriate time, the Lama is said to have replied. When king Prithvi Narayan Shah had brought the erstwhile city-states of Kathmandu, Patan, Bhaktapur and Kirtipur under his rule, the Bhutanese Lama returned to Nepal, and reminded the king of his father's promise. Prithvi Narayan made a land-grant to the Lama including the right to conduct the affairs of the Swayambhunath stupa.

Kasthamandap and Around

Did you know that the present day Nepal valley was known as "Bhaayul", Deopatan as 'Kanchi', Lalitpur as Lalit Pattan or Ashoka Pattan, Kirtipur as Thencho Gram, Banepa as "Bandipur" and the Swayambhu hillock as "Gopuchhe" in earlier days ?

That the word Kathmandu itself has been derived from *Kaastha Mandap* is too well-known a story to deserve repetition here. What needs to be clarified in this context, however, is that the credit for constructing the *Kastha Mandap* (otherwise also known as *Maru Sattal* or the "Rest House at Maru") around which the legend of Kathmandu has been built, has been wrongly placed.

Contrary to popular belief, which ascribes its construction to a 17th century king, Narasimha Malla, this edifice finds mention even in an eleventh century ms., entitled *"Nama Sangiti"*. A century later, another verse-composition categorically recorded that "Janarakshita (i.e., the Buddha) resided here". These records, therefore, push back the antiquity of *Kastha Mandap* by many a century more, at least six !

It may also be mentioned, in passing, that Kathmandu was also known, at different times of history, by such names as *Kali Daha* (Black-water Lake), and *Naga Daha* or *Naga Hrad* (Lake of Serpents), both of which obviously refer to the area having been water-filled; a fact which has since found geological and scientific corroboration. Also, the legend of sage Manjushree, who is credited with the draining of the lake-water and establishing civilisation here, is borne out by another name, Manju Pattan, given to it.

The local Newars, who are a dominant majority in the Valley, still refer to Kathmandu as *Yan*, presumably an abbreviation of its old-time names such as Yangal or Yambu. That this city originally owed it existence to an ancient community such as the *Kiratas* can also be conjectured on the basis of some Lichchhavi records which are said to refer to two separate principalities -- namely Yambu proper and Yangwal. The Chinese Blue Annals have also made reference to both these principalities, it is averred.

Another tradition has it that Kathmandu city of the old was divided into three separate zones or areas, with the upper (or northern) part being known as *Thon*, the middle part (between the present-day Asan and Makhan) as *Dathu* and the lower part, south of Hanuman Dhoka, as *Kwon*. Kantipur is yet another name given to it in more present times as is evidenced in, among other things, the writings of Bhanubhakta, popularly known as the father of Nepali literature (19 century).

Patan, another sister-city in the valley, (currently known in administrative parlance as Lalitpur) is believed to be a derivative of Lalit Pattan, afterwards abbreviated as Patan Another ancient name given to it was Yupagram (in the Lichchhavi period), while the popular Newari name *Yala* by which it is referred to by the locals, also points to its possible association, as a capital, with the *Kiratis,* the most ancient historically known rulers of the Kathmandu valley. The word Yala itself, in turn, could be an abbreviation of

Yalambar, one of the more notable Kirati kings (3rd century A.D.), who may have laid the foundations of Yambu and Yangwal as well.

Bhadgaon or Bhaktapur (literally, The City Of Devotees'), in its turn, is known in local parlance as *Khwapu*. Knowledgeable sources aver that this is a derivative of Khopring, itself again a possible Kirati word.

Slightly beyond the ancient Bhaktapur principality lies another better-known settlement, Banepa, known in earlier times as Bhonta (Bhotay?) in Newari. One explanation given to this term is that it denoted a major stop-over and supply centre for travellers and caravans passing to and from Kathmandu and Tibet (also known, to the majority of Nepalese, as "Bhot").

Similar explanation is given to the term Sankhu, yet another township to the north of Kathmandu, from where also caravans used to take off for Tibet. The prefix "Saa", it is said, stands for Tibet. Both these townships, it is also held, could have been named after the many mongoloid settlers in the northern high-hill Nepal belt, including the Kiratis, who are sometimes referred to by the Kathmanduites as Parbatays or Bhotays, thus possibly indicating that both Banepa and Sankhu used to be the strongholds of non-Newar, high-hill tribes till late in history.

If the *Kastha Mandap* (literally, a 'Wooden Shrine' or Holy platform), a 66-feet square by 65.4 feet high shrine-cum-rest house at the heart of Kathmandu, was built out of the timber of a single tree, Kirtipur, another of the earliest fortified settlements in the Valley and a separate principality till as late as the Malla rule, was, in its turn, believed to have been originally built out of the stone of a single boulder ! But, unlike that of Kathmandu, the ancient names given to Kirtipur do not go to support the contention of its being the product of a 'single boulder'. On the other hand, the terms Padma Kastha Puri ("City of Lotus Timber") or Madhyam Kastha Giri (Middle Hill of

Wooden Timber?), as it was said to be known in ancient days, clearly indicate its origin as a 'timber-city' rather than a boulder-born one. It was also known in earlier days as Bar Gad, possibly meaning a fortified citadel.

Another very ancient pilgrimage centre in the Kathmandu valley, known for, among other things, some rare inscriptions dating back to the Lichhavi times, is the Changu Narayan near Sankhu. This shrine, it is said, was referred to in earlier days as, the "Dola Sikhara Swami"(or the 'Lord of the Dola Hill-top') and also Champaka Narayan. The first name obviously refers to the 1540 m. high Dolagiri or Doladri hillock after which the Sankhu settle ment was also said to be known,and the second to the fact that it was possibly built out of *Champak* timber.

Lastly, the famous "Buddhist Sphinx" or Bodhnath temple is perhaps the single most multi-epitheted monument in the Kathmandu valley. Said to have been originally built by a Lichchhavi king Shiva Deva, it must have been rebuilt or renovated upteen number of times. While romantic nick-names such as the "Temple of Dew Drops" have their own legendary backing behind them, some other names that have been given to it at different times or by different communities include Khasti or Khasha Chaitya, Mahakal Chaitya, Khash Chibaha, Khasa Tirtha, Jhyamung Khasgor Chhorten, Thasu Chhen and, of course, Bauddha !

And how about "Bhaayal"? Many a Tibetan record, it is said, has often referred to Nepal as Bhaayul (possibly meaning the Land of Garuda) and Bhutan as "Druk-Yul" or the Dragon-country !

The Simplest Divorce ?

Divorce, it is often claimed, is a Western innovation. It may, therefore, come as a news to many that Nepal not only has some of the world's simplest traditional divorce-procedures, but also that some such procedures had actually been codified into a law at least a hundred and forty years ago! King Surendra Bikram Shah's *Muluki Ain* (Legal Code), 1853 A.D., is an instance in point. But more about it later.

The common word for divorce in Nepal is *paar paachuke*, or simply *paachuke*. Some hill communities also call it *Sinko-paango*, which perhaps indicates that a divorce can be as simple as snapping a Sinko or tiny twig! Amongst the Limbus of eastern Nepal, divorce from the husband's side is known as Khemjong and that from the wife's as Naajong. Many other hill communities like the Newars, Gurungs, Sherpas and Tamangs also take a couple's right to obtain divorce for granted, and not much fuss is made over it. Amongst the Terai people, the Satars are particularly known for securing a divorce by simply making a token payment known as pon, or price. A satar wife, for instance, can return an amount equivalent to the *pon* (bride-price) she may have recieved from the groom at the time of wedding. In case the initiative for divorce comes from the husband's side, he has to pay the wife double the *pon* amount. It's as simple as that !

Even simpler, in the sense that it involves no financial burden, is the Newari custom. A Newar wife, for instance, can customarily walk out of a wedlock by simply slipping, under her husband's pillow, some split betel-nuts and sullking away from his house ! Is it not as simple as, if not simpler than, uttering the word "Talaak" thrice under the Muslim law ? What is even more remarkable is that a Newar husband, in his turn, doesn't seem to enjoy a similar privilege !

What has thus been an ancient tradition-- how much ancient it is difficult to determine-- received a legal recognition, as mentioned above, in the year 1853. There are nine different clauses enshrined in the Legal Code made in that year, 7 of which are as follows :

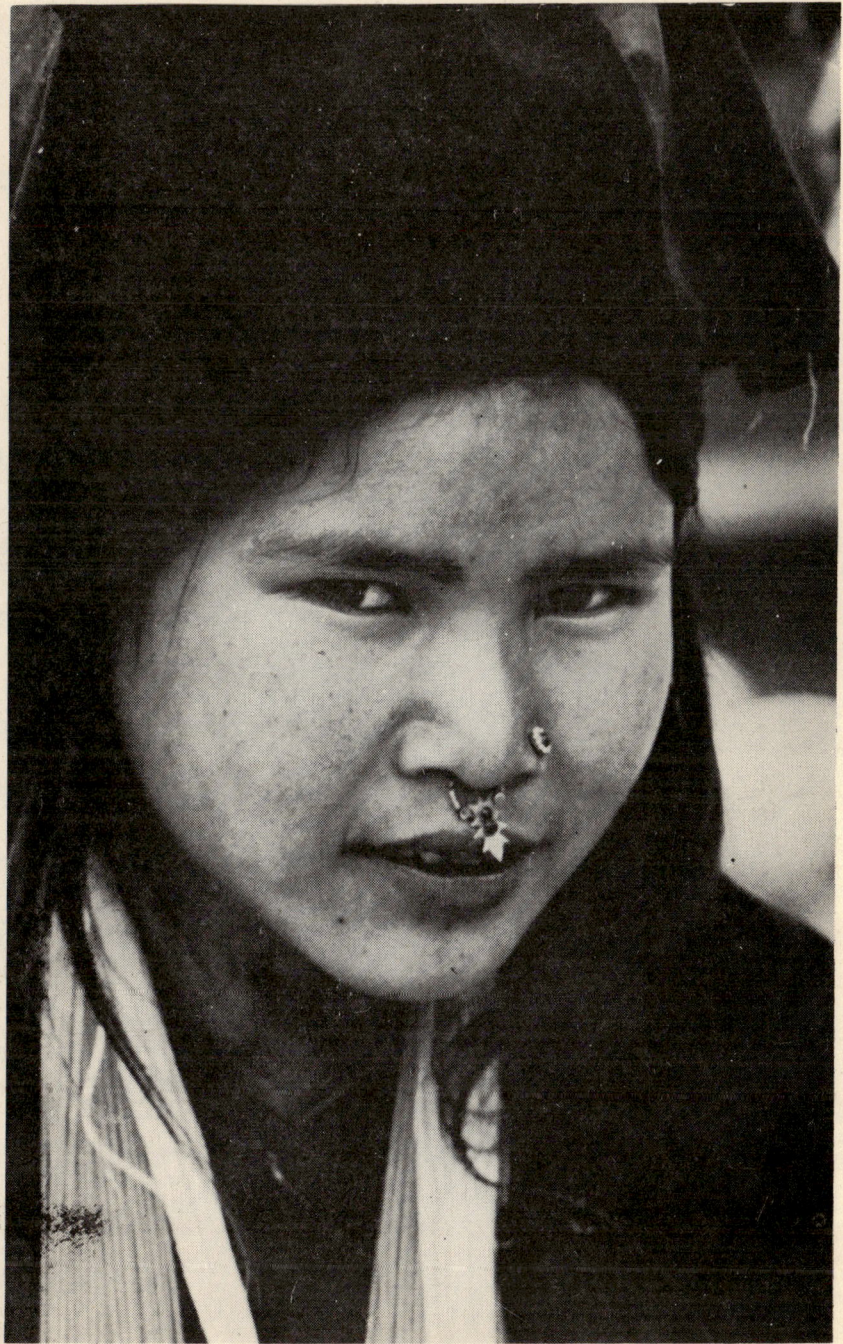

Photo by *Yeti Photos Centre*

Photo by Yeti Photos Centre

Photo by *Laxman Shrestha*

1. If a Newar woman, on being left at home for long periods by her husband without making adequate arrangement for her upkeep during the period of his absence, or on her being made to stay at her parental home for three years after marriage, or on her being left behind when he opts for settlement elsewhere, lodges a complaint to the effect that she no longer wants to remain his wife, the concerned authority shall grant her a divorce forthwith !

2. Likewise, if a Newar woman, on being left alone by her husband who is convicted of a crime and is fleeing from the law as a result, comes to the court and expresses a desire that she no longer wants to remain his wife, she shall be granted a divorce.

3. In the event of a Newar husband "keeping" another woman in addition to the legally married one, or on his driving the latter from his residence or neglecting her as a consequence of his being enamoured of a prostitute, the concerned court, on receiving the wife's complaint to the effect, shall grant her a divorce .

4. If a Newar husband becomes a *fakir* (ascetic) or "loses his caste", no divorce proceedings are even called for and the woman's parents can have her married elsewhere without inviting criminal punishment for so doing.

5. If a Newar wife complains that her husband is the victim of an incurable disease, or is lame, dumb, blind or otherwise impotent, the concerned court shall grant her a divorce; the husband cannot force her to live with him against her will.

6. A Newar married woman shall not "return the betel-nuts" and walk out of a wedlock simply on the ground that her husband is seriously ill; nor shall a Newar husband be granted a divorce on the mere ground that his wife is under the "cast of evil stars"; the "returning of betel-nuts" by a wife during her husband's illness shall be nullified by law and the concerned court shall return her to the custody of the said husband.

7. The '*dastur* (court fee) payable by a Newar woman on her being granted a divorce on the aforesaid grounds "shall be Rupee One; no larger amount shall be charged," etc.

The progressive liberalism as reflected in the above and such other provisions, can be matched with that of the Newar ancients who also invented and developed suitable social institutions that guaranteed, right from the beginning, a young man or woman's inherent right to freedom in matters such as divorce. The well known institution of "*Ihi*" is an instance in point.

Must we, therefore, continue to suffer from a 'backwardness' complex in every sphere of life ? I dare say no !

Lifestyles

CHAPTER FIVE

'Mityaari'

To say that ours is a culture which imparts divinity to every single living being is an understatement. In fact, our ancestors, who were little aware that trees or plants had a 'life' in the modern sense of the term, nevertheless saw divinity in them too, as is evident in their tree-worship and other ritulas.

The *Bar* (Banyan) tree was, for them, the incarnation of Vishnu; so was *tulsi* or the Basil plant. The *Peepul* tree, in its turn, was an incarnation of Lakshmi, the goddess of wealth. Why, even inaminate things like stones didn't fail to receive their share of worship or oblations.

The concept of the *Aatmaa*, when it meant the 'self', resulted in worshipping one's own body, as highlighted in rituals like the Newari *Mha Pujaa* and, the same term, used in a broader sense as the 'soul', would regard even the minutest form of life, such as an insect, as a divine being, worthy of respect--nay, of outright worship too!

No wonder, therefore, that the Nepalese see divine virtue even in the simple act of striking a friendship--and make a religious ritual out of it. A ritual friendship so established is known as the *Mityaari* and the person with whom this relationship is struck is known as the *Mit*. By extension, the parents of the *mit* are, not unlike one's own parents, known as *Mit Babu* and *Mit Amaa*, (meaning *Mit* father and *Mit* mother respectively), the ritual friend's elder brother is a *Mit Dai* and his or her younger sister is a *Mit Bahini*, etc. And so on its goes.

A *Mit* is also known as a *Saina*, particularly when a ritual friendship is established between women or girls. In the villages, where the *Mityaari* relationship is common, a man or woman can have as many *Mits* and *Mitinis* (female *Mits*) as one would like or could afford to have. For, establishing a *Mityaari* friendship isn't just a matter of striking acquaintance or intimacy. It is much more than that and calls for a religious ritual, a celebration, a feast and exchange of gifts !

If two persons, often of the same age and sex, decide to become one another's *Mit*, they go through most of the processes that are called for in organising a holy ceremony like a *Pujaa*. Other friends and relatives are asked to join the celebration; a goat, a chicken or a duck is sacrificed; and delicacies distributed amongst all of those present. Some gifts are also exchanged as mementoes. And, much like in wedlock, the tail-ends of one another's gar ments may be tied into a ritual knot, while, if *Mityaari* is established between women, the long tresses of their hair are joined together to form a common plait, as a part of the ceremonial ritual.

Establishing a *Mityaari* is not without its obligations too. One may not, for instance, address one's *Mit* by name. The death of a *Mit* calls for a ritual mourning, much as one would mourn a death in the family. If one's custom calls for the touching of a parent's feet in salutation, a *Mit*-parent may not be treated differently either.

The uninitiated may not immediately realise how utterly signifi cant this otherwise simple ritual of 'touching the feet' is. The rural Nepalese community is highly castecompartmentalised into the *Taagaadharis*, the *Matawaalis*, the *Achhuts* and the like. The first- named are the wearers of the holy threads and form the highest strata of society -- they cannot even sit at the same table with the latter categories when it comes to partaking of food such as rice. And the last-named, the so-called 'untouchables', are even expected to side-step along a trail when they accost the higher-echelon Hindus lest they come into physical contact and 'pollute' the latter !

Seen against this orthodox social backdrop, the institution of the *Mityaari* must be regarded not only as a 'great level ler' or 'unifier'. For, a *Mit* need not belong to one's own caste or social strata. A *Bahun* (priest class) youth can strike a *Mityaari* with a *Matawaali* (the liquor-drinking, and, by implication, a lower caste) counterpart on almost 'equal' terms. The concept of the Mityaari, therefore, is nothing short of revolutionary !

That the *Mityaari* has come in handy in commercial and even diplomatic relationships is evident. In the Nepalese countryside, for instance, it is not unusual to find a tradesman building up his 'empire' based on *Mityaari* contacts with more than one local bigwig or influence-peddler at a time. And, in politics, king Prithvi Narayan Shah, Nepal's great unifier, had a *Mit* in the person of king Ranjit Malla of Bhadgaon that helped smooth his conquest right up to the Kuti pass, the north ern limits of the then Bhadgaon 'empire'. One can imagine that the history of Nepal wouldn't have been what it is, but for the bond of intimacy provided by Prithvi Narayan's statesmanlike *Mityaari* with the Bhadgaon royal household !

How Many Husbands ?

Those that have regarded as curious the story of five Pandava brothers married to one Draupadi, will find this mythological story re-lived in parts of mountainous Nepal this day. For, over a large area of the Nepal Himalayas, fraternal polyandry is as much a reality today as are the Himalayas themselves. In this sort of polyandry, the wife comes to live with a group of brothers in their house, as distinguished from the matriarchal type, where she remains in her own house and the husbands come to live with her by turn as casual visitors. Property under the fraternal polyandry, in its turn, passes from father to son and not, as in the case of the other type, down the uterine line.

Among the Dolpos, for instance, brothers usually marry a common wife, no matter what the number of brothers be. In some cases, even two friends have been seen living with a common wife. The Manangbas, another tribe that has got its name from the Manang Bhot area in north-west Nepal, practise polyandry too.

The Sherpas, famous the world over as sturdy mountain-climbers, present a slight variation in theme in the sense that, amongst them, just two brothers, not more, marry a joint wife; if there are four bothers, the third and fourth may take a second joint wife.

Interestingly, two such brothers go out together in the same wedding procession and take part in the rituals, thereby establishing equal rights over the wife and the parental property.

The Rais of eastern Nepal practice what in technical jargon is known as junior levirate and junior sorrorate, that is, a Rai young man may marry his elder brother's widow, his deceased wife's younger sister or his wife's brother's daughter. A Satar or a Dhimal youngman of Nepal's eastern Terai isn't averse to marrying the elder brother's widow either; while, in the case of the Sherpas, younger brothers would consider it a matter of birthright, so would a young damsel lay claim to the hand of her deceased elder sister's husband. And, in the latter case, should the widower have some other girl in view as his second spouse, the formality of a permission of his younger sister-in-law must needs be met.

The Baragaunle people living between Mustang and Thak regions in north-western Nepal also practise polyandry, but, in their case, only the eldest brother need go through the formalities of mar riage, his younger brothers joining in later as they come of age.

Freedom in the choice of mates is taken for granted in many a Nepalese tribe. In order that a suitable environment be created for the purpose, the Gurungs of western Nepal have devised a unique institution--the *Rodi Ghar* which, in other words, means a village youngsters' club.

Young girls of marriageable age, attending such 'clubs' after their daily chores are over, may even make a night-long affair of their repartee with the visiting young men, generally under the surveillance of elderly club-keepers or leaders known as *chivas,* the girls generally providing liquors and other delicacies and the boys helping defray the expenses.

If the Buddhist community, for example in the Tenang village, even go to the extent of organising the annual festival of *dyokyapsi,* in autumn, where it is virtually incumbent for their young girls and boys of marriageable age to spend five nights at a stretch together, the affairs the participants may have had on such occasions hardly, if ever, prejudice the pros pects of their future marriage with somebody else !

"Unhampered by the trammels of caste", writes a well-known authority on Nepal after observing such amusing practices, "the Gurkha women of the hill districts enjoy a greater measure of freedom than is allowed to their sisters in the Indian plains, and they are able to take an interest in life and what's going on around them in a manner more approximating to that of the women of Europe".

Some Mores and Manners

There are certain customs and manners that the faithful consider as bearing enough religious merits, if not also salutary benefits. And perhaps it is time we cast a more than cursory look into some of the so-called superstitious customs and try to ascertain if it is mere orthodoxy, ignorance or blind faith that has been sustaining them, after all.

An instance that comes readily to mind is the ancestral taboo imposed against sweeping houses after nightfall. But it stands to reason that some tiny yet valuable items that may have fallen on the floors could unwittingly be swept off in the dark --and hence the taboo. The fact that one could conveniently overlook such tiny items--like a useful needle, for example--in areas denied of modern electricity-fed brightness (which is the rule rather than an exception in our part of the world) makes it especially mean ingful for us to desist from sweeping the floors after nightfall, no ?

Our ancestral tradition of taking off footwears--even clothes in many *Bahun* (priestly) households--before we enter the kitchen to partake of food is another instance in point. It is not for nothing that our ancestors enjoined us to don a freshly laundered *Dhoti* or at least to remove the work-a-day ensembles as also to thoroughly wash our hands and feet before we squat down--crosslegged and on *pirkaas* placed on the kitchen-floor -- to eat. Is it difficult to appreciate that a simple sense of hygiene demands that we observe such practices ?

Our elders never entered their homes unwashed and unbathed, on returning from funerals. The simple logic behind the idea of taking a bath on such occasions could not have been anything but to help rid us of any infection we may have contacted while accompanying a corpse to the funeral grounds. Additionally, they also made it a point to stand over a bunch of fuming *titte-paati* leaves placed at the threshholds or at cross-roads on the return journey from a funeral procession. That the *titte-paati* juice often comes in handy as an antiseptic or a blood-coagulant when we have minor cuts and bleeding sores, is known to many. The idea, per haps therefore, was that burnt *titte-paati* leaves could help disinfect people as they passed through the ritual of inhal ing the fumes!

Be it a *Bada Dashain* or *Diwali*, a Full Moon day or a New Moon one, a child-birth or a death in the family or whatever, the custom is to smear house floors with a *gobar* (cow-dung) paste. What's more, a sip of *gomutra*, premixed with a pinch of cow-dung, is even believed to ritually purify us on many a 'polluted' occasion. These customs are regarded by many as unhygienic and, therefore, abhorrent. Yet, a recent write-up suggests that fresh cow-dung contains a large proportion of vitamin B-12 which, it is said, is essential for maintaining normal health of the humans—especially because deficiency of this vitamin produces a pernicious type of anaemia. If so, one would perhaps be justified in saying that our forefathers wanted to be fortified with small doses of vitamin B-12, either in the shape of the *gawoont* or *gobar.*

It is again an age-old tradition in Nepal to wear some sort of a *topi* (cap) or *pheta* (turban) particularly when out-doors. Even if such traditions are increasingly being given a go-by in cities, they persist in the rural areas. But there is an increasing evidence in favour of wearing such headgear in order to provide an effective canopy that acts as a protection against sun-stroke, particularly if one works in the farms and fields during the day-time.

Why do our elders enjoin us to sleep with our legs pointing towards the north or the south, but not east and the west? One traditional explanation is that *Yama* or the Lord of Death is said to reside in the north. But some probes, seemingly car ried out by scien tists, go to suggest that there is ample justification to support this practice too.

"The human body", reads the write-up above-referred,"contains iron and if all of it is collected in one place, it could be wrought into two large nails. It is a known fact that, if an iron rod or a nail is hung north-south in the geomagnetic field for a long time, it automatically attains magnetic properties..."

It is said that the value of magnets in curing many of our physical ailments was known to the ancient Greeks and Egyptians as well. Why, even the famous Cleopatra is said to have perennially sported a *tika* on her forehead, which, it is believed, was nothing but a tiny magnet and was instrumental in helping her maintain the beauty of face and figure that have become so legendary.

Do our traditions of sleeping north-south or of wearing a *tika* assume a new meaning and significance in view of these scientific findings? If so, could there be more than meets the eye in these 'meaningless' manners?

A Requiem for Customs !

Of many ancient customary 'signs' of Hinduism that we have learnt to leave without, the most noticeable is perhaps, the missing *Tupi*! Called the 'pigtail' by westerners for lack of a more appropriate and better term, it was, even as late as some two decades back, the sign and symbol of orthodox Brahminism *par excellence*. One would even be tempted to compare it with an epaullette or a shoulder-star worn by a soldier or policeman as a certificate of having made the grade !

Another close cousin of *Tupi*, also conspicuous by its present-day absence, is the moustache--be it of the handlebar variety or of the walrus one! Yet, alas, time was when only parentless youngmen were allowed to go around *sans* the moustache!

Little do we come across, too, people who sport a gold-foiled tooth. One is constrained to say that this is also another evidence of our generation having moved further away from our religion--or from the fear of having to land in hell. For, the precise reason why most Nepali predecessors favoured the practice was that, somehow, gold had come to be associated with an 'eman cipator' of sorts. The belief of yesteryear being that a dying man or woman needed to be 'fed' with gold-washed water as a safe guarantee to a passage to heaven, and with a golden tooth already inside one's mouth, a mere dropping of water on top of it was the most leak-proof guarantee to ensure his or her safe transcendence heaven-wards !

Of course, we no longer bother whether a Bahun or a Chhetry en twines his holy thread, the *Janai*, around his ear while on his way to attend a call of nature. Why this is so, is obvious— most houses, at least in the urban areas, are equipped with toilets that ensure adequate privacy.

Cigarettes are also a twenty-first century innovation, at least in 'official' Nepal, which is already in the year 2048 that is, at least 57 years ahead of the westerners. The great social leveller of the yesteryear was the *Hookah* (again, for lack of a better expression, the westerners call it the hubble-bubble!) or the *Kakkad* that used to be passed around for a puff, at least among equals.

What about soaps? We were used to the *Rithaa* fruits, the ash and the *Kamero* clay! Of course, they were much more effective than the present-day soaps at least in so far as killing the lice was concerned. Boil the garments along with *Kharani* (fuelwood ash) and the lice have not a chance! But, the soap-invasion has marred any such prospect, alas!

As you may have read in most of yesteryear's accounts of Nepal of course penned by the 'perplexed foreigner-- the Nepalese hardly locked their doors when away from houses. That we owe to the Tibetans the practice of locking our doors is evident from the fact that locks we first used--the oncethat most of our rural people use to this day-- are known as the *Bhotay Taal chaas*, meaning "Tibetan Locks", of course! Have you ever seen their enormous sizes? They are just to be seen to be believed!

Our ancestors would simply have laughed at 'contraptions' like the Dairy Development Corporation. For, to them, selling of milk was a sin against god! By implication, the selling or buying of a milch-cow or a milch buffalo was a taboo too!

Did we have matchsticks? Of course not! Every household had an *Agenaa* (a fireplace) which kept on smouldering the whole day and night--for fuelwood was aplenty. Raising a new fire involved a mere reviving of the semi burnt-out embers, not a re kindling of new fire. In case the fire was extinguished in our own house, the neighbours were more than willing--and ready--to lend you a burning ember. So, where was the necessity of a match stick?

Now, to conclude, let's dwell upon salt. Those were the days when we sang in praise of "*Bhotako Nuna, Lhasako Suna*", meaning thereby that both our salts and gold came from Tibet. Indian salt was known as 'Saabari' (remember) Mahatma Gandhi's Sabar Dardi 'anti-salt' movement?), but Saabari salt was meant for animal consumption alone!

A 'Picnic' Month

Traditionally, the month of *Mangshir* (November-December) is also a 'picnic' month for the Nepalese hillfolk. Why a particular month in a year should be so specified and why most people should make it a point to go for routine and organised group-- outings during these 30-odd days may appear curious, if not intriguing.

For one thing, *Mangshir* or *Maargashirsha,* in an cient times, was regarded as the first month in the Hindu calen dar year. Otherwise also known as *Agrahaayan* (the Terai people still refer to it as *Agahan*), it literally stands for the First Month (*Agra* preceding, *Haayan* month.) It is not for nothing that Lord Krishna, while referring to his various personal attributes, says in the *Geeta*: "Among the months. I am the *Maargashirsha*".

It is often said that the Hindus are guided by the Lunar calendar as far as their religious observances are concerned. We have, for instance, our *Aunshis* (new-moon nights) and *Purnimaas* (full moon nights), our *Shuklapakshas* (bright fortnights) and *Krishnapakshas* (dark fortnights), etc., that guide us throughout the year.

But, a more than cursory glance at our ancestral practices will make it abundantly clear that the solar calendar had been as much in vogue in the olden times as the lunar one. Only that, while the lunar calendar -- year started with the festival of Lakshmi *Puja* (otherwise also known as *Diwaali* or *Ti haar*), the solar one started from the month of *Chait* or *Chaitra* (March-April).

It is also of interest to note that the *Vikrama* Era or *Samvat* (the Nepalese official calendar) used to mark its beginning with the *Lakshmi Puja* day (in the fall) itself, unlike, as in the present, with the First of *Baisaakh* (April-May). The calendar year beginning in *Chaitra* was the *Saka Sam vat*.

Another point worth mentioning here is that, it was often the *Amaavashyaas* (Aunshis) that marked the completion of a particular month, and not the *Purnimaas*. The months were thus known as Amantas (literally meaning ending in *Ama*, or *Aunshi*).

That the completion of the dark fortnight on the *Lakshmi Puja* day also heralds the beginning of the first month of the follow ing calendar - year is also evidenced from the way *Tihaar* is celebrated in many Hindu communities. For the Newars, for in stance, it is the New Year's

Day, as is familiar to anyone living in Kathmandu and its suburbs. The Marwadi and Bengali tradesmen also close their annual business accounts on this day and start operating new ledger books, befitting a New Year's Day.

"Ringing out the old, ringing in the new", is a common-enough saying in the West. Church bells, ringing in the midnight, pro nounce the advent of the new year elsewhere in the world. People in Nepal say it with *Deepawali* (Festival of Lamps), the bursting of crackers, and the like.

Are these New-Year festivities limited to the living ? It seems not. For, judging by what goes on in many households during the month of *Kaartika*, one would imagine the heavenly deities and ancestors also make a beeline to the Land of the Living in order to witness the mirth and merry-making. The tradition of lighting *Aakaash Deeps* (literally, 'Sky- Lamps') is an instance in point.

These sky-lamps are often colourful festooned paper-box lanterns hung a top long bamboo poles placed on house-tops. It is said that these lamps which are oil-fed and lit every evening, serve as sign-posts for the dear departeds to locate their erstwhile earthly abodes as they descend from the heavens ! This phenomenon of *Aakaash Deep* is fairly popular in Kathmandu, too, to this day.

That these festivites should coincide with the months of *Kaartika* and *Mangshir* is understandable otherwise too. For this is also the paddy-harvesting time, a time when the granaries are full, when the year-long toils in the fields are over--a time to rejoice.

In fact, the word *Lakshmi* ('Goddess of Wealth') aptly conjures up memories of the bountiful Mother Earth. Lakshmi, according to the *Rig Veda,* resides in the cow-dung, which, in turn, is the principal organic fertiliser that ensures better harvests. It stands to reason, therefore, that the Nepalese have set apart two days in the 5-day long

Tihaar festival for the worship of the 'dung-giving' mother-cow and the bull-- the latter, incidentally, being the farmer's principal aide in ploughing the fields.

The *Tihaar* festivities over, what next ? The time now is, of course, ripe for outings and community-feasting! What's more, this is a season of "mellow fruitfulness"-- with the trees laden with guavas, citrus fruits, persimmons and what have you-- and relaxation. It is appropriate, then, that the Nepalese have set aside a whole month--the month of *Mangshir*--for picnics!

Women Wedded To Gods

We hear of beautiful women consecrated to ancient Babylonian temples in order "to entertain the gods", probably by indulging in erotic activities, besides other chores. The custom was also prevalent in ancient Greece, Rome and Egypt.

The ancient Hindu religious scriptures, in their turn, are replete with references to the *Devadasis* or temple-maids. *Padma Purana*, in which the earliest reference to this institution is found, avers that "one who offers a beautiful woman to god at tains heaven for one full *Kalpa* (43,20,00,000 years)". While the *Bhavishya Purana* prescribes similar virtues of such consecration of women to the Sun-God, the *Shiva Purana* categorically states that temples to Shiva should be provided, among other things, with hundreds of beautiful girls proficient in the art of singing, dancing and entertainment.

But these are tales of a long bygone era. To see, therefore an institution of the *Deokis* existing to this day in some villages of remote Baitadi, Dadeldhura and, to some extent, Doti, Salyan, Humla and Jumla districts in western Nepal is a curious spectacle indeed. Like their *Devadasi* counterparts in some South Indian temples (such girls, curiously enough, being absent in the north-Indian ones), these young "hand-maids of gods" in these areas are consecrated to temple-service which normally includes dancing, fanning the idols on ceremonial occasions and other related activities. But the remuneration they receive in return calls for supplemental income by being too meagre, and the sale of favours either to affluent local people or visiting devotees comes in handy, particularly since they aren't supposed to marry, at any rate not permanently, or seek succour elsewhere, for fear of divine wrath.

Often dedicated to the village deities by promise of the parents even before they are born, their ranks are also said to be largely increased at times by other means; the reported case of an aged *Deoki* having kidnapped a village-girl in order to procure a successor and a maintenance may be cited as a typical example of modern-day defilement of this 'sacred' institution.

A Nepalese researcher in anthropology would have us believe, following a survey of the Baitadi region, that this institution, otherwise alien to the Nepalese social milieu, found a foothold in the country during the heyday of the Ranas who ruled Nepal for an unbroken spell of 104 years till 1950. The roadless and climatically unkind regions of Nepal hills, especially in the western districts, posed a peren nial administrative problem in the absence of willing civil servants for postings there. Elderly personnel would abhor the prospects of such postings, while nothing in those remote areas would sufficiently allure the youthful officials; the possibility of their families accompanying them or of their rejoining their wives or children back home for months, if not years, at a stretch, was ruled out. The invention, or rather the import, of this institution, therefore, was possibly a clever ruse of the Ranas in collusion with religious leaders of the day.

Others would ascribe the prevalence of this custom to the emigration, into these areas, of the displaced Hindu potentates and their courtesans from north India following the advent of the Muslim rule. And with feudals like the Chands and the Pals of western Nepal still tracing their ancestry to the erstwhile Rajput nobles, an atmosphere favouring a fertile transplantation into Nepal of this institution from elsewhere may be said to have existed a few centuries ago.

Many are the examples, holds the researcher, of young government officials of yester-year who, after having accepted postings in these areas, found this institution enthralling enough to virtually forget their families back home for long years--to the utter relief of their Rana bosses ! Not a few actually kept these *Deokis* as concubines and settled there for life.

The affluent amongst Nepalese would fulfil their promises -- made during an emergency to propitiate local divinities -- by buying off girls from poorer families of the localities and sending them to local shrines as promised offerings. The indigent would offer their own off-springs.

With instances of *Deokis* having settled into a married life later or, more often, as concubines of the wealthy set, they have, over the years, earned an acceptability in society. What's more, their apparent affluence as reflected in resplendent dress es and finery befitting their vocation, also earn for them a certain respectability amongst a generally poverty-ridden popu lance.

Deokaas, the male offspring of unmarried *Deokis*, could adopt any vocation, but daughters generally followed their mothers' mode of life and were called *Deokis* from their very childhood, whether consecrated to any divinity or not. Both, however, were denied paternal inheritance, should the male par entage be known.

A 1950 law banning this institution has been effective in gradu ally relegating it to past memory. However, religious instincts, traditions and superstitions die hard in a backward country like Nepal and especially in the more backward areas like Baitadi and Doti. As such, a whole village full of *Deokis* in Dadeldhu ra was reported as late as in 1970. And the census - enumerators, it is said, have found it a standing puzzle whether the *Deokis* be entered as married -- by virtue of their be trothal to the temple-deities -- or just as spinsters !

How Do You Do ?

In the West, taking off your hat is a public display of private respect. In Nepal, accosting a superior with a head bereft of a cap is, to the contrary, a sign of great disrespect. Here then, once again, never the twain may meet!

Again, unlike in the West, the traditionally stratified Nepalese society has allowed itself the Luxury of numberless forms of greeting applicable to a person in a variety of circumstances or to different people under similar circumstances.

By virtue of their position at the apex of the caste-hierarchy, the Brahmans literally make the rural folk touch their feet with their foreheads, while the former condescendingly grant the favour of taking off their shoes or raise one leg after another for the benefit of their 'parishioners'! This mode of salutation is generally accompanied by expressions *Paulagi* (May I be allowed to touch your feet). *Ashirvad*, the Brahman priest may retort, and this roughly answers to the English "God Bless You".

A more familiar scene these days would be to see people slightly bowing their head forward to meet the extended hands of the Brahman priests. While touching the head of the *Jajaman* (client) thus, the Brahman keeps the palm partially open and upturned; for superstition has it that the palm of a Brahman exudes fire and he intentionally upturns it so as to avert the possibility of his devotee going up in flames !

Unlike certain Indian societies, notably the Bengali, Nepalese women are not expected to touch the feet of their elder men-folk except those of their husbands. Public kissing too is a taboo, even by way of a greeting, and even when only women are involved.

Some of the Tibeto-Mongoloid people in the high hills stick out their tongues when accosting a superior personage. This, it is said, is purported to mean that they bear no evil designs against such a person and that their intentions are as clean as their sticking-out tongues!

Get off your horse-back or *Woling kath* (palanquin), you idiot, whenever you accost a person of higher status, socially or castewise, is the lesson a Nepalese child learns early in life. And if he comes from a socalled 'untouchable' caste, he even learns to "get off" the road itself so that his shadow may not fall on the socially superior souls!

The menial classes also raise a cupped hand in salutation accompanied by the word *Jadau*, meaning "May my lord be victorious".

I couldn't say if it is a legacy of his fire-worshipping culture, but we see that a Nepalese hardly forgets to salute even a lamp when it is lit, irrespective of whether it is a candlelight, a kerosene lamp or even an electric one! If a group of people are sitting together in the evening and a lamp is lit, the practice is to first "Namaskar" the lamp, followed by exchange of similar salutations amongst one another.

Where the Twain does meet, however, is in considering it in bad taste to turn one's back upon a guest or a visitor. In extreme cases, a Nepalese may even, while leaving the presence of a great personage, walk backwards until he or she is out of the latter's immediate presence. Similarly, it is a great rarity to see a servant, when accompanying his master, be it on foot or on horseback, going ahead of him, except when specifically ordered.

While custom demands that married women, particularly amongst Brahmans and Chhetris, either pull down a veil or cover their heads with the *sari* when they accost elderly men from the husband's household, it wouldn't be considered anything but extreme politeness even if they turn their backs on such men ! Here is a case, however, of an exception proving the rule !

For the Dear Departeds

If it is the soul that leaves the body of a man when he dies, the Satars of south-eastern Nepal, an aboriginal tribe, believe that it literally needs some suitable exits. So, when a family-member is breathing his last, they keep all their doors and windows open to facilitate the soul an unhindered passage to heaven!

The Rais of eastern Nepal, in their turn, lose no time in slaughtering a chicken as soon as there is death in the family, the sex of the bird being determined by that of the deceased person. Some feathers plucked from its wings are then placed underneath the dead man's armpits; ostensibly to help him fly smoothly to heaven !

Noise, on the other hand, becomes synonymous with a Newar funeral in Kathmandu valley, where the tendency appears to be to collect as many persons as possible to keep on wailing and crying as the hearse is borne to the site of cremation. The *Guthiars* (members of a traditional co-operative institution, *Guthi*) come in handy on such occasions--attendance by member-families being obligatory. But even otherwise "professional" mourners are cheaper by the dozen!

Some Gurung's of mid-western Nepal consider a metal- preferably a gold or silver coin-- a must, along with some food and liquor, to be put on the mouth and chest of the dead person before the grave is filled. Those who cremate do so in a hollow, round structure built with holes near the bottom from which firewood can be thrust.

Pa-ye, the final Gurung rite for the dead, is performed any time up to a year following death. It consists of making an effigy of white cloth on bamboo sticks, 3 feet long. This effigy is draped with gold ornaments and is known as *pla*, represent ing the dead person. The *Ghyabre* or priest addresses the spirit of the dead that is thus ritually sent to heaven.

The relatively longish interval between death and *pa-ye* may give an occasion for the dead man's spirit to trouble the surviving members of the family, should the latter fail to erect a small shrine up on the hill and regularly offer food and liquor to the spirit. This shrine is pulled down after *pa-ye* is completed, as the spirit is then supposed to retire to *langsa* (heaven).

While the *pa-ye* is being conducted, the members of the family tie the *pla* effigy to one end of a rope, while the other end is taken outside the house to the courtyard and tied to a lamb. The sex of the lamb must be the same as that of the deceased person. The lamb is fed during the service and finally taken to a crossroad of the village for ritual slaughter.

Animal sacrifice is also the Chepang's way of appeasing the dead, the number and variety of sacrificial four-footeds acting as a status-symbol.

"On one occasion", reports an expert, "the village headman sacri ficed six goats, one buffalo and five chickens at the funeral of his wife. The six goats and 5 chickens were gifts brought by the headman's sisters and daughters. The headman, in return, gave them gifts at the end of the day."

The Dhimals of Jhapa display a sound practicality by burying the dead during rainy season and cremating them during the dry months!

For the Dhimals, as also the Dhangars of eastern Terai, death pollution lasts for 12 days and is terminated by shaving the heads of all the males and cutting the nails of all the immediate female relatives.

In Dolpo, a district in north-western mountainous Nepal, the body of the dear departeds may lovingly be thrown into the river or cut into small pieces to feed the vultures.

The Tamangs of eastern Nepal would have their dead once sit cross-legged and upright, have them put in huge cauldron-like metal containers, and have them carried to the cremation ground amidst chanting of Lamaist hymns, beating of gongs and blowing of trumpets. A feast may follow at the cremation ground itself, while the corpse burns in a nearby *pyre*.

The Tharus, a plains people, bury their dead face down in case of a man and face up in the case of a woman. For cremation the dead body is liberally smeared with clarified *ghee* (butter) before it is put on the *pyre*.

The twain--east and west--will not meet, we said elsewhere while discussing Nepalese modes of solutations. If black is the colour of mourning in the west, in Nepal it is white--and here too will not the twain ever meet !

Till Death Doth Us Part

"... as Jonathan, with desperate energy, attacked one end of the chest, attempting to prize off the lid with his great *Khukri* knife, he (Mr. Morris) attacked the other (end of the chest) frantically with his bowie...

"... on the instant, came the sweep and flash of Jonathan's great knife. I shrieked as I saw it shear through the throat (of Dracula); whilst the same moment Mr. Morris's bowie knife plunged into the heart"

---

* A Passage from Bram Stoker's celebrated horrorfication describing Dracula's end.

The setting: a partly real, and mostly magical obscurity of a nineteenth century Europe-- a village where wierd-witchcraft found a gullible public and a fertile field to thrive. The weapon too, in order to match the eerie setting, had to have an aura of popularly ascribed otherworldliness about it and Stoker's choice of the Gorkha knife could hardly have been bettered.

Admittedly, the Gorkhas with their otherwise tiny handmaid, the *Khukri,* had already inspired awe and reverence beyond all proportions to its size or exploits, in the battle arenas of the world, including mid-nineteenth century Europe. The valiant Gorkhas, many thought and still think, owed their exploits to the legendary *Khukri,* due, in no mean measure, to despatches like the following, sent by Col. Rand, a one-time British Resident Representative at the court of Kathmandu:

"In one instance, Lt. Young with a force of 2,000 men was easily defeated by two hundred Gurkhas. They fought superbly, those little men... with the terrible *Khukri.*"

Or this eye-witness account, corroborated by author Hassoldt Davis:

"A full-grown and able-bodied Hun was split open from scalp to pelvis by a five-footer (Gorkha) with one stroke of his two-foot blade."

To such approbatory descriptions of the Gorkha and his *Khukri,* the passing decades, time and distance helped weave an ever-increasingly charismatic halo of seeming outworldliness. And it worked ideally--as far as Stoker's purpose was concerned.

Thus, if the world has come to regard the Gorkha and the *Khukri,* as an inseparable twosome, it is not for nothing. For, the *Khukri* is an implement which a Gorkhali home virtually cannot do without and hasn't ceased looking upon with a certain reverential awe. It is even deified, particularly on occasions like the *Dasain* or *Dussera*, their great est national festival, when the *Khukri* literally even adorns the household altar of worship, and receives votive offer ings of flowers, vermillion powder, delicacies and blood of the animals sacrificed with it, or without.

But the hitherto all-too-familiar portrait of a Gorkha soldier with his *Khukri* dangling down his uniform-belt or that of a Nepalese hillman holding his *Khukri* snugly against the belly with the help of a *Patuka* (waist-sash) has increas ingly been receding to the bylanes of memory.

Deservedly, however, some unusually heavy and ap- parently unwieldy *Khukri* specimens of the historic past have found an appropriate place in Nepal's national museum. Two of these have drawn particular approbation at the hands of the onlookers; one of these weapons, reputedly belonging to Kalu Pandey, one-time high civil and military official in the 17th century Nepalese court, exudes a seeming aura of awe by its sheer size and weight; the other, said to have belonged to Colonel Bahadur Gambhir Singh, whom, as the legend displayed beside the weapon mentions, the Prince of Wales presented a claymore in 1875 "for his bravery demonstrated while fighting against the Prince's own forces" !

Worthy of mention, also, are two other little accompani- ments of the traditional *Khukri*. In its sheath, which can be either of plain wood or of wood wrapped with leather, are invariably included items of utility like a *Kardo* and a *Chakmak*, both mini- replicas of the bigger weapon. The first of these is used for chores like the paring of nails or shaving the hair of the hand (not the head itself !) off, and the second, which is devoid of a sharp edge, is the Gorkha's heredi tary and traditional "match-box". With a piece of flint and some cottonwool for which also virtually every *Khukri* has an extra provision in its sheath, this flint-lock comes in handy in producing impromptu fires in Nepal's remote recesses where match- boxes are a rare luxury, if not a completely unavailable item.

A unique companion for life, thus, the *Khukri* even accompanies many a Gorkha to his grave ! For it is not uncommon to see a man, a sleek and shiny *Khukri* kept at the ready in his hand, walking as a vanguard in a Gorkha's funeral procession. Such a man, preceeding the cortege, keeps on waving his naked *Khukri* in the air supposedly slashing imaginary enemies, which, superstition has it, are the evil ghosts and spirits that tend to block the dead man's safe passage to heaven !

The Gorkha's trust in this tiny metallic handmaid is, therefore, unique, and could be a matter of envy either for the Spanish stilletto or the Sikh kirpan. It is, in fact a Gorkha's life and part of it.

Horse Racing in Mustang

How the word 'Mustang' came to mean a 'horse' as far west as in the Americas is beyond my comprehension. To us in Nepal, too, the word 'Mustang' conjures up memories of horses, of horse- riding, and horse-racing often of the 'bare-back' variety !

In Nepal's remote Mustang district is located the shrine of Muktinath. To its south lie the towering snows of the Annapurna and Dhaula giri ranges while to its north rises the sheer vertical steepness of the ridge beyond Kagbeni, and on to the Muktinath peak.

While a peak is by definition the highest point of a given area, the shrine of Muktinath itself is situated slightly lower--at 12,000 feet. A steep goat- track led us above a deep vertical gorge, below which the Kali Gandaki river (Tibetan name: *Tsangpo* or "The Clear One") roared past. Looking across the gorge and the expansive, mountainous desert land, we could only see some tiny, scattered, thorny, leafless bushes. This vista was in complete contrast to areas south of the Annapurna ranges like, for instance, the Ghodepani crest that we had seen earlier and that boasted of countless varieties of rhododendron and other trees whose pink trunks were veiled in moss and whose branches supported dozens of white and dark-blue orchids besides different strains of grass, moss and ferns.

For more than three days, from Tatopani onwards, we had crossed and recrossed, skirted or waded across the Kali Gandaki. At other times we had simply marvelled at the "deepest gorge in the world"-- a gorge said to be far deeper and more impressive than that of the one-mile-deep Grand Canyon, for, in parts, it (the Kali Gandaki gorge) is fully "three miles deep". But once we were at Muktinath, the Kali Gandaki was so small indeed that we could easily jump across it, and wondered again if it was the same river that formed the "world's deepest gorge".

We were now in the very heart of the Muktinath area, and the climate here was a good deal cooler than either at Jomosom (incidentally, meaning a "frontier fort" in Tibetan) or at Kagbeni. Also, we were safe, in the sense that we were beyond the pale of the howling and pebble-kicking gale that had almost chased us all along the river-trail. No more were we obliged to hug the steep rocky riverbanks to find shelter from the whistling wind that swept up the gorge every day.

Once we were through with our visit to the Muktinath shrine, called *Chumiq-Rgat-Sa-Gye* (the "108 Spring-spouts"), we witnessed preparations afoot for the most popular "Summer Festival of Great Men" (that is what, we were told, the *Pompo Yartung* meant) jointly organised by the nobles of Puran, Luprak and Jharkot, with the villagers of Kagbeni, quite some distance away, reportedly joining the festival every alternate year . The year that we were in Mustang happened to be the *minus*-Kagbeni one.

Caravans of colourful people, dressed in Tibetan fineries and *Chubas*, had started arriving-- the men on horseback and the women on foot. Tents had been pitched around the rest-house next to the Ningma gompa, some to serve as lodges and others as restaurants. Local delicacies were galore with a profusion of *Chyang* and *Arak*.

The broad road-like open space, some 35 feet wide and ten times as long, stretching in front of the rest-house, served as the 'race- course'. The race was on soon after the Jharkot chiefs had arrived and sportive expertise in horse-riding, often bare back, was in full evidence as sturdy Mustang youngsters galloped to and fro at fastest possible speeds.

The principal attraction of the festival appeared to lie in testing the horse- riders' skill in picking up, while still atop galloping horses, medieval knights- style, odd bits of articles like coins and *Khaadaas* (the ceremonial white Tibetan scarves) off the ground. We were given to understand that the *Khaadaas,* placed at various places along the route, con tained money put in as 'stakes' by the spectators. It was a sheer marvel to witness some of the riders, apparently as drunk as can be, gallop past the stake at breakneck speed, while, at the same time, trying to lift the *Khaadaas* off the ground with one hand outstretched for the purpose. Losing one's balance in the process and falling off the horse-back could mean a physi cal disaster!

The spectators applauded with gay abandon every time a rider succeeded in his herculean effort. It was also not unusual to see the panting and perspiring mounts, with flaring nostrils, suddenly go berserk and rush like mad at the surrounding, shouting and clapping crowds, scaring them out of their wits and making them run helter-skelter for cover in the process !

The climax of the festival was known as the *Drazur* — a dance in which the nobles of Jharkot (i.e., the Pompos), those of Luprak and the Pohyog (or the com moners) participated in a wide-circle formation. In the centre stood a man, as colourfully attired as the others (*bakhu,* boots and hat) and holding a long spear. The drums beat, the horns blew and the crowds shouted as the men, each holding a whip, danced around him in a slow, rhythmic movement. At inter vals they rushed towards the central figure, simultaneously striking his hand-held spear with cracking whips. At the final closing-in rush, they lifted the spear-wielding man off the ground. This, it was said, was a gesture of solidarity amongst the representing villages, the person so lifted being a Jharkot 'royal' priest of old times and the spear he held representing the Jharkot ancestral deity, the *Abse Dungsara*.

It was almost dusk when we, enthralled and exhilerated at the day's proceedings, wended our way back to Kagbeni for a night halt. But the wild horse-racing was still on even as darkness descended. The crowds would disperse only the next morning, we were told.

Handkerchief Mile, Elephant Mile

Rural Nepal has curious but popular methods of measuring dis tances-- the unit of linear measurement sometimes fluctuating according to the time of the day, season of the year or the idiosync racies of the man or beast involved in the assessment.

Akosh that normally means two miles, for example, may denote twice or thrice that distance if the *kosh* referred to is the *Hatti-kosh* (literally, "Elephant-mile") ! For it is a unit of measurement assessed in terms of the distance cov ered between two voluntary stops by an elephant.

Then there is the *Rumale-kosh* ("Handkerchief mile") which is the distance supposedly measured in terms of the time taken by a wet handkerchief, fluttering from a walking stick, to dry. And almost akin to the handkerchief-mile is the *Shyaulee-kosh (Shyaulee* meaning a twig); here, as you have rightly guessed, distances are reckoned in terms of the time taken by a twig, held aloft by a traveller, to wither and wilt !

Bundles carried on men's heads or the backs of pack-animals must have been the pioneers of any exact system of weighment in the days of yore, but you needn't be caught unawares if, in your jaunt to a remote Nepal village mart, the vendor were to peddle his wares in terms of a "palmful" (*muthi*) or the "double palmful" *(anju li)* !

Aunlas or *anguls* (finger-breadths), *bittas* (spans) and *haths* (cubits) are the other units of length in local Nepalese metrology; "handy" at all times and anywhere, these units hold good in many a linear measurement, be it of a piece of cloth or a piece of land !

Our Mr. Nepal (plebeian) is least bothered if it was Abul Fazl, a scion of the historical Mughals in India, who enumerated 5 spe cies of the Yard, the long yard being equivalent to a row of 192 barley corns and the short yard of 144 barley corns. He is perfectly happy with his own Auble of length that gces something like this :

12 *Aunlas*	=	1 *bitta*
2 *Bittas*	=	1 *hath*
2 *Haths*	=	1 *gaz* (yard), etc.

Flaunting your "sanskritic" credentials, you may be led into arguing that the Nepalese *kori* is but a derivation of the Sanskrit word meaning a crore; nothing of the kind. It simply means twenty and make no mistake if the Nepalese reckon your greying 65 years in terms of three *kori* and five!

How we miss our traditional double-purpose gold *Asharfis* and pure silver *rupiahs* that served both as a unit of currency and weight ! Even now, when it comes to measuring valuables like gold, we would still like to go by our old generation *rupiahs*, mohurs (50 pice coins) and *sukis* (25 pice ones); but no nonsense like modern-day alloys !

The traditional cup-measurements do not seem to go away from Nepal either. Rice, wheat and other grains are still sold and purchased, despite the current academic fetish for metric weights, in terms of *manas* (half-a-kilogram, roughly), *pathis* (eight *manas*) and *muris* (twenty *pathis*, roughly a quintal). *Dharnis* (about 2.5 Kilogram) and *pawas* (one-twelveth of a *dharni*) are similar to other measure ments applied in the case of salt, sugar and ghee (purified butter), as also milk, oil and liquids.

Land measurements, particularly in the hills, still go by *mato- muri* (mato is soil); one *mato muri* is the area of land that takes a *muri* (about a quintal) of grainseeds. In urban areas, however, land is measured in terms of the *hath* (cubit) and *ropani* (roughly 75 feet square), while in the *terai* plains the units are the traditional *katthas* and *bighas*.

But with all this, now a bit of news. "Backward" Nepal learnt to live with the decimal system of coinage about five decades ahead of India and six ahead of the United Kingdom!

The Numbers Game

In the western world, number seven is associated with good omen as much as number thirteen is associated with the unlucky or inauspicious.

The orientals are no less steeped in superstitious beliefs of their own respective brands. We have our own auspicious or inauspicious days of the week, our own ideas about a good omen or bad. We may not be sharing this 'game of numbers' but then number seven holds quite a different kind of significance in our own ethos too!

A random instance that comes readily to mind is provided by river-names like the *Sapta Gandaki* (comprising the Tadi, Madi, Marsyangdi, Trishuli, Kali, Seti and Budi Gandaki) and the *Sapta Koshi* (the Sun, Tama and Dudha Koshis besides Arun, Barun, Tamor and Indravati).

Similar lumping together of river names has also persisted in the South Asian sub-continent from very ancient times as in the case of the *Sapta Ganga, Sapta Sindhu* and the like. Under the *Sapta Ganga* are bracketed together such better-known rivers as the Ganges, Yamuna, Godavari, Saraswati, Narmada, Kaveri and the Indus; and, under *Sapta Sindhu* are included the Ravi, Chenab, Sutlej, Jhelum, Vyas, Saraswati and again, curiously enough, the Indus !

Our infatuation with number seven does not end here. Talk of ancient Hindu sages known for their eminence and erudition, for instance, and we come across *Saptarishi* (literally, the seven rishis)--Kashyap, Bharadwaj, Atri, Gautama, Vasistha, Vishwamitra and Jamadagni. Likewise, our ancients have counted seven continents such as Pushkar, Saka, Salmali, Kush, Krauncha and Jambudvipa--the last denoting the sub-continent south of the great Himalayas. If we have seven *Swargas* (heavens), we also have seven underworlds (some say they symbolise the earth's layers) like Atal, Bital, Sutal, Mahatal, Talatal, Rasatal and Patal !

How about the elements of nature ? Seven, including the Sun, Wind, Water, Fire, Sky, etc. The sun-god itself, it is believed, traverses the sky in a chariot drawn by seven horses, every day. A ray of light, in its turn, is said to comprise seven hues, known as *Saptavarna*.

A well-known religious exercise undertaken by Hindu households is known as *Saptah,* which also denotes a week. This ritual, to be completed in seven days, comprises the narration of the *Bhagavat purana*. The seventh day of *Navaratra*, heralding the advent of the year's biggest Hindu festival, is known in Nepal as the *Phulpati* day and calls for, among other things, a colourful procession and a *badain* marked by salvoes of gun-fire, at least in Kathmandu.

The Hindu nuptial ceremony is marked by *Saptapadi* (meaning the circumambulation of the holy fire seven times) as one of the most crucial rituals, while, not unoften, the bridal pair is also made to worship the *Saptakul*-- a conglomeration of seven supposedly holy mountain lakes.

We also have the *Saptak* meaning a combination of the musical seven *Swaras*. And then, among the Hindu female divinities, the *Sapta Matrikas* (literally seven Mother- Goddesses) are well-known.

It is not only the number Seven that assumes such religious overtones in the Hindu scheme of things, however. Numbers eleven, ten, eight, five and three are also among those which are equally successful in attracting our reverence and ritual appli cation. *Yama Panchak*, meaning the 'five days of Yama (the Death-god)', for instance, is the more appropriate appellation for the *Tihar* festival, considered by many Nepalese as being even more important than the *Dasain*, the greatest annual festival. Five mythical ladies (namely, Ahalya, Draupadi, Kunti, Tara and Mandodari) are lumped together as the *Pancha Kanyas*, meaning five 'virgins'- -a little anomalous a term though, because some of them even had more than their share of husbands each (Draupadi, for instance) !

We also have terms like *Pancha Buddha* meaning the five celestial Buddhas (Vairochana, Akshobhya, Amitabha, Ratna Sambhava and Amoghasiddhi) at one time and the mythological or human Buddhas (Vipashwi, Sikhi, Krakuchhanda, Kanakamuni and Kashyapa) at another. And, of course, the *Pancha makaar* (or the 'five Ms' associated with the *tantrik* rituals, the *Panchasheel* (or five principles of co-existence) and the traditional Nepalese orches tra played on ceremonial occasions known as the *Panche Baja* are well known.

Of the several *Dasamis* (or tenth days of the lunar fortnight), the most important, of course, is the *Vijaya Dasami*, otherwise also known as *Dasai*. Then there are *Dasa Daan* and *Dasa Dikpal*, which mean, respectively,

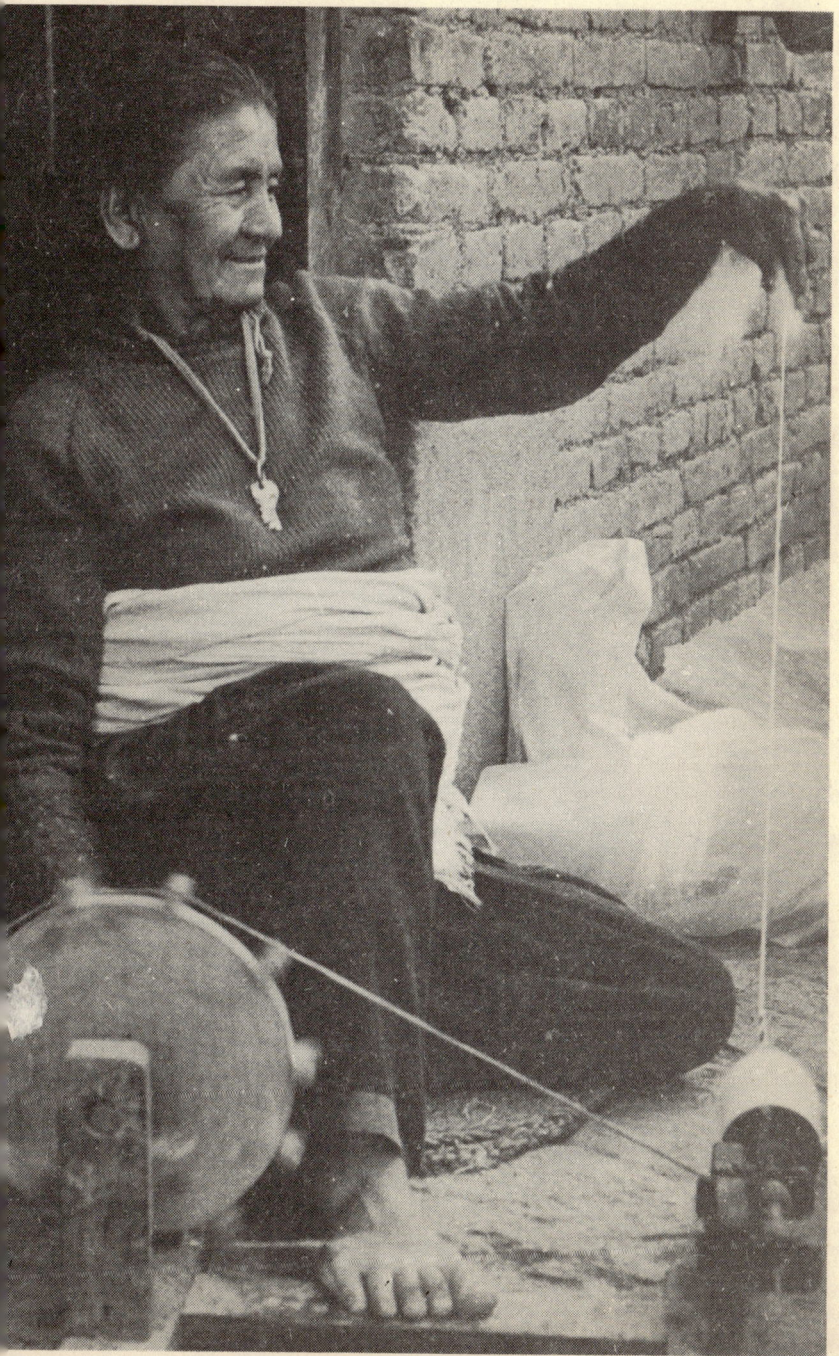

Photo by Laxman Shrestha

Photo by Laxman Shrestha

Photo by *Yeti Photos Centre*

the ten ritual gifts and the deities traditionally believed to be the guardians of the ten cardinal points or directions.

Coming to number nine, we come across terms like *Nava graha* or the nine planets, *Nava Durga* or the nine incarnations of the Mother-Goddess worshipped during the *Nava Ratra* (Nine Nights of Durga) and *Nava Ratna* or the nine precious stones considered ritually auspicious and important.

Among *Asthamis* (eighth days of the lunar fortnight), the birthday of Lord Krishna, known as *Krishnashtami*, is well-known. Not so well-known, however, are terms like *Ashtakul* (meaning the eight mythical and holy *Nagas* or serpents) and *Ashta Dhatu,* i.e., a combination of eight religiously significant metals.

The Sanskrit term for eleven is *ekadashi*, and the *ekadashi*, meaning the eleventh day of the lunar for + night, is the most auspicious day for prayer and fasting for any religiously- inclined Hindu. And, even among these *ekada shis* when animal or bird slaughter is a legal taboo in the Kingdom of Nepal, *Hari Sayani* and *Hari Bodhini* are the two holiest ones in the whole year. The first, falling sometime in the months of June-July, is the occasion when lord Vishnu is believed to enter the nether-world (*patal*) for a four-month- long annual slumber. The second, in its turn, is the day of his ritual 'waking-up', sometime in November-December. The four intervening months are known as the *Chaturmas*. There you are, when even number four, which we had left in our earlier reckoning, assuming a religious significance of its own !

The importance of number three cannot be over-emphasised either. The idea of time has traditionally been imparted to us by terms like *Trikal* (past, present, future). The principal Buddhist scriptures (like Vinaya, Abhidhamma and Suttapitaka) are grouped together as

Tripitaka. And, of course, who doesn't know about the holy Hindu *trinity* or *Trimurti*, meaning Brahma, Vishnu and Shiva ? Likewise, *Triratna* means Buddha, Dharma and Sangha; *trilok* the sky, earth and the netherworld; and *trishul*, the holy trident of lord Shiva. We thus have not only our own notions of the 'Lucky Seven' but also of many other 'lucky' or holy numbers. In short, you name it, we have it !

Language and Literature

CHAPTER SIX

Literature by Accident

About three generations earlier, one young man, a 'holy' Brahman at that, had been shoved off to a Kathmandu prison on charges of mis-appropriation of state funds; only that the offence was not his, but that of his grandfather, long dead and gone !

But the succeeding Nepalese generations were grateful to these ancient law-givers that such a fate did come to pass for Bhanubhakta, that Brahman youth from Tanahun in mid-west Nepal, even if they wouldn't be too grateful if they were themselves in his shoes! For hadn't it been so Nepalese literature would have been all the poorer for absence of verses like these :

Day after day I behold thy face, delight without ceasing,

The evenings I pass in revelry and dance, pleasure ever increasing,

The mosquitoes, the bugs and fleas, their company I keep,

The fleas dance, mosquitoes sing, and I watch without sleep.

But this wasn't just a casual verse; more, it was part of a petition complaining to the jail authorities against conditions in the prison. No wonder, on reading the petition, the humane jail-warden didn't keep Bhanubhakta there for long.

Yet this poetic propensity in Bhanubhakta wasn't known to any, including himself, till quite late in his life. And, were it not for a severe mental shake-up he received while he was a pampered idler of a youth, the poet within him would perhaps have remained buried under his otherwise easy-going temperament.

The story of the chance accident that turned him into a poet goes somewhat like this. One day, while young Bhanubhakta was lazying it up in a midday siesta, as was his wont, near a murmuring hill rivulet, a disturbing element appeared in the person of a grass-cutter who had got down to business quite close by. The idler's first instinct at having been awakened was to fly into a rage at the grass-cutter, but he thought the better of it, and in order to while away the time, dragged himself into a reluctant chat with the old man.

"I see you toil very hard, my man," he began. "What use do you make of the money you so earn ?"

"I hardly earn enough to make two ends meet", replied the grass-cutter, "but what little I scrape up as my life's saving, I have been keeping aside with a view to get a well dug for my village-folk".

"Got dug a what ?" asked Bhanu, half-believing what he had heard.

"A well", repeated the old man, "to meet the villagers' need for drinking water". Later he added philosophically, "Mortals as we are, we have got to go one day. The only thing that sustains our memory for posterity is the mark we leave behind us in the sands of time. It is the works of charity that alone endure."

It was an utterly metamorphosed, if inspired, Bhanu that emerged from this otherwise casual *tete-a-tete*. For all his family erudition and relative affluence, he felt utterly belittled before the noble spirit of the indigent grass-cutter. He felt like cursing himself and he did — in an eight-line improptu versification, Tennyson-style, which concludes in the follow ing strain :

How come the grass-cutter enlightened me
                             this day,
I fie on this life of mine, nameless and
                             unworthy.

The seemingly inherent poet in Bhanubhakta thus sparked, he embarked upon an ambitious venture to "found" a literature for his people. And a life-long dedication to the cause resulted in literary creations of many hues, climaxing in the adaptation, in the "lay-man's language", of the well-known epic, the Ramayana, *a la Valmiki*.

Prior to Bhanubhakta, the language he chose as a literary medium had all along been derisively described as a mere dialect, unwor thy of scholarly attention. As such, if Bhanubhakta is reverent ly remembered today as torch-bearer and a trend-setter, it was because he challenged the established norms of literary creation, despite heavy onslaughts from the orthodox and powerful sections who held that writing in any medium other than Sanskrit, "the Gods' language", wasn't worth the ink spilt over it. But Bhanu stuck his ground.

Much like Wordsworth in his later works, Bhanubhakta found noble inspiration in moral poetry. Religious by tradition and training — he came from a family of priests-- he wrote almost entirely in defence of established religious norms. Despite this, however, he simply could not help reverting to his old, youthful and romantic self and betrayed an occasional Khayyamik streak in him; for instance, he went into raptures on first seeing Kathmandu's Balaju gardens when he was already on the wrong side of forty, thus:

Ah, be it mine the writing delight,

A verse here, for a maiden fair and bright,

To dance in its rhythm, and else

Would what I wish, when paradise I create !

Next only to king Prithvi Narayan Shah, the unifier of Nepal into one nation, Bhanubhakta is acknowledged on all hands as the greatest single influence in shaping the Nepalese nationhood. His *Ramayana*, a monumental work, has remained the bible of virtually every Nepalese home for about a hundred years now.

A Modern Milton

September 1959 saw Devkota, Nepal's non-drinking but chain-smoking Dylan Thomas, tossing in the agony of death at Kathmandu's lonesome Bagmati riverside. The pre-historic Pashupatinath kept vigil over his last gasping days, as it has eternally done over so many of His dying devotees. Amongst those that shared Devkota's painful last moments there was the now famous Dom Moraes.

Devkota's premature end was preceded by months of acute suffering resulting from a cancer of the polyrus. Earlier, he had been taken to a Calcutta hospital for treatment. Then followed a trip to Moscow, also for treatment, and, still later, once again to India. It however, fell to the lot of a Kathmandu missionary hospital to wage an unsuccessful last-ditch battle against Devkota's destiny.

---

*Apart from figuring in a Moraes memoir "Gone Away", Devkota also received a pensive homage at the former's hand in the form of an article in the London "Observer" which was reproduced in the Hindustan Times dated August 14, 1960.

A series of blood transfusions later Devkota himself realised the futility of fighting against an unrelenting fate and begged that he be removed to the banks of the holy Bagmati. "I grew tired of drinking human blood", Devkota is recounted as having told Moraes, "So I have come here to die."

Thus passed away Nepal's most versatile literary genius of this century. And, as the years go by, Nepal, almost with a smitten conscience, is increasingly realising that, in the person of Devkota she had produced — and callously lost — almost all that epito mised the spirit and achievement of the twentieth — century Asian literary resurgence in this country. For, in his works we can discern the very spirit of renaissance-- expansive, humourous, powerful and, above all, human.

Most of Devkota's one hundred and fifty written works are yet to be published; but the dozen or odd that have seen the light of the day are enough to set his name firmly on the saddle of fame. Devkota's uniformly high standard of published works cover a wide range from epics to erudite essays, from prattle to politics, and ele gant translations. What is more, all these were products of the rare moments of leisure amidst a hectic and penurious life of Devkota the college and school teacher, and Devkota the rebel-politician.

His prolific creativity is attributed to his pronounced Tennysonian capacity of writing poetry at instant notice.

Devkota, a publisher once noted, had agreed to write twelve short stories for a proposed collection. But when the publisher called on him on the appointed day, the promised stories had not been written, not even one. Devkota had perhaps forgotten, as was his wont. "But would you mind, "Devkota asked, "if I dictated a few right now ?"

"When I emerged from Devkota's residence five hours after", said he later, "my platter was full. But that I could not bring all the twelve was not because Devkota's dictation had been slow or halting; it was I who could not write fast enough. I wish I knew stenography."

On another occasion, the perennially penurious Devkota, when in need of some urgent cash, wrote a two-hundred-page verse-lyric called, "Kunjini", almost overnight. But again, as was his wont, forgot all about it soon after.

Some years later, a local group of stage-enthusiasts adapted the same story in the form of a play and invited Devkota to witness the show. When the play was over, Devkota was asked to comment on the performance. "It is very well written", the poet retorted but, forgetful as ever, asked, "Whose work is it ?"

When he learnt it was an adaptation from one of his own works, Devkota was amazement personified !

The two epics *Shakuntala* and *Sulochana* are among Devkota's major literary creations. The first-named, a volumi nous work, he reportedly completed in three months, but when some doubting Thomases challenged him to produce another epic of similar quality and proportions, he did. That was "Sulochana", another equally remarkable work, written in just over ten short days !

A law graduate from the Patna University, Devkota had been to Calcutta during the Thirties, presumably to complete his Master's degree. There, it is said, he got a taste of the Bengali literature and became enamoured with it, especially with Tagore and his works like the "Gitanjali". He is said to have kept himself confined to his room for weeks at a stretch, studying Tagore. Apprehensive of a developing mental derangement in him, friends tried to break this spell and despatched him, post-haste, to the Ranchi Mental Hospital. There, perhaps, his real literary 'flowering' began...

Back home on recovery, Devkota himself called that spell of derangement a "bursting forth" of his latent talents, as summed up in "The Lunatic", thus:

"In the frigid winter months I basked

In the first white heat of the astral light

And people called me crazy...

Shocked by the first streak of frost

On a fair lady's tresses

For a length of three days

My sockets filled and rolled---

And they called me one distraught !

... ...

I laughed with the tempest one day

And the wiseacres of the world

Despatched me promptly to Ranchi !"

The well-known Indologist and Hindi scholar, late Rahul Sankrit tayana, compared Devkota's poetic genius to that of Valmiki and Kalidasa and added that Hindi literature had yet to see a poet of Devkota's calibre. "One of the greatest sons of the Himalayas", wrote Sankrittayana in his well-known work, *Ateet se Bartman* (Past to Present), and at once equated Devkota to the famous Hindi literary *trimurti*–Prasad, Pant and Nira la. A more lavish commendation from a scholar who was a well-known Hindi litterateur himself, is hard to conceive.

Devkota led his country's delegation to the two Afro-Asian literary meets at New Delhi and later at Tashkent. The signs of a failing health, however, were already becoming gravely apparent in him and, in response to invitations from the writing fraternity in India and Russia, he made a trip to these countries for treatment.

But, ironically enough, his own countrymen were too slow, or indifferent, to come to his rescue even during these last days when precious life was fast ebbing out of him. It took much, indeed too much, time for the then Nepalese authorities to grasp the gravity of the situation. Considering that late B.P. Koirala, the then Nepalese prime minister, was himself a life-long associate of Devkota, both as a litterateur and a fellow revolutionary during the long years of the country's struggle for democracy, it was utterly callous of him not to have been smitten by a qualm of conscience till a vociferous and widespread popular protest forced him to act. Act he then did, but it was almost far too late in the day.

To Dom Moraes, the dying Devkota described this phase of his life cryptically yet pathetically thus : "I went to Russia and they called me a Communist...Alas, I was a mere poet".

Utterly unconventional in his approach to God and spiritual values, Devkota's poems are often reminiscent of the revolutionary fervour of the Nazrul school of Bengali literature. In the "Song of the Storm", for example, Devkota almost speaks the language of Nazrul when he writes:

The wild flight of the smoke-like locks

Of the Doom Dancer, Shiva

I bear the standard of deluge;

My flight is frantic free.

Untamed in an upward sweep,

I rage over ocean and heaven

Sweeping them in a wild commotion
In a mighty swirling motion.

Like a Lady of Terror,
Pleased with my own dread beauty,
Beaming with my smiling flashes
And, apparelled well, I swing,
Then I sing, my sorrows maddening
With laughters that sting
And let loose the furies of the wind.

He also blazed a new trail in Nepalese literature by his satire of the accepted human values and human civilization. In "The Donkey Speaks", Devkota subjects human civilization to the satirical scrutiny of a donkey, thus:

Have you the power to create grass
Without its seeds, out of the Law
Master Man Hee-hee-haw, hee-hee-haw !
What is the meaning of the Vedas four,
Before the twin principles of man,
Hunger and lust
A spark in a glow-worm's tail
And a nut of the squirrel ?

I have my fantasies too, Master Man,
But I speak not, write not, pour not,

Like you I belch not;

Look at your cruel idols,

Wreathed in skulls

Hee-hee-haw, hee-hee-haw !

In your worship of the Earth

And of the phallus, Master Man

The sides of my stomach swell and burst,

Hee-hee-haw, hee-hee-haw !

Though not an outright skeptic, Devkota was a freethinker all the same; the wheel of his ideals apparently turned a full-cycle only towards the end of his spasmodic but short career. The almost incredible tale of woe and agony were writ large on his face when I met him in his Calcutta hospital shortly before his death. His prolonged illness had reduced the five-feet eight sturdy build of a Rugby forward to a mere skeleton. "What you see before you is the carcass of a man", he said, "I once weighed 175 lbs. Now I weigh fifty two". His eyes were two liquid pools, full of tears.

Death, perhaps he knew, was lurking too perilously close before him, and his words sounded like a pathetic confession: "Perhaps my life-long atheism is at the back of my suffering...I have suffered both at the hands of man and God".

To Dom Moraes, he said, "My poems were too materialistic...they were too much of the world. But I will not renounce them". And, in concluding these lines, he etched his own epitaph, as it were: "I am the most unfortunate of the writers of Nepal".

One of his very last poems summarises this disillusionment and is hauntingly elegiac :

Void and empty,

In a fire of repentant thoughts burning,

Like a hot grain of desert sand

In eternal dumbness I toss

Dying and burning.

Ladies with the Pen

It is only rarely that we come across wielders of pen among Nepalese women. And, it is as it should be, considering that women have, for ages, been deprived of the benefit of education and have been relegated to the role of wives and mothers, limiting themselves to the four walls of the household.

Yet, once in a long while, we do come across some women who have broken the tethers of social limitations and have shot into literary limelight. One leading torchbearer of this genre in the 19th century was Lalita Tripura Sundari Devi, the youngest wife of king Ranbahadur Shah, who is said to have translated the "Rajdharma" from Sanskrit into Nepali. She died in 1831.

Next to her came Bhagawat Kumari Pande, Prem Rajeshwari Thapa (1920--), Lokpriya Devi, Goma and Vidya Devi Dikshit (1905-85). Goma, moulded in the traditional cast, wrote a number of poems which were published in the literary magazine, "Sharada". Like wise, Vidya Devi, a poetess of the old school, started writing around 1927 and has three collections, namely *Sankalan* (Collection), 1961, *Naniko Ankha* (The Child's Eyes), 1962 and *Indra Dhanu* (Rainbow), 1963. But then, Rajeshwari's poems, being of reflective kind and with an adequate dose of pathos, stand out more prominently.

Another lady poet, who has stopped writing since, is Sashikala Sharma.

Among poetesses of the present generation, names such as Chandni Shah, Prema Shah, Parizat, Banira Giri, Kundan Sharma, Chhinnala ta, Toya Gurung, Anita Tuladhar, Binita Singh, Sabitri Sundas, Punya Prabha Devi Dhungana, Kunti Devi Sharma, Sushila Koirala, Vijaya Sharma and Lakkhi Devi Sundas come readily to mind. Chand ni Shah, particularly, breaks new grounds in lyrical poetry by doing away with the traditional yet redundant rhyming of lines, thus:

"When your eyes speak out and express,

The feelings that lie fathomed at heart's bottom,

My entire worldly being shrinks and fits itself

Into a single pupil of your eyes, and

I see myself everywhere in them,

In you--and all around you."

Prema Shah and Parizat may be said to have shaken their innate shyness in coming out with poems that exploit emotions of a sexual and amoral nature with a boldness that is rare. While frustrations are often writ large in their poems, Parizat, for one, would have us believe that god and his ilk have no place in her system of values. Says she:

"The death of god

I have fonded in my lap,

Throughout a cat's hairy furcoat

I have experienced the confident coldness of death:

If this too is a self-realization

I constantly feel such an emotion

That is peculiar and unique."

She has come out with a collection of her poems, "*Akangchha*" (Aspirations, 1957), but her short poem, "*Lahurelai Ek Rogi Premikako Patra*" (A Sick Lady-love's Letter to A Soldier) touches one's innermost chords with its pathos and poignancy.

Chhinnalata's lyrics and poems are also finely woven. They have been published in two volumes, "*Antar Bhavana*" (Inner Feelings,1971) and "*Amar Taranga*" (Deathless Ripples) preceding it.

Banira Giri (1946---) is, however, the most voluble woman poetess who has a grasp of the feminine psyche and expresses it with a finesse that is as rare as it is novel. Her satires are subtle too. *Jiwan Thaya Maru* (1977) and *Euta Jiundo Jung Bahadur* (One Live Jung Bahadur) are here better-known works. Kathmandu is, to her:

"A sizeable epic

Filled with interesting stories, sweet and sour,

This darling Kathmandu

Auspicious ritual-song of high-sounding speeches

From the leaders,

A chorus of people's wants and deprivations

Comedy of salary enhancement

Tragedy of spiralling inflation

A perennial struggle for kerosene and sugar

That appear now and disappear again

What is not there, here ?"

The toils and tribulations of life do not only move another younger - generation poetess, Toya Gurung, to tears but also make her urge others to jerk themselves free. Her *Tears In Every Street* is a poem in this vein:

"Stand up, ye pillars

How innocent of you to crash down on your own ?

...   .

...   .

Tears of every heart

Have started flowing down

In every street,

In as many queues". *(From Galli Gallika Ansuharu)*

More recent additions to this list are Usha Bhattachan, Binita Singh, Arati Rai, Sushama Moktan, Padmavati Singh, Indira Prasai, Usha Dikshit, Sarala Bista, Sashi Tiwari, Sita Pande, Bhagirathi Shrestha, etc.

Novel and Short Story

The tradition of the novel, given a good start by Ambalika Devi (Upadhyaya) with her *Rajput Ramani* (1932), has been kept alive by, among others, Parijat, Krishna Kumari Rai, Geeta Keshari, Pavan Kumari Devi, Sarita Pradhan and Banira Giri.

Parijat is by far the best-known woman novelist Nepal has pro duced to date. She has about seven novels to her credit so far: the prestigious Madan Award winner, *Shirisko Phool* (which has also enjoyed the distinction of being the first Nepali novel to be translated into English, under the title *The Blue Mimosa)* was published in 1965. Others include *Mahattahin* (Insignificant, 1968), *Bainsako Manchhe* (Man of Youth, 1972), *Parkhal Bhitra, Parkhal Bahira* (Within The Walls, Outside The Walls, 1978), *Antarmukhi* (Introvert, 1979), etc.

Parijat, once again, emerges as one of the most successful weav ers of the short-story yarn, as is evidenced by, among others, her collections so far published. Maya Thakuri and Banira Giri, re-migrants into Nepal, also have two collections each to their credit.

Earlier, Prema Shah, Dev Kumari Sinha and Sashikala Sharma had shone in the literary firmament with quite a brilliance. But while both Shah and Sashi seem to have gone into premature retirement, the one lady that keeps on holding the torch aloft is Dev Kumari Thapa (*nee Sinha*), a weaver of tales for the young and not-so-young.

A Martyr to Literature

It is said that corn or *makai* was a virtually unknown commodity in Kathmandu till the 18th century. A story has it that the Kathmanduites not only called it an 'evil' grain, but also, following a famine in the wake of its introduction into the valley, king Jagat Jyoti Malla of Bhadgaon had even issued an edict that any *makai* grain seen in his kingdom was to be destroyed forthwith!

The story may or may not be true. But another story, which says that a young man, whose "crime" it was to write a booklet on the "Cultivation of Maize," had to pay for it with his dear life, is not merely a fiction. It is a sad fact of Nepalese literary history.

Accounts of the *Makai Parva* (literally, "the Maize Episode") make an interesting reading. This *Parva* was, in fact, the first major event in the 30-year-long history of Nepal's march towards freedom and democracy that culminated in an armed insurrection in 1950. What's more, another literary episode that sparked off a political upheaval of an equal magnitude is difficult to find in the annals of any country, let alone Nepal.

As far as can be ascertained, a group of middle-class youths, bitten with the literary bug, used to hold indoor meetings at regular intervals at the residence of Krishnalall Adhikari at Kamalakshi, near Kathmandu's Asan

Tole. What is also notable is that most of these youths were, like Adhikari (a 'Subba' at the 'Kausal'), higher-cadre government officials. Not only were their sessions held in *camera*, but, once the participants entered the upper-floor living-room of Krishnalall, all the doors and windows, including the outside entrance-gate leading to the house, would be 'locked from inside', to keep off those outside the selected coterie !

It was seemingly in the course of one of these deliberations that Bhojraj and Krishnalall came forward with a project to jointly author the *Makaiko Kheti*. What was Bhojraj's contribution to the completion of the project is not exactly known, but since it was Krishnalall who received the punishment, it is safe to assume that the latter was instrumental in the final editing and publication of the book.

That the book had hit the then authorities where it hurt them most and that they were bent upon forfeiting and destroying every single copy of the publication, is not difficult to imagine, because the three additional years of jail term meted out to Krishnalall was for the otherwise simple offence of "not producing the last one copy," out of the presumed 1,000 copies, of the book !

But what was it in the book that irked the officialdom so? Or, in other words, what was there in the contents of *Makaiko Kheti* that the then rulers found so utterly objectionable ? It is said that, while discussing the different aspects of maize cultivation, the book also dealt with the various insects and termites that could destroy a maize crop, and, in doing so, had used the term "red-headed pests" and "black-headed pests". Those terms were somehow interpreted as being directed not towards the insects in a technical sense, but towards the higher-echelon Rana officialdom that wore caps bearing these colours as parts of their respective official uniforms.

Krishnalall, thus, quite eminently fits into the description of "a martyr to the cause of litterature", for the simple reason that he died before his 9-year prison term ran out. Some other litterateurs of the period who were also variously charged and convicted included the well-known poet, Sambhu Prasad; he was dismissed from government service for having composed some verses incorporated in the said book. Another notable literary person age, Somnath Sigdyal, was sentenced to a fine of Rupees fifty for the "offence" of editing the book. Krishna Prasad Koirala, father of late B.P. Koirala, and an anti-Rana political activist, may also have been associated with the publication directly or indirectly, but he escaped punishment simply by virtue of the fact that he was already living in exile in India. It is also said that it was Koirala who had instigated the writers of *Makaiko Kheti* to give the contents a political colour because of his inherent animosity against the Rana regime. Others who lost their services and suffered iniquities as an aftermath of this episode included one Upendra Bahadur Basnet, Kharidar Chudamani, Subba Rishi Bhakta Padhya and Durganath Pandit, besides thirty-three other persons.

But exactly how many persons were involved in the writing and publication of this book is a mere matter of conjecture today. Also, as long as a copy of this seemingly harmless booklet, that nevertheless caused a historic furore, is not available, it cannot be ascertained why it was regarded 'seditious' enough to invite such patently disproportionate punishments to its author or authors, and col laborators.

Comparisons are useless. But it is difficult to come across another story of a man dying for the cause of literature the way Krishnalall did. Yes, he was no Socrates and drank no hemlock. But nor was he a Galileo to be "forced" to recant whatever he wrote. He simply accepted the prison sentence as calmly as he could, and died, almost unlamented, before his jail-term ran out. Martyrs, one can imagine, are made that way.

Nepali, Hindi and English

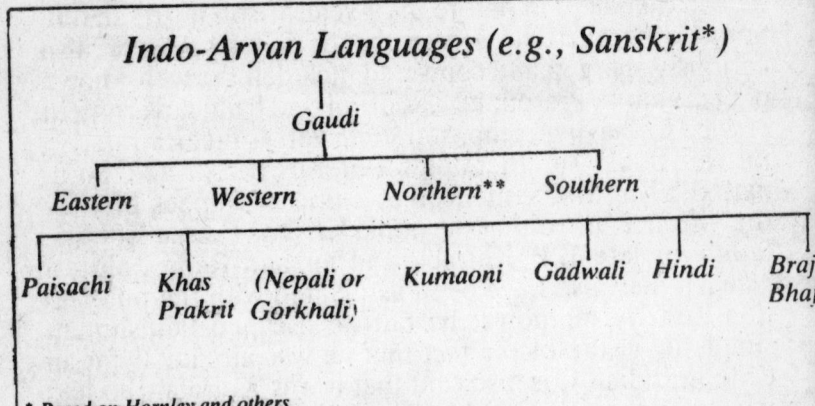

* Based on Hornley and others
* Related to Saurseni, an ancient prakrit lingo prevalent in Surasen (the 'middle' country including Mathura and surrounding areas)

To say that the Nepali and Hindi languages have enjoyed sisterly relations for a long time in the past is to repeat an age-worn cliche. Nepal's close geographical proximity with the Hindi-speaking north Indian States, added to the fact that a large section of the Terai population speaks dialects such as Maithili, Bhojpuri and Awadhi, besides Hindi proper, explains this Nepali-Hindi affinity. What's more, the Nepali and Hindi languages trace their origin to a common parent-stock, namely the Indo-European family of languages and the Vedic Sanskrit. But that is not to say that Nepali is a derivative of Hindi. And it is pertinent to examine, in this context, where exactly these two more or less similar tongues feature in the aforesaid family of languages, and how this affinity came about.

In earlier days, Nepali language was also known as *Khas* or *Parbatiya* (Eastern Pahari). The *Khasas* were a people probably of Scythian origin that hailed from areas around the Caspian Sea (*Kashyap sagar*)? Later, they are said to have migrated to Khasgar (meaning, perhaps, the Home of the Khasas), Khasmir or Kashmir, and then to the erstwhile Sinja area in western Nepal. Some people like the late Mahananda Sapkota even hold that the Khas language was not in fact a branch of the Indo-European family of languages, but a tongue of an earlier origin. This assumption, however, has not been proved, let alone widely accepted.

Besides Hindi, the modern Nepali language is closely linked also with Bengali, Maithili, Bhojpuri and Awadhi, as well as Kumaoni, Garhwali and Gujarati. The Kumaon and Garhwal areas, besides being considered a stronghold of the Khasa people, had also come under the sway of the Gorkhas for quite a while. Professor Guiseppe Tucci holds that the Khasa people ruled over an extensive kingdom with their capital as Sinja and Dullu around the 12th century. Capil la, Krachalla and Ashok Challa were the better-known 'first' kings of this dynasty.

The kingdom of Sinja was divided into two provinces, Jadan and Khasan. The people of Jadan spoke a Tibeto-Burman tongue, while those of Khasan spoke the Khasa language. Some of the inscriptions found in the Sinja area are also said to feature Sanskrit at the top and Nepali at the bottom.

Thus, it appears that the Sinjali language developed into modern Nepali which, in its turn, admits of three classifications, namely, Western, Central and Eastern.

Sinjali or the Western group may also be termed Medieval Nepali as can be seen in the copper-plate inscription of one Dhawakar matha (15th century). A linguist further classifies the Western group into *Orpachhima* (Near-Western), *Maajh Pacchima* (Mid- Western) and *Para Pachchima* (Far Western). According to this analysis, persent day Nepal areas like Achham, Bajhang and Bajura districts would come into the first, Doti and Dandeldhura in the second and Baitadi in the third.

The central Nepali has also been classified into dialects such as Lamjunli, Asirdali, Tibrikoti, Humli, Raskoti and Dolpali. And the Eastern Nepali, in its turn, is said to include the Khasaan (Rapti and Bheri areas), Parbati (Dhaulagiri, Lumbini and Gandaki areas) and Gorkhali (east of Gorkha right up to Darjeeling and Assam areas of north-eastern India). The existence of the East ern dialect in the Kathmandu area is evidenced by the inscrip tions of king Laxmi Narsingh Malla (1611 A.D.), Jagatprakash Malla (1673 A.D.) and Pratap Malla (1650 A.D.) that are much before the unification of Nepal by king Prithvi Narayan Shah. These inscriptions, thus, give the lie to the widely-held conception that Nepali language entered into Kathmandu valley only on the advent of the Gorkhas.

Following the unification of Nepal at the hands of king Prithvi Narayan Shah and the shifting of his capital from Gorkha to Kathmandu, this language also gradually came to be known as Nepali proper. Thus, the Khas language transformed itself into the Gorkha Bhasha and, subsequently, into the Nepali language.

A cursory glance at the position of Nepali on the one hand and some European languages on the other will go to show the link persisting between English and Nepali as well. To begin with, the Nepali langauge is as much a branch of the Indo-European family of languages as eight other branches of this family, namely, Celtic, Germanic, Tutonic, Italic, Helenic, Tokharian, Hittite, Albanian and Balto-Slavic which are spoken in Europe and the remaining two, namely, Armenian and Indo-Iranian, spoken in Asia. Six of these languages fall into the Kentum category and the last four in the Satum category, such as Nepali.

The Vedic Sanskrit language also traces its link to the Indo- Iranian family of languages. The transformation of Vedic San skrit into Nepali is said to have taken place through the *Prakrit* tongues, such as Sauraseni, Magadhi. Paisachi, etc., though a school of thought would have us believe that *Prakrit* was not a successor, but a predecessor, of San skrit. Sauraseni *Prakrit* belonged to the Surasen area and it was from this Prakrit that the modern Hindi, Gujarati, Panja bi, Sindhi and Nepali were born. The Nepali-Hindi link is put into better perspective thus.

The Nepali language, in its earliest form, can be dated back about six hundred years. As mentioned earlier, the inscriptions of kings Prithvi Malla (1356 A.D.) and Aditya Malla (1321 A.D.) indicate its prevalence in the Sinja area at the time. In other words, Nepali language is as old as, if not older than, Hindi.

Religions

CHAPTER SEVEN

Phallus Worship

As is well known, the word "Nepal" has lent itself to various interpretations. A relatively unheard one, however, is that the founding of Nepal can be linked with Daksha, an ancient mythological chieftain. According to this view, Yama, the Hindu God of Death, was married to the daughters of Daksha, one of whom gave birth to the twins named Nip and Pal. These two kings jointly ruled over an area that possibly included the valley of Kathmandu, and which, after them, was named Nip-pal or Nepal. While this goes counter to the other and more widely held view that Nepal got its name from a mythological sage, Ne Muni, there is no evidence to back either and, as such, we can at best treat them as mere conjectures, except to add that the Nip-Pal connection finds mention in the works of some noted historians also.

Interestingly enough, the same Yama is also represented at times as antigods, that is, anti-Aryans. And, when it is said that *Rudra* (later lord Shiva or Mahadeva of the Hindu pantheon) was the second son of Yama and his wife Basu, it is easy to see why *Rudra* also was initialy opposed

---

See also another essay, "Nepal" in these pages.

to the philosophy of the Aryans. As a protector of the local people, such as the Nagas, he is said to have been derided by the Aryans as anti-Vedas and the story of Daksha having been killed at the hands of Shiva's *ganas* is symbolic in this context. Daksha Praja pati, as the story goes, invited all the Gods to a *Yagna* sacrifice he had organised. When Sati, a daughter of Daksha and the first wife of Shiva, asked her father why her husband had not been invited, Daksha is said to have used abusive words against Shiva, calling him "anti-Gods", among other things. Sati, unable to bear the insult of her husband in public, immo lated herself in the sacrificial fire. This incident so infuri ated Shiva that he avenged his insult, as also the death of his wife, by butchering Daksha at the very spot. That he subsequently married Parvati, the daughter of a Himalayan chieftain (possibly another non-Aryan) is symbolic too.

Was Rudra the name of one person at all ? That is, could this be a generic name as implied by expressions such as *Sata Rudra* (a Hundred Rudras) in *Yajur Veda*? Other texts have also named at least eleven Rudras. Rudra images, it is said, have been discovered in Harappa and Mohenjodaro, while *Satapatha Brahmana*, another text, holds that "all the gods of the outly ing areas" were known as Rudras, such as, for instance, the son of Prajapati and Usha Devi. Whatever their number and variety, however, they were perhaps opponents of the Aryan "Gods" and many non-Aryan heroes, like Ravana, sought Rudra's blessings in their war against the former.

That lord Shiva is to this day regarded as the "Destroyer" amongst the holy Hindu Trinity is also symbolic in this context. "Shiva was not only a non-Aryan deity, but also a pre-Aryan, most probably a Dravidian, or the deity of the mighty Kirats", notes Dhoosyan Sayami, in his treatise, "The Lotus and the Flame". Ancient Hindu scriptures are replete with instances of continuous power-struggle be tween the invading or "exotic" Aryans and the indigenous non-Aryans like the Kirats. It goes without saying that the terrible Rudra wreeked havoc many a time on the Aryans, which explains not only the epithet of a "Destroyer" as given to him, but also his various terrifying *Bhairava* aspects, so famil iar till this day in Nepal.

The worship of this great god of the Himalayas -- some people even refer to him as "Adam" of the Kirat people--in the *linga* (phallic) representation is also indigenous to the Orient. Scholars have tried to prove that the earliest reference to phallus worship can be traced among the Greeks. But the abundance of *lingas* in the Indus Valley civilisation sug gest with certitude that it was Asia which gave the world the phallic cult. Even granting that the Greeks were familiar with a form of phallus worship in their heyday around the 6th century B.C., it is common knowledge that the Indus Valley civilisation flourished some 3000 years before Christ. The western research ers may well have attributed the Greek and/or the Romans with the origin of almost every single thing, but the need today, for us, is not to look at things through tinted glasses.

Granted, for argument's sake, that the "Shiva" of the Himalayas--the deity that ultimately found his way into the Vedic or Puranic pantheon--was too far removed from *Rudra* of the Indus Valley era, both distance-wise and time-wise. Granted, too, that the Kiratas, possibly a prehistoric people of the Tibeto-Burman origin that dominated areas lying between the Himalayas and the Ganges, could not have been associated with the Indus Valley civilisation, as held by many scholars.

Yet, the Kiratas of the Himalayan belt do find a mention in such ancient texts as the *Vedas*. They are referred to, for instance, in the *Yajurveda* as also in the *Atharva veda*, not to speak of the later *Puranas* and epics such as the *Mahabharata* and the *Ramayana*. Now, even the most authentic dating of the *Vedas* puts their authorship to sometime between 2500 B.C. and 1500 B.C. By this reckoning, too, the Kirata civilisation, if there was any, antedates the Greek one by at least a few hundred years.

And lord Shiva as a Kirata deity must have lived sometime around the Vedic age, if not earlier. How the phallic worship originated in this part of the world is a different question, but to ascribe its invention to the Greeks is a far-fetched *imagination*.

There is another way of looking at it too. The *Vamshavalis* (geneaologies), which are the major source of pre-historic information about Nepal in general and the Kathmandu valley in particular, also suggest that the Kiratas were the original settlers in this region. The *Vamshavalis* give us a list of some 29 Kirati kings who had ruled the Kathmandu val ley, and some of them have ever been treated as contemporaries of Lord Buddha. Agreed that these *Vamshavalis* have yet to find archaeological or epigraphic corroboration to prove their authenticity. But till such time that counter-evidence is forth coming, we will be justified in believing, after the *Vamsha valis*, that the Shiva-worshipping Kirata civilisation flour ished in Nepal around 3000 B.C. As such, even in the present state of our knowledge, sketchy as it is, we can question the contention that the phallus-worship originated in ancient Greece and Rome.

Fusion of Faiths

That in a tolerant Nepal the Hindu and Buddhist deities brush shoulders or share a common temple-roof is a common-enough cliche. Also well-known is the patronage received by Buddhist shrines and deities at the hands of devout Hindu royalty and laity alike. How far in the past do the roots of this Nepalese heritage lie ?

One of the more remarkable inscriptions at Patan *Gairi Dhara*, it is said, dates back to 659 A.D. and is attributed to Narendra Deva, a Lichhavi king. This inscription records, among other things, the fact that the devotees had been enjoined to associate even *Pasupat* Brahmans (another Hindu sect) in the community feasts organised on the occasion of the Buddhist *Vajareshwa ra* festivities.

Now, presuming that the *Pasupats*, besides being Hindus, were *Brahmans* who donned the *Jogi* attire, and that lord Vajreshwara was verily a Buddhist deity, it's obvious that this royal exhortation was aimed at bringing about an increasing rapport between the Hindu and Buddhist commonality.

It is fairly well-known that the *Vaishnava* and the *Shaiva* Hindu sects were in the ascendancy in the Lichhavi social echelon. It is, therefore, of no mean significance to note that some Lichhavi kings took a lead in constructing Buddhist *viharas* on their own. The *Kwa-Baha* in Patan, for instance, is credited by some to king Bhaskara Deva, while the *Chuka Baha*, another notable Lalitpur landmark, is said to have been named after the famous Lichhavi king, Manadeva, its builder. Also, a Thakuri king, Guna Kama Deva, is believed to have revived the ancient Buddhist tradition of the *Mataya* festive procession, now popular in Patan. Why, even the so- called "Buddhist Sphinx", or Bodhnath, Nepal's largest chaitya to-date, was originally built by another Lichhavi king, Shiva Deva, who is also said to have built the *Uku Baha* in Patan, according to a tradition.

The *Nepal Mahatmya*, a chronological but mostly undated account, has found wide acceptance as a source of the kingdom's history. And, if one were to go by it, its emphasis on the desirability of a Hindu worshipping at the Swayambhu *chaitya* can only be matched by the *Swayambhu Purana*, which, in its turn, underscores the virtues connected with the worship, by its Buddhist adherents, of lord Pasupati nath.

It is traditions such as these that find expression, till today, in the worship of, among others, lord Machhindranath and of the 'vestal-virgins' (*Kumaris*) even by ruling Nepalese Hindu monarchs on the one hand, and the thronging, by the Buddhists, of Pasupatinath on *Mukha Ashtami* day when the *Shiva Linga* there is made to don the coronet of Five Buddhas (*Pancha Buddha*), every year.

Not uncommon, also, is the practice of giving separate names to the same deity. The 'Red' Machhendra (also known as *Bunga Dyo*), for instance, is regarded by Nepalese Buddhists as Padmapani Lokeshwara (or Karunamaya) himself. But the fact that the *Nath* appellation has been added to "Machchhendra" goes to suggest that this happened somewhere along the course of history when the Hinduistic *Nath* sect had been in the ascendancy, 12th century onwards.

The *Seto* (or White) Machchendra *Jatra*, likewise, couldn't have been anything but a Buddhist festival initially. Two factors go to suggest that this was so. Firstly, that the deity is still known as the *Jana Baha Dyo* in local parlance, the term, Baha, in its turn, being a derivative of the Buddhist *vihara*. And, secondly, it is the *Gubhajus* (Buddhist priests) who take precedence in officiating over this *jatra*. But these facts do not deter the Hindu laity from worshipping this deity with all devotion and gusto.

Taking this line of argument a bit further, we come across almost a similar situation when it comes to propititating Manjushree. Well, it hardly needs reiteration that Manjushree is often regarded as a Chinese savant who is credited with the founding of civilisation in the Kathmandu valley. The mythical savant, also known as Manju Ghosha, has been identified by some with Bodhisatva Amitabha while there is another school of thought which has, of late, laid claims to his having been a local saint hailing from Sankhu.

Be that as it may, however, the Hindus, to this day, are confirmed in their belief that Manjushree is an incarnation of goddess Saraswati and worship 'her' accordingly, year after year, on the *Basanta Panchami* day. Interestingly also, the object of worship in this case, be it for the Buddhists or the Hindus, is one and the same image located in the vicinity of Kathmandu's Swayambhu temple!

Namura, otherwise also known as Namo Buddha, is a holy Buddhist pilgrimage centre near Banepa. The place is believed to have been hallowed by the visit of lord Buddha in person some 2600 years ago, as the name itself also implies. Thousands of devotees, Hindus and Buddhists alike, make a bee-line to the place, particularly on occasions like the full moon day in the month of *Kartik*, when an image of Harihara, flanked by Lakshmi and Parvati, is carried around on a *Khat* procession. Interestingly enough, Harihara is also a name given to lord Shiva, a Hindu deity, but here he is regard ed as the Buddhist deity, *Maha satva* or *Dharmapala*.

While most gateways of the Buddhist *viharas* (known also as *Bahas* and *Bahis*) in Nepal are not unoften "guard ed" by a "Hindu" Hanumana statue, their centre courtyards also invariably feature a *Dharma Dhatu* supposed to symbolise the thunder-bolt of lord Indra, the king of Hindu divinities. It is also no less interesting to note that the *Baha Puja*, a popular Buddhist ceremonial procession, almost always ends up with a worship of lord Ganesha, with the Buddhist householders, who organise such *Pujas*, often paying a visit to the Koyna Ganesh near Chobhar.

But this tradition of accommodating the Hindu and Buddhist deities in one and the same pilgrimage centre isn't limited to the Kath mandu valley and its vicinity alone, as is generally believed, but has been a common feature almost everywhere in the kingdom. The famous *Kankre Vihar* in far-west Surkhet, for instance, doesn't lag behind any others in the sense that images of both Shiva and Buddha have shared the same shrine together for many a past decade.

The First Great Yogi

Two basic criteria that determine a *Yogi* Hindu ascetic are said to be *Vairagya* (non-attachment to worldly objects) and *Yoga* (meditation). And both these attributes single out lord Shiva as the greatest of all *Yogis*, past or present, it is said.

From the standpoint of his devotees, here is a divinity who is pleased and satisfied by the offering of a mere *bel* fruit or leaf, nothing more. He wears no garments either, except for a tiger skin wrapped around his loins. A frequenter of graveyards and cremation grounds, he doesn't even have a home to call his own. He is also often pictured as a vagrant, smeared with ashes or adorned with skulls and snakes. His only possession is the *trishula* (trident). He is thus the arch *Yogi* who sits atop the Kailash mountain, oblivious of the world around him, rapt in meditation.

As is known to many, the origin of *Yoga* as a life-style is attributed to Patanjali, author of *Yoga Sutras* (fifth century A.D.), with Vyasa (6th century A.D.) as the earliest commentator on it.

Unlike the *Sankhya* school of philosophy, which is mainly theoretical, the *Yoga* school is thoroughly practical. The system is not so much concerned with the nature of the soul as with the con crete steps one can undertake to liberate it from the mundane bondages of life.

Yoga, by implication therefore, teaches a system of mind and body-training that helps one obtain release from the cycle of births and deaths. *Vairagya*, one of the primary Yogic attributes, arises out of a conviction of the evil that is life, and a realisation of its ills.

Yoga or meditation, the other attribute, is a system of training, moral as well as physical attributes, that aims at imbibing in the trainee such virtues as: (1) Non-injury (*Ahimsa*), (2) Truthfulness (*Satya*), (3) Abstinence (*Asteya*), (4) Celibacy (*Brahmacharya*), (5) Disowning of possessions (*Apari graha*), (6) Purity (*Sucha*) (7) Contentment (*Santo sha*) (8) Fortitude (*Tapasya*), (9) Study (*Svad hyaaya*), and (10) Devotion to gods *(Isvara-Bhakti)*.

This training has two stages: the first comprises *Aasana* (bodily postures), *Pranayama* (control of breath) and *Pratyahara* (withdrawal of senses from the objects around). The second includes *Dharana, Dhyana* and *Sa madhi*-- different forms of concentration. Of these, *Samadhi* is the highest stage of Yoga. In this state, which is also the highest and most desirable, the mind is so controlled as to enable the *Yogi* to lose all consciousness of the outside world as also of self, and virtually to pass into the realm of mysticism.

The occult powers of a true *Yogi* are said to be tremendous. Powers, for example, of making himself invisible at will and suspending himself in mid-air. Such claims may appearexag gerated but there is little doubt that a Yogi can exercise remarkable control over his nervous system, his mind and his body. There is no dearth of 'eye-witnesses' who have seen Yogis raising themselves two or three feet above the ground and remain ing suspended in the air for quite a while, or burying themselves underground, with air and water-supply cut off for hours, or even days, with no visible ill-effects, let alone death. It is said that a Yogic teacher of Ranjit Singh, a Sikh king of India, remained thus buried for 45 days and then emerged alive!

Nepal-India, Nepal-Tibet

In the dim darkness of pre-history, a number of ancient holies are either said to have visited Nepal or gone out from here to distant India and Tibet primarily for religious pilgrimage. It is commonly held, for example, that Dharmakara, a disciple coming along with the Chinese savant, Manjushree, was probably the first ruler Kathmandu valley ever had and that king Prachandadeva, from Gaud (Bengal), came here to become the disciple of another legendary saint, Gunakara.

Coming to history proper, Shankaracharya figures prominently as an eighth-century Hindu savant from

Photo by *Yeti Photos Centre*

Photo by *Yeti Photos Centre*

Photo by Yeti Photos Centre

Photo by *Gyanendra Das, Das Colour Lab*

South India who is said to have visited the valley on a seemingly self-appointed mission to re-instal Hinduism (more precisely, Shaivism) back on the pedes tal from which it had more or less been dislodged by competing local cults.

Not that we are in a position to contradict this account, appear ing primarily in our *Vamshavalis*. But what should be stated rather categorically, at least in order to set the record straight, is that the accounts dealing with Shankaracharya's own holy travels do nowhere mention Nepal in the list of countries visited by him. As such, we aren't prepared to believe, merely on the basis of legends and tales, that Shankaracharya did, in fact, set foot in Nepal. Nor has it been proved that Dharmadduta, a king of Coonjeeveram, also in south India, was the person to build the famous temple of Pasupatinath, as the chroni clesaver.

But we have evidence to suggest that there were some other Shaiv ite savants who had visited Nepal sometime or other in its history. One of the better known among them was, for instance, Acharya Amritamitra, a priest and pilgrim hailing possibly from Varanasi. He is also said to find mention in *Kulottara Tantra*, dated Nepal Sambat 289 (1169 A.D.)

That such visiting pilgrims go to form a link in the long chain of Nepal-India relations and religious exchange is undeniable. What's interesting also, in this context, is to note that not only laymen but also kings from distant lands made it a point to visit Nepalese holy places.

Dharmapal, another king of Bengal, for instance, is said to have made a pilgrimage to the then famous Shaivite religious shrine of Gokarneshwar near Kathmandu. Also, one Lakshmideva Som, a "great" Brahmin scholar from far off Maharastra in south India, not only visited Nepal for a pilgrimage but also had an image of Shiva cast and set up here, along with an inscription dated N.S. 534 (1414 A.D.). Evidence such as this go to indicate that Nepal's fame as a pilgrimage centre wasn't limited to its neighbouring principali ties but had spread almost up to the shores of the Indian ocean-- it had become, in other words, verily a centre of international repute. Likewise, Dr. Jagadish Chandra Regmi, a well- known researcher in history, mentions of a pillar in the vicinity of Balaju bearing an inscription in what he believes is a south Indian, possibly Kannada, script, leading to the presumption that pilgrims coming here from far away Karnataka may have set up the pillar and a possible Nandikeshwar image adjacent to it. The inscription is dated N.S. 705 (1585 A.D.).

The Damodarpur copper-plate inscription (said to belong to the period of Buddha Gupta, a king of India's Gupta dynasty) bears reference to a land-gift made by one Ribhupal in honour of *Kokamukha Swami*, "of the Himalayas". Now, eminent Indian historians like Hem Chandra Roy Chowdhury and Dr. Radha Kumud Mukherjee tend to agree that the inscription alludes to Baraha Chhetra in the Nepal terai, till this day a well-known religious centre believed to be hallowed by lord Vishnu in his boar incarnation. Ribhupal not only visited this holy land of the Vaishnavites and made the aforesaid gift, but also drew inspiration to set up a replica of the *Varaha* image in Dinajpur in Bengal (India) for the convenience of his kith and kin who couldn't afford the arduous trip to Baraha Chhetra, it is said.

If Nepal was thus a cynosure for the eyes of Hindu pilgrims even in ancient times, it was no less significant as a Buddhist pilgrimage centre. We have, of course, heard about sages like Manjushree who came here all the way from China. Stories of Vipashwi Buddha, Sikhi Buddha, and Viswambhuva Buddha having preceded Manjushree in making a beeline for Nepal are also common. The last of the human (*Manushi*) Buddhas, Siddhartha Gautama, it is said, also came to Kathmandu and Banepa, wor--

shipped at a place which is known to this day as Namo Buddha or Namura, named after him. Also, it is very widely held that the four stupas existing till today at four cardinal points outside Lalitpur town were built by none other than emperor Ashoka himself who came to the valley along with his daughter, Charumati. Why, even the present-day township of Chabahil and the nearby Devapattan are said to have been founded by Charumati and her husband Devapala, respectively.

Nepal was a leading centre for Buddhist learning in the medieval ages, if not also in the ancient. One of the two noted Buddhist scholars to visit Nepal was Basu Bandhu (ca. 4th century A.D.) and Atisha Dipankara (10th century), while Buddhist scholars who fanned out to different directions from Nepal with a mission of spreading the Master's messages included such famous names as Shantibhadra (ca. 1055 A.D.), Bimalashri, Anantashri, and others. Ratna Rakshita and Ravindra were two other scholars of repute who had drawn better-known Tibetan *Vikhsus* like Dharmaswami to Nepal for a study of Buddhism. Dharmaswami, in his turn, is said to have gone on record saying that he had seen a large number of Tibetan students undergoing religious training in Nepal in the thirteenth century A.D. Roerich has penned a "Biography of Dharmaswamin" which provides a greater insight into him as a man and a scholar.

Hardly less interesting, although not as much highlighted hitherto, is the role played by the medieval Malla kingdom in western Nepal in the promotion and propagation of Buddhism. King Ashoka Challa, for instance, is credited with having left the legacy to posterity in the shape of two inscriptions at Bodh Gaya (India), indicating that he had made seemingly lasting arrangements for the worship of Buddha there besides probably making land and other grants to a Kashmiri priest for the purpose. Some other kings of the same dynasty, namely, Ripumalla, Punya Malla and Prithivi Malla, were also great patrons of

Buddhism and were said to have contributed their mite for its propagation and promotion.

According to the well-known Indian scholar, late Rahul Sankrittyayana, a notable personality to visit Tibet during the reign of king Shrong Tson Gampo and help translate many a Buddhist scripture into Tibetan was another Nepalese, Shilamanju. By so doing, he is said to have made outstanding contribution towards the propagation of the faith in Tibet in the 7th century.

Other Buddhist luminaries to follow the trail blazed by Shilamanju included Bodhi Gupta (ca. 967 A.D.), Bagishwar Kirti (ca. 1003 A.D.) a resident of Pharping near Kathmandu (according to Surya Bikram Gewali, another noted historian), Shanti Bhadra, Ananta Shree and Gautam Shree. Shanti Bhadra and Ananta Shree are particularly noted for their contributions in getting a number of Buddhist scriptures translated into the Tibetan language. Gautam Shree, in his turn, was not only known as "Maha Pundit" (great Buddhist scholar), but was also credited with the construction of the Saptapur Mahavihara, according to an early 10th century inscription at Guit Vihar, Lalitpur. Two other better-known scholars referred to in the same inscription include Shuva Shree and Rabindra Dev. According to Dr. Kamal Prakash Malla, a well-known scholar, "Ratna Kirti, Virochan (and) Kamalshree were well-known names at (India's) Vikramshila University...(where) Bagishwarkirti later on became a *Dwara pandit* (Head of the Department).... his disciples there in cluded scholars like Niropali Sen (Bengal) and Marpa, founder of Kagyu cult in Tibet. It was not an isolated instance but was a moment in Nepalese history which naturally reminds us of the Renaissance in Europe."

Dharmaswami, the Tibetan pilgrim referred to earlier, is said to have credited one Rabindra, possibly another Nepalese, with having taught him the Buddhist scriptures. Dr. Jagadish Chandra Regmi is of the opinion that

Rabindra and "Dasabal Labinha", as referred to by the famous lama Taranath in his treatise "History of Buddhism in India", could have been one and the same person.

Acharya Kshemendra was also another well-known teacher of the Vajrayana tradition in the fifteenth century. Some other seeming contemporaries of his were Sri Jayananda, Gyan Kirtisen and Acharya Subodh Jiva. As the term Acharya applied to most of them is an honorific appellation suggesting great veneration, we can assume that these were no ordinary mortals but Nepalese savants of great repute, despite the scanty references handed down to posterity by history till this day.

A Brahmin Disciple of Buddha

Brahmins, as is well-known, consider themselves to be patriarchs of Hinduism. To see a Brahmin scholar following the footsteps of lord Buddha and, that too, more than 2,500 years ago therefore, provides yet another sidelight into the beginnings of Hindu-Buddhist culturalfusion, so much a part of Nepal's heritage of religious synthesis since time immemorial.

As far back as in the 7th century A.D., the well-known Chinese pilgrim-historian, Yuan Chang, had eloquently portrayed this spirit of the fusion of faiths thus : "Buddhist convents and temples of Hindu gods touch each other (in Nepal)."

Sariputta and Modgallayana are perhaps the best-known two immediate disciples of lord Buddha. But the credit of being the first, or the "Eldermost", of lord Buddha's disciples goes not to either of them but to one Kaundinya.

"Fortyone *Bhikshus* attained special position during lord Buddha's lifetime, 'Gyata Kaundinya' being the foremost of them... Gyata Kaundinya *mahasthavir* could achieve the most covetable position of 'Ratragya', i.e., the eldermost disciple of the Lord," says one authority.

But the story of Kaundinya also provides an indication that is, at best, enigmatic. Or, in other words, if we are to believe in the legends surrounding prince Siddhartha Gautama, we may also be led to wonder if Buddhism, as a faith, did not exist even prior to himself !

Batukrishan 'Bhushan', for instance, has this to say :

"An astrologer *par excellence*, he (Kaundinya) had forecast, on the very day of Siddhartha's christening ceremony, that the prince "would attain Buddhahood". This leads one to presume that the terms like Buddha and Buddhahood were perhaps popular even prior to prince Siddhartha's advent on the earth.

We have also heard of or read about the *Aadi Buddha*, the *Dhyani* Buddhas and the *Manushi* Buddhas. The *Aadi* (literally, the primordial) Buddha, also known as *Panchagyana Aatmika*, is believed to have revealed himself in the form of the legendary "Flame of Light" at Swayambhunath and credited with the creation of the five *Dhyani* Buddhas, also known as *Tathagatas* or *Arupadakas* ("Those Without Parents")? They are cha racterised as 'Celestial' or heavenly and, by implication, immortal. Yet another group of Buddhas known as *Manushi* (human or mythical), include Vipashwi, Sikhi, Krakuchhanda, Vishwabhu, Kanakamuni, Kashyapa and Sakya Simha (also, perhaps, Dipankara and Ratnagarbha, making a total of nine).

The term 'Lord Buddha', as is well known, almost invariably refers to Siddhartha Gautama. But some accounts hold that our historic Buddha of the Shakya clan, born in Lumbini, son of king Suddhodhana, himself had accepted at least three of the *Manushi* Buddhas, namely, Vipashvi, Sikhi and Bishwabhu, as his 'forerunners'.

That this is so has also found corroboration in yet another independent source, this time a Tibetan *Terma* text attributed to the great guru, Padmasambhava (8th century), which, in the course of a legend in respect of the Bodhnath Stupa, has this to say: "In a bygone age countless *kalpas* ago, the Boddhisatva *Mahasatva*,... vowed at the feet of his *Guru*, the Buddha Amitabh, to liberate all beings from the misery of this world.

To turn, then, once again, to Kaundinya. He was a Brahmin by birth, was older than prince Gautama, as is alluded to by a legend which says he had 'forecast' the future of the prince even while he was just a new-born. He is said to have hailed from a Brahmin village, Dronabastu, in the vicinity of Kapilavastu, also known as Tilaurakot in recent times. Kaundinya came of a very wealthy Brahmin family of the area. He had a sister called Mantani.

Kaundinya was not only one of the 108 Brahmin priests whom king Suddodhana had invited to his palace at the christening ceremony of Gautama but was also the youngest member of a select band of eight experts to be assigned the task of name-giving. Seven priests out of these eight forecast, on the basis of astral calculations, that, should the new-born choose to settle down as a householder or a man-about-the-world, he would rise to the position of an all-powerful king or *Chakravartin*. Kaundinya, however, did not subscribe to this consensus and held that a person of the new-born's attributes was least likely to lead the life of an ordinary domestic or a family-man but would most certainly quit his home and 'become a Buddha'. The name *Siddhartha* was based on this interpretation of Kaundunya, it is said.

Not only that, Kaundinya is also said to have declared, at the very time, that he would 'follow the footsteps' of Siddhartha once the latter attained Buddhahood. And when he heard that prince Siddhartha had quit his home and had started residing in the Uruvela forest in Bodh Gaya, he proceeded to meet the sons of the seven Brahmin priests (his ertswhile colleagues at prince Siddhartha's naming ceremony) and said :

"Had your fathers been alive, they would have followed the footsteps of Siddhartha and become his disciples... Should you be interested to follow suit, come along with me to the Uruvela forest."

But only five among the eight decided to follow him to Uruvela. It is these five, led by Kaundinya, who have come down to Buddhist legends and history as the *Pancha-Vargiya*.

The point that is sought to be made here is that Kaundinya, a Brahmin priest, was not only a contemporary of prince Siddhartha but was one of the latter's first disciples. What's more important, his forecast that prince Siddhartha "wouldn't but be a Buddha" goes to give further credence to the belief that Buddhism as a religion was not something prince Siddhartha 'invented' but had been there even prior to his advent on earth.

The Shiva Linga Legends

There are several legends explaining the origin of the Shiva *linga* as the symbol of lord Shiva and as an object of worhip. The *Padma Purana*, for instance, holds a curse pronounced by the sage Bhrigu as being instrumental in the proc ess. It is said that sage Bhrigu was once deputed by other sages to find out who of the three gods, namely Brahma, Vishnu and Shiva, was the greatest. When Bhrigu came to Shiva's abode and tried to enter into Shiva's room, he was stopped from doing so by an attendant who said that his master was with Devi, his consort. Not seeing Shiva emerge even after a word had been sent, a patently furious Bhrigu cursed Shiva thus : "As thou, O Shankara, hast preferred Parvati to me, your forms of worship shall be the *linga* (phallus) and the *yoni*."

The *Vamana Purana*, in its turn, says that the Shiva *linga* became the object of worship as a result of curses uttered by several sages. When his beloved wife Sati died at her father Daksha's sacrifice, Shiva was driven to madness with sorrow and anger and, dancing demented, even naked, in one hermittage after another, he offended the resident *rishis* (sages) who cursed that Shiva would have his *linga* forfeited as a result. But meanwhile, at the intervention of Brahma and Vishnu on his behalf, the sages agreed to withdraw their curse on condition that Shiva should be represented by the *linga* which would become an object of worship.

A third legend contained in the *Shiva Purana* would have us believe that a demon named Bhima received a boon from Rama that made him invincible in war. In order to test his newly-acquired prowess, he laid seige over Kamarupa, a state in north-eastern India, conquered its king and took him prisoner. The latter, however, turned out to be a verygood devotee of lord Shiva whom he used to worship every day. One day, as he was engrossed in profound meditation before the *linga*, one of the demon's guards espied him and reported the matter to Bhima, who naturally became furious. Sword in hand, he entered into the prison and demanded: "Why dost thou worship the *lingam*? It is an evil thing to do in my domain". Undaunted, the king replied, "In truth, the *linga* is none but lord Shankara himself and I do always worship it, come what may." A sword-weilding Bhima then said, "Witness now the power of thy Lord," and struck the *linga* with it. As soon as the sword touched the *linga*, however, *Hara* (a sound) emanated from it which converted itself into a terrible roar: "Behold, I am verily the *Ishvara* (god) who appears for the protection of his devotees, anytime, anywhere". Also simultaneously, Bhima and his armymen were instantly reduced to ashes by the flame of fire shooting out of the *lingam*, leading posterity to worship lord Shiva in the form of the *linga* ever since.

And then there is this story: Brahma and Vishnu were fighting for their supremacy on a particular occasion when lord Shiva emerged from the depths of the earth in the form of a flame shooting up from a colossal *linga* which covered the entire sky. Unnerved at this unique phenomenon, Brahma and Vishnu decided to find out the beginning or the end of this flame. Vishnu assumed the shape of a boar and started to dig the base of the *linga* while Brahma took the shape of a swan and flew up into the sky to discover its top, but without success. In order, however, to establish his superiority over Vishnu, Brahma uttered an untruth to the effect that he did reach the end of the glorious fire. For evidence, he said, a holy cow was his witness. The cow apparently confirmed Brahma's statement by nodding her head while, at the same time, wagging her tail to imply that she was refuting the 'statement' thus made ! Lord Shiva then appeared in the scene and held that Vishnu was truthful enough to admit his failure while Brahma was not. As such, Vishnu would be worshipped in the same manner and to the same degree as Shiva himself was, while Brahma would be denied worship at par with the two. That is why, it is said, the cult of Brahma has no independent existence of its own in today's society. Also, since that time the worship of the Shiva in the phallus form has been permanently established on earth!

Environment Worship

A conservative estimate puts the annual depletion of forests, in the tropical countries alone, to the tune of 8 million hectares. A staggering figure indeed. In our own country too, experts presume, there may be no forests left towards the turn of this century if the present pace of deforestation goes unchecked. Even such fearful predictions, however, seem to have raised little general alarm, at least among the common people. Improved nature-conservation practices often receive no more than a lip-service, if they are not given a complete go-by.

It is worthwhile pondering, in this context, how the modern view of ecologists and nature conservationists finds ample and elo quent support in our religious texts, legends and lore. Our ancient sages and seers evolved a system of faith which imparts divinity to almost every plant, tree and even grass. They have also enjoined, at the same time, that we should consider plant life as being equally valuabe as human life. The need to restore the balance between Man and Nature, or, at least, not to disturb the ecological balance, is highlighted, for instance, in scriptures like the *Matsya Purana*, which, it is said, not only exhorts all people to plant trees in order to earn heavenly merit, but also warns, on the other hand, that any harm done to any plant life amounts to a religious sacrilege, a crime of the magnitude of murder itself !

That the Hindu and Buddhist philosophy of life imparts divinity to various plants and trees is evident from the esteem and reverence in which we hold the *Bar* and *Pipal* trees, among others. Both these trees are regarded as being the incarnations of lord Vishnu and his divine consort, Lakshmi, or of lord Shiva and his consort, Parvati. The *bel* tree, likewise, serves as the very substitute of lord Shiva, to be literally worshipped both during the annual *Shivaratri* ("The Night of Lord Shiva") festival and in the course of the month-long *Swasthani* fasting festival in the month of *Magh* (January-February). Why, the Newar community even regards the *Bel* as the incarnation of the Kumar (the Eternal Bachelor), as is evidenced in their popular social and religious ritual, the "Ihi", organised in order to mark the attainment, by the Newar girls, of puberty.

And there is the story of *Kalpabriksha*. This tree, which the Hindus believe was planted in heaven, was supposed to bring all human wishes, including immortality, to fruition. Another focus of attention in many a Hindu myth and legend is the *Parijat* tree and flower, also known as the *Rudilo* or the Jasmine. A legend woven round Kathmandu's famous *Indra Jatra* festival has it that lord Indra had once attempted to steal the *Parijat*, and had, with that end in view, taken a human form. The Kathmandu people caught him in the process of stealing, however, and had him imprisoned, but realising later that their prisoner was no other than lord Indra himself, they not only let him go scot-free, but also organised the festival in his honour.

The banana and bamboo plants, in their turn, are said to symbolise the *Vatsu Devata* (God of the Household), and are regarded as indispensable in decorating houses and shrines as and when an auspicious ceremony, like a wedding, takes place. There is also the *Pancha Pallava*, a combination of five leaves or sprouts, that figure in our holy altars or form a leafy canopy over the puja *Mandapas*. Nor is a Hindu religious ritual complete without either the *Kusha* grass or the *Dubo* (Durva). In fact, a whole day in the annual Hindu calendar, namely the *Kushe Aunshi* (sometime in July-August), is even exclusively reserved for the ritual propitiation of the *Kusha* grass. The *Dubo*, in its turn, is said to represent lord Ganesha, or the elephant-headed deity. Likewise, a Nepali *Dasain* festival without the omnipresent *Jamara* leaf and sprout growing from a receptacle, placed near the family altar and nurtured with love and devotion for nine consecutive days ending in the *Tika* day, would be difficult to imagine.

We can see, thus, that our ancestors have tried their utmost to inculcate in us a love and respect towards plants and trees of almost every hue. How else could our elders and predecessors have developed a spirit of adoration and reverence among their progeny towards the plant kingdom, given the generally unlettered and superstition-ridden society that ours is ? The *Jatakas* and *Puranas* have also woven out countless stories designed to teach us nature conservation through the medium of religious rituals. Some of these stories are designed to impress on all people the absolute need for desisting from destroying natural heritage on the one hand and to plant, love and rear trees and forests to the utmost possible extent, on the other.

The disastrous impact that lies in store for human civilisation as a result of our rampant and reckless destruction of the eco- system could perhaps be better explained to the generally unlettered majority of our people with a mix with the mystic. The cultural and religious susceptibilities of the common man should not be given a go-by, that is.

The Shaligram :A Divine Stone

Up on the other side beyond the massive, snow-capped silveriness of the Annapurna, Dhaulagiri and Nilgiri mountains, along the upper--and surprisingly, wider-reaches of the Kali Gandaki, people go hunting for the legendary multi-hued stone-pebbles known as the *Shaligram*. So seemingly do the sturdy *Bakkhu*-clad muleteers who drive hordes of yaks, mules and donkeys either on their way up towards Jomosom or down towards Tatopani. The famed *Shaligram* is a kind of smooth and shiny, often oblong like a bird's egg, fossilised ammonite, so dear and sacred to all Hindus.

They also are, according to science, an extant order of mollusks, some 100 to 200 million years old ! In Kathmandu, one often hears tales of the "one-eyed" or "one-mouthed" *Rudraksha* rosary-beads and "one-eyed" *Shaligrams* being the rarest of collectors' items and fetching enormous prices if only one can lay hands on them. And, curiously enough, the Pasupatinath temple is reputedly the sole repository of the only extant pieces in Nepal, of both such a *Rudraksha* and *Shaligram*. The "eyes" in a *Shaligram*, believe scientists, lead to air- chambers within that permit the shells to "swim" to a certain degree.

We find reference to *Shaligrams*-- as also their antiquity and the high religious esteem in which they have been traditionally held-- in many *puranas* like the Skanda, Padma, Varaha, Bramhanda and Narasimha. Scholars hold that the origin of *Shaligram* worship in this part of the world dates at least to 2000 years. It is said also that the *Vajra-Kit* (a worm as strong as the *Vajra*) that remains embedded in a circular form, like a coiled-up snake, inside the *Shaligram* stones, represents lord Vishnu himself. Also, the number of *Chakra* coils found inside them is believed to be a measure of their relative 'holiness'- a single coil representing the *Sudarshan*, a double one representing Lakshmi-Narayana, and the like. A total of twelve or more coils, one spiral stop the other, is said to exist inside these stones.

Besides their value as rare curio items or their inherent religious characteristics, the *Shaligrams* are also much sought after, commercially, on the strength of the popular belief that grains of gold are found inside them!

Shaligrams are believed to come in many hues--white, black, red, yellow, grey, etc. Many of them also bear long, thread-like streaks of white or grey appearing all around the outer casing; these streaks, the devotees believe, represent the *Janai* or holy-thread worn by lord Vishnu or lord Shiva, as you please :

Despite the age-old Nepalese belief that it is *sinful* to trade in *Shaligrams*, this traditional taboo is seen to have been observed more in violation over the decades. Nepalese history is replete with instances where successive governments have, time and again, found the futility of imposing restrictions on *Shaligram*-trading at the hands of irreverent traders at exhorbitant prices. The *Mulki-Ain* (legal code) promulgated in 1910 B.S. (1853 A.D.), for example, set the price of the Lakshmi Narayan variety at Rupees one hundred a piece-not a pice more!

Also, with a view to discouraging the rampant practices of breaking-up of *Shaligrams*, edicts seem to have been issued, occasionally, by Nepalese authorities. The last one to come to our notice in the form of a stone inscription dates back to 1898 A.D., (some 93 years ago), issued by premier Bir Shumshere. In fact, it seems to have been prompted by the constant and repeated floutings of many earlier edicts and official circulars on the subject. The text of the said stone inscription, in the Muktinath area, has been reproduced by the well-known scholar savant, Yogi Naraharinath, in one of his publications. Any further violations of the order, the edict is said to have read, will lead "to the arrest and imprisonment of the accused for two months."

How important a place *Shaligram* worship has occupied in Nepalese culture (both Hindu and Buddhist) is also evident from the fact that at least four ancient and published Sanskrit manuscripts on the subject have been found to exist in the National Archives to this day. There have been, scholars hold, many other books besides these, which include a full-length *Shaligram Upanishad*, a *Shaligram Nighantu*, and a *Shaligram Mimamsha*, among others.

Controversies

CHAPTER EIGHT

The Yeti Stories

Wangdi and Pasang were two Sherpas who joined F.M. Smythe's expedition in 1937 which took the first-ever photograph of the huge Yeti foot-prints at a height of 16,000 feet in the central Himalayas. It is said to have actually visited their base camp at 5,170 meters. To quote:

"We, Wangdi Norbu Bhotia and Pasang Urgen, were accompanying Mr. Smythe over a pass when we saw tracks which we know to be those of a *mirka*, or the Wild Man. We have often seen bear, snow leopard and other animal tracks, but we swear that these tracks belonged to none of these."

Such stories about the *Mirka*, or *Shokpa*, or *Metoh Kangmi*, or *Dremo*, or *Ragshi Bonpo*, or *Mitre*, or Yeti--Nepal's legendary and prize fauna--are galore.

Long before Western man came to the Himalayas to climb them or to explore, a belief in the existence of the Yeti, also known after Henry Newman's translation in 1936 of *Metoh Kangmi* as the Abominable Snowman, persisted in the minds of the Nepalese. Many a mountain monastery displays somber likenesses of the Yeti, while the Khumbu monastery, at the base of the Mount Everest, even preserves what the pesple believe to be a Yeti scalp.

The scientific interest in the Yeti began as early as in 1899 when Waddel reported to the West about the trail of the "hairy wild man" of the Himalayas. Howard-Bury's report of having seen Yeti footprints on the 21,000 foot Lhakpa-la pass followed (1921) and was confirmed by what Ronald Kaulback said were "five sets of tracks which looked as though made by a bare-footed man" in Upper Salween at a height of 16,000 feet. Since then many Westerners including W.H. Tilman and John Hunt (1937), Eric Shipton (1951), Wyss-Dunant (1953), Abbe P.Bordet (1954), Tom Slick (1957), Neel Barber (1959) and Sir Edmund Hillary (1961), amongst many others, have tried a tryst with the Yeti, but with little success beyond further sightings of the proverbial footprints. Some members of the Japanese Sendai Club expedition to the 7,219 meter Annapurna South peak in October 1975 held that the Yeti actually visited their base camp at 5,170 meters !

But, whether or not the explorers will ever come across the Yeti, the Nepalese mountainfolk will continue to believe in its existence as long as hair-raising stories about the "experiences" of their own people remain in popular circulation, as they do to this day--stories, for example, of a neighbour having gone to live with a female Yeti, or of a Sherpa girl having been kidnapped by a *mirka*, only to return from the wilderness with a baby, that looks less like a human offspring, in her arms!

Meeting the barefooted bogeyman, the Nepalese argue, is an unwelcome adventure. However, a man is able sometimes to worst a Yeti encounter simply with the help of a torch or a firebrand which, with all their hair, the Yetis dread being burnt and simply lope away. It is easy, too, to elude a female of the species; you simply run down-hill, for her enormous drooping breasts and long hair (covering her eyes) hinder her downward movement, the Sherpas say.

Huge and hairy, the body of the *Shokpa* bulges with muscles. He looks like a cross between man and ape, but walks erect and more like a human - being than an animal. Some specimens are as tall as 2.5 meters--much too big to be a Himalayan human--with arms reaching their knees and hands powerful enough to crush a human skull to smithereens ! A slightly conical head with small expressionless eyes sits on an enormous chest. His calls are weird and nerve-shattering but a musky odour emanating from him and permeating the environs he stalks will scare a nervy Nepali miles away ! He leaves oversized footprints, some measuring up to 40 cms. in length, on snow and mud, but what fools the uninitiated (god help him !) is his turned-about feet, it is said !

Marriages between the Yetis and human-beings aren't unknown, if you believe the stories ! At Chilankha, a village three days trek north of Kathmandu, a very tall and robust man, his monkey-like facial features still driving a chill down the local's spine, claims a *Shokpa* ancestry on the father's side--three generations away. People who have seen him vouch for his enormous strength by saying that he easily lifts weights meant for three average porters. Another family in Tarkeghyang in the Helambu region to the north of Kathmandu, is also believed to be a progeny of a Sherpa mother and a *Shokpa* father, while yet one more family in Melumche village is said to claim the reverse, that is a *Shokpa* mother !

Any harm done to this shaggy mountain monster recoils on the humans or on one's own family, so runs a local Nepalese belief. The *Shokpa* therefore, is held in awe and reverence by the lamas and the laity alike. A prevalent superstition has it that whoever encounters a *Shokpa* may die an instant, violent death. So, if a Sherpa, even by chance, comes across a *Shokpa*, he will instinctively shut his eyes with his hands or turn back and run away !

Yogi Naraharinath, a famous mendicant-scholar of Nepal and a widely travelled man, even lays claim to have personally come across the Yeti while he, along with a group of pilgrims, was trekking laboriously up beyond the Sarsyu *Gompa* (monastery) on way to the Manasarovar lake beyond the Himalayas.

"It was about eight in the morning", says Naraharinath. "At the height we were at, any likelihood of coming across a living creature was a virtual impossibility.

"Suddenly, I was face-to-face with the most unprecedented and unique life-time experience-- for, along a snow-covered ridge there stumbled, with a sure-footed downward move towards the banks of the Shivaganga river, a gigantic, awe-striking snowman !

"He turned his head to glance towards me, but didn't stop. He crossed the path and proceeded in the direction of Mount Kailash, western flank.

"I stopped breathlessly short and, when the rest of the party caught up with me, all I could do was to point a finger towards the *Shokpa* and ask, "What on earth is that ?"

"The arrival of my friends," continues the *Yogi*, "helped me gather courage enough to take a box-camera from my pack and to take a shot at the *Shokpa*, who, however, was only half visible by then in the thick, drifting snow-mist". The resultant photograph, naturally not a sharp one, is still in his possession, claims the *Yogi*.

This intriguing, if incredible, sighting was later discussed by the pilgrims with other people of *Chiu Gompa* and *Mul Gompa* lamaseries as they journeyed along, but the locals thought nothing much of it, since, according to them, *Shokpas* were nothing uncommon in the area.

To those that dismiss the stories that the Yeti could be an offshoot of the pre-historic man and that the Yeti tracks could simply be bear-ones, one may simply quote M. Heurelman's candid opinion as expressed in *Science at Avernir* in 1952. Says he, "One need only look at a track to see if the big toe is on the inside or the outside to decide whether it was made by a primate or a bear". To this Mr. James Schuman adds, "Scientific annals are littered with the tarnished reputations of men who dismissed initial reports of the existence of the giant squid, the gorilla, the Okapi and the giant panda".

Thus it is that the Nepalese aren't normally prone to raise sceptical eyebrows at the Yogi's story-- or, for that matter, at the very many *Shokpa* stories circulating amidst them. Well, who knows if, one day...

Mystery of Buddha's Death

"All humans are equal", said the Buddha and, by so doing, let loose a storm that, more than sending jitters down the spine of a traditional caste-ridden Hindu society, swept himself off his feet !

Hindusim stood for casteism and Buddha opposed it. It was noth ing for Buddha to partake of the food offered by Sujata-- a lowly untouchable girl as far as the Hindus were concerned, thereby drawing hordes of people of her ilk towards him, and away from Hinduism. What's more, Hinduism was based on sacrifices and rituals; Buddha had no respect for them. Hindus believed in a transcendental soul; Buddha did not support this belief. Thus, wasn't Buddha against almost all the basic tenets of the then prevalent Hindu faith ?

Obviously, Buddha had thus hit the citadels of Hindu norms and beliefs where it hurt them most. And, for all that he did to demolish the well-nurtured and cherished Hindu beliefs and insti tutions, he would be made to suffer, sooner or later.

This Hindu-Buddhist tug-of-war is brought into sharp focus even by the composition of the devotees and mourners gathered to collect the Master's relics on his death. We hear of representatives from Rajagriha, the Lichhavis of Vaisali, the Shakyas of Kapilvastu, the Bulis of Alkappa, the Mallas of Pawa and the Koliyas. Similarly, amongst the people who set up *Stupas* to preserve the Master's relics were the Mauryas of Pippalivana, the Nagas of Kalinga and even people of far-away Kandahar. But representatives of most Hindu principalities which were by far the largest in number (except one Hindu priest, Drona, and another Brahmin from Banadwipa) were conspicuous by their absence.

About Buddha's death itself, which took place in completely mysterious circumstances, this much is known: he had taken shelter in the house of one Chunda, a blacksmith. There he was treated with a dish containing *Sukar Mardava*, which is said to have brought about his end. Once school of thought holds the view that *Sukar Mardava* was a kind of mushroom, perhaps of the poisonous variety. The other holds that it was pork (ham or bacon).

An advocate of non-voilence throughout his long religious career, Buddha may well have abhored pork or, meat at all costs, except by mistake. What, therefore, he ate at the house of Chunda was more likely a dish of mushrooms, either poisoned or naturally poisonous. The question should now be asked: it they were poisoned, how far it was intentional; and secondly, had it been intentional, was Chunda's a lonely sadistic hand in the apparent conspiracy or was he just a tool at the hands of powerful enemies of Buddha, conspiring to do away with him?

Part of the answer may be gleaned from the proceedings of the Buddhist Council following the Master's death, where, conspicuous by his absence (at least at the initial stages), was Ananda, the otherwise well-known life-long friend and favourite disciple of Buddha. According to Tibetan scriptural sources, he was later charge-sheeted on seven counts, three of which were as follows:

(1) that Ananda had refused water to Buddha even as the Master lay dying and had requested Ananda thrice for it;

(2) that, immediately after Buddha breathed his last, Ananda disrobed him and exposed his naked corpse, including his genitals, to public view; and

(3) that, while wrapping the coffin for cremation, Ananda had disrespectfully stepped on the Master's body.

It is also said that Ananda had been struck with apparent remorse after the Master's death. What precise reasons led Ananda to weep over his "doings", we are not sure. Was it that he had been in the know of the conspiracy, had there been one, even if he had no hand in it himself? The following words of the dying Buddha, addressed to the repentant Ananda, are eloquent and reverberate in our memory with a resounding note :

"Ananda, futile it is to weep over me now. Whatever is born in this world is destined to death and destruction... ...I hope you will also rise above petty interests and may one day attain salvation"...

Not only this. The Council is also understood to have awarded a very severe punishment to one Channa, a charioteer of Buddha, with what in those days was known as *Brahma Danda*, besides expelling him from the Society of Buddhists. This step taken by the Council also leads us to strongly suspect Channa's role in that mysterious affair.

Agreed that all this is legend. Agreed also that legends do not make history, as history has to have the sanctifying touch of evidence, such as epigraphy. Our story has no such sanction behind it. But how about the contrary version-- the version of a natural death ? What do we have but the historian's word for it-- mere words at that and no evidence?

Who Was Hazrat Mahal?

Nana Saheb Peshwa died in Nepal, says one story. Begum Hazrat Mahal was born in Nepal, says another.

Both seem to have remained unsolved mysteries. "One of the unsolved mysteries of Asiatic history", wrote Percival Landon in 1928, "will always be the exact date of the death of Nana Sahib and the manner of his ending". The other one, if at all we can call it a mystery, is in respect to the birthplace of begum Hazrat Mahal.

Now, first Nana Sahib *alias* Dhandu Pant. He was a relative adopted by Baji Rao, the peshwa of Poona, and a representative of the Maratha claim to the empire of India. During the Sepoy Mutiny--later known as the First War of Indian Independence-- of 1957 A.D., this rebel leader had earned the nickname of "Devil Incarnate" at the hands of the British. Chased by the Britishers from his stronghold in Kanpur, he, along with his 13-year-old wife, Kasi Bai, and the widow of Baji Rao, crossed into Nepal in December of that year.

They were received at the Nepal-India border by Kedar Narsing, a Nepalese general, who had been specially deputed from Kathmandu for the purpose. Others who entered into Nepal along with Nana Saheb included rebel leaders like Tantia Tope, begum Hazrat Mahal, Benee Madhoo and the Raja of Gonda, Munnoo Khan. The Nepal authorities took upon themselves the responsibility of providing shelter to the Begum of Oudh, the two wives of Bazi Rao II the wives of Nana Saheb and Bala Rao whom they escorted to Kathmandu. Not only that; they were also given a monthly subsidy of Rupees four hundred each and a residence at Thapathali.

It is alleged that Kathmandu had given asylum to the rebel leaders partly because of their immense wealth which they had brought with them from India. Of course, as could be expected, most of the jewellery of the rebels was bought by, among others, premier Jung Bahadur. Why should he not ?

But there are also instances of Nepal helping some indigent rebel leaders with free gifts of land and offers of jobs. Col. Law rence, the then British Resident in Nepal, himself reported that "the Nepal Durbar had conferred a *jagheer* (free-hold land) on Surfraz Ali Khan", a rebel leader. Also, "Surfraz Ali's son was given employment in the Nepal Durbar with a pay of Rs. 200.00 a year", writes Ashad Hussain, another researcher on the subject.

The very act of providing asylum to the anti-British rebels was like tiny Nepal challenging the British lion. But challenge she did, as eloquently put by the noted historian, Dr. Tara Chand, who writes : "The plots which were hatched in different parts of India received encouragement from the neighbouring countries, especially Nepal...while (the Gurkhas) maintained minimum rela tions with the British envoy in their country". And this is corroborated by the British Resident himself: "The more I hear and see what is passing at this (Nepal) Durbar, the more con vinced I am that the sympathies of the *Sardars* and the army are with the rebels rather than wth us".

While most historians believe that Nana Saheb died of *Aul* (Malaria) at Deokhuri in west Nepal as reported by Lt. Col. Ramsay, the British Resident in Kathmandu, in his letter dated October 8, 1859, it is still a mystery whether it was actually Nana Saheb who had died there or someone else ! For, even as late as in 1895, various stories of Nana Saheb having surfaced up at this place or the other, at one time or the other, kept on circulating !

Now to turn to begum Hazrat Mahal. A tomb near Ghantaghar in Kathmandu, still extant, is believed to contain the mortal re mains of Hazrat Mahal. But little do we know that this historic personality, a leader of the Indian Mutiny in her own right, had expressed the desire to "return" to Nepal because she hailed from this country in the first place. Here is how the story goes :

"Wazid Ali Shah, the last Nawab of Lucknow, sat on the throne in the year 1847. Given to the pleasures of life, he was very fond of dance, songs and music. Around that time, some local courte sans came across a beautiful Nepali girl in the streets of Luc know. They took her with them, had her trained in the arts of the muses, and took her to the palace of Wazid Ali Shah. In the course of time, this Nepali girl rose to the status of one of the *begums* (queens) of Wazid Ali and was named begum Hazrat Mahal. That was a time when the wave of Sepoy Mutiny had been sweeping across the length and breadth of India."

"Wazid Ali, arrested by the British on February 7, 1856, was imprisoned at Metiabruz in far away Calcutta. It was then that Hazrat Mahal rose up in arms against the Britishers...

"Wazid Ali died while still under British custody at Metiabruz on September 1, 1887 at the age of sixty-eight. On his death, begum Hazrat Mahal expressed the desire to spend her last days in Nepal. Mangal Pande, the brain behind the Sepoy Mutiny, was put to the gallows on April 8, 1857. Bujhawan Pande, a close relative of Mangal Pande, in collusion with the Gonda king, Devi Bak Singh, undertook the mission of taking begum Hazrat Mahal to Nepal".

A slightly different, also more elaborate, version of the Hazrat Mahal story reads as follows:

"Nawab Wazid Ali Shah once fell in love with one of his mother's beautiful slave-girls. This slave-girl, a Nepali, had (earlier) been bought off the Lucknow market for Rupees seven and, after having been trained as a courtesan, was resold to the Nawab's palace.

"Sometime later the Nawab suddenly fell ill...Astrologers divined his illness as having been caused by one of the 28 palace slave-girls bearing *kundalis* (an evil omen in the shape of hair-curls?) at their napes... and suggested such signs be done away with. Most of the slave-girls, save the Nepali one, fled the palace out of fear.

... The nape of Hazrat Mahal's neck was branded with red-hot iron rods, but she suffered the resultant pain with surprising equanimity. Wazid Ali was so impressed as to fall in love with her and, braving his mother's protestations, married her. Soon she bore him a son who was named Birjis Kadir (Quadr).

"...When the Nawab was taken into British custody on February 7, 1856 and later removed to Calcutta as a war-prisoner, begum Hazrat was among the very few not to lose their cool. She not only stood her ground but also mobilised all her subjects into an army in order to fight the British invaders of Awadh--thereby earning for herself great acclaim as one of the foremost leaders of India's First War of Independence.

"On the 5th of July 1857, she also enthroned her son, Birjis, as the Nawab.

"...The war waged to shake off the British yoke continued till February 1858. ...But this prolonged struggle had sapped the vitality both of the begum and her subjects... Ultimately she had perforce to leave her Kesarbagh palace and ultimately to seek refuge in Muhammadabad (March 16, 1858).

"But Sir Colin Campbell would not let the queen escape unharmed and trailed her wherever she went. ..At long last, she and Birjis were safely escorted to Nepal by (rebel-leaders like) Bujhawan Pandey and the king of Gonda, Devi Baksh...

"The begum breathed her last at a place called Nuwakot in Nepal on April 7, 1879."

Where Was Kailashkuta ?

The recent HMG-ISMEO archaeological excavations in Kathmandu's Handigaon and Dhumbarahi areas have once again underscored the importance historical researchers have attached to this archaeo logically potential area. Articles discovered there included a *purnakalasha,* some ancient figurines, Lichhavi coins, *Makara* spouts and the like, thus alluding to the possibility of still richer treasures that may be unearthed later and that may unravel an ancient mystery.

One such mystery-- if it can be called one-- surrounds the celebrated Kailashkuta palace of Angshuverma and its possible location, and controversies haven't ceased raging amongst scholars and historians on this issue.

The more common belief is that the present-day Kailash ridge above the Pashupatinath temple is, in fact, an abbreviation of the word Kailashkuta, and, as such, no ground for raising any further controversy exists. Not all scholars support this contention, however.

But before we try to find out what historians have to say about its alternative site, a physical description of whatever little is available to us may be in order. A stone inscription at Bungamati, credited to the 6th century king Angshuverma and dated Manadeva Era 29 (V.S. 562 or 505 A.D.?), is said to describe the palace as the "cynosure of all eyes", whose splendour kept people gazing at it in awe and appreciation ! So utterly beautiful was this structural marvel that it could be likened to a *tika* on the "forehead of the Mother Earth," reads the account.

"This most exquisite of the world's palaces is a feast for the eyes and resembles a snow-white mountain, washed with moon-shine, and rising high into the sky", goes another description.

Even foreigners, it is said, used to gape in wonder at the sight of this marvellous piece of architecture. A Chinese pilgrim, for instance, has been quoted by a noted researcher on the subject, Gyanmani Nepal, as having expressed his appreciation in the following vein :

"So huge was the *Kailashkuta Bhavan* that it could accommodate 10,000 persons in the upper storey alone. It was surrounded on three sides by other palaces, each, again, seven storeys high !

"The roofs," continues the approbation, "were made of copper; golden water-spouts placed at the eaves and roof-corners were shaped like the snouts of crocodiles that kept on emitting fountain-springs of water. The supporting beams and pillars, windows and walls, were inlaid with costly stones like *muga*, pearls and the like....Nowhere else could one come across as beautiful and artistic a palace as this one."

A school of historical thought holds the view that, of the two famous palaces during the rule of the ancient Lichhavis, one was *Mana Griha*, attributed to emperor Mana Deva himself, and the other, Kailashkuta, possibly built and occupied by Angshuver ma as the prime minister. It is said that *Mana Griha* was located around the present-day Mangal Bazar in Patan and Kailash kuta near the present-day Deopatan, at the base of the Kailash ridge above-referred, on the banks of the Bagmati.

Another stone inscription, said to have been discovered at Naksal Narayan Chour some six kilometers west of Deopatan, and first deciphered by the noted historian, Levi, however, points to the possible existence of a citadel or *drung* at the same spot and a "so-called" Maneshwar village nearby. Mr. Nepal holds, on the strength of Levi's findings, that the site of Kailashkuta palace couldn't have been far removed from the temple of Man Maneshwari (or the present-day Handigaon near Bishalnagar), should this temple be identified with its namesake village of Maneshwar.

This later contention seems to find further corroboration in the fact that two more stone inscriptions, both attributed to Angshuverma, have also been discovered and lie embedded on the walls of a *dabali*-platform nearby, and date back to Manadeva Era 30 and 32 respectively.

Two years prior to this, i.e. till the year 28 of the Manadeva Era, Angshuverma had, it is said, been issuing edicts in the capacity of a minister of the Lichhavi king, Shivadeva. The 'fact' that he started issuing edicts not from Managriha (or the palace of Lichhavi kings) but from a separate Kailashkuta palace some two years later goes to indicate, according to Mr. Nepal, that in the period intervening, Angshuverma must have assumed the regal title himself and probably moved on to his new official residence, namely, the Kailashkuta Bhavan.

Concludes Mr. Nepal, "Those two stone inscriptions, unlike all others attributed to Angshuverma, bear no *dutak* (or medium ?) and thereby go to indicate that they had been placed nowhere other than the palace-precincts itself. Which, in its turn, is proof positive that, despite it having been lost to posterity due to the ravages of time, the Kailashkuta Bhavan was located at the same place and no other."

Added to this is the fact, says the author, that some bricks with the word 'Angshuverma' inscribed on them, have also been unearthed recently near Handigaon. But are these enough to put an end to the long-raging controversy ?

Was Bharavi a Nepali ?

"*Upama Kalidasasya, Bharave arthagauravam,*

Dandinah Padalalityam, Maghe santi trayogunah"...

The above is a Sanskrit couplet believed to be quoted from Udbhata's commentary on the *Kavyalankara* of Bhamaha.

Roughly translated, it reads:

"Kalidasa (is known for his) similes, Bharavi for his profundity of thought and meaning, Dandi for beauty of diction, and Magha (represents) the combination of all three attributes."

There have been countless Sanskrit poets and writers throughout history beginning from such ancient epic-writers as Valmiki and Vyasa, of the *Ramayana* and *Mahabharata* fame respectively. Coming to the middle ages, considered the most creative phase of classical Sanskrit literature, we come across many eminent poets and authors besides those named above, including Harsha, Vana, Bhartrihari and Bhavabhuti, to name just a few, who have shone across the literary firmament.

But, that the noted commentator, Udbhata (ca. 8th century A.D.), ignored scores of them by bracketing together just the four, Kalidasa, Bharavi, Dandi and Magha, in his above couplet goes to establish their unquestionable pre-eminence. And, as far as Bharavi is concerned, his qualities of head and heart is reflected in yet another quote, as follows:

"Despite virulent criticism and unpardonable glosses, Bharavi has survived with us for his most quotable quotes, profundity of thoughts, sublimity of diction, faithfulness of his description of men and nature, and for the 'feast of reason and the flow of soul'............."

This brief write-up, not purporting to present a critique of this famous poet and his immortal poetry, merely seeks to deal with the question of Bharavi's life and times, particularly in respect of his place of birth, lineage, etcetera. Where, in other words, was this celebrated author of *Kiratarjuniye* born, where did he live, who were his mentors and patrons and during which period of history ? All these have been subjects of diverse conjectures, speculations, claims and counter-claims at the hands of literary critics. It was only recently, that is' as late as in 1956, that Professor R. Gnoli's reading of a Nepalese inscription revealed, to the pleasant surprise of all concerned, the name of Bharavi in connection with the delimitation of the boundary of a monastery on the bank of river Manumati or Manohara near Kathmandu. This inscription is said to indicate that the poet appears to have begun his career as a religious acolyte during the Lichhavi rule in Nepal !

Writes Kaisher Bahadur K.C. in "The *Kiratarjuniye* by Bharavi" (1972):

"Although the date of this inscription was illegible, yet circumstantial evidence indicates that this was, perhaps, the last inscription proclaimed in the joint names of king Siva-deva I and Amsuvarman....This was the first indication that Bharavi....was born and brought up in Nepal and further that the poet was ante rior to king Siva-deva I and Amsuvarman."

But a note of caution seems to be in order here. For, the well known author of *India* (1959), Herman Goetz, is said to have made out a point, on the basis of the evidence of the 7th century poet Ravikirti's inscription in Magauti in south India, that Bharavi was the protege of a Pallavaking, Mahendra Varman (ca. 600-630). K.C. also alludes to Bharavi's references to Kanchi in south India, but that does not deter him from pointing out that "the poet was a much travelled man and that Nepal had contacts with the South Indian ports and cities" at the time.

The aforesaid dedicatory slab belonging to the Lichhavi period and bearing the name of Bharavi itself seems to have passed through a chequered 'career' in recent times. While the noted historian and researcher, Nayaraj Panta, had 'seen it' sometime in 1940 A.D. (at Harigaon ?), he and his colleagues were mysti fied to find it missing when they visited the site subseqently for a more detailed study. What seems to have happened, in the meantime, was that a neighbour of one Rajman Kusule, a local tailor, had the slab removed from the Harigaon platform in order to pave the foundation of his own house !

It must be said to be a sheer fortuitous accident, then, that K.C. ran across Rajman while doing the rounds of

Harigaon in search of the missing slab some 20 years later, in February 1967. And thanks both to K.C.'s perseverance and his chance-meeting with Rajman, this priceless treasure of antiquity was rescued and reportedly deposited in the Nepal Museum soon after.

On the strength of his reading of this stone inscription, K.C. asserts that it bears "northern Brahmi characters and Sanskrit language of early Lichhavi period" and that it "was inscribed by the order of Bharavi in order to commemorate the construction of a water- conduit (d*hara*) in honour of his grandfather, king Mana- deva I...through his daughter Vijayavati (and her 'Shiva- like' husband, Vartta, i.e., 'officer' Deva-labha)."

To quote K.C. further : "This *dhara* of Bharavi, which is situated in a secluded place to the north of the temple of what is known today as Satya-Narayana, has survived with a very an cient bas-relief of Uma Mahesvara, Makaras (mythical creatures with the face of a crocodile), Nakula (mongoose) lid-covers and chaitya to bear testimony to the poet's faith...This particular water-conduit spurts deliciously cool, clear and uncontaminated water as it has been described in the inscription of Bharavi." Delving in to the famous poet's geneaology further, K.C. adds that "Vijayasvamini (Dhruvasvamini) was the grandmother of Bha ravi."

It is further assumed that during the "dark period" marked by a power scramble following the death of king Mana-deva I and Vi jayasvamini, Bharavi's father Deva-labha may have lost his life and his wife put the poet in a monastery to pursue his career as a *Shramana*.

But the term *Shramana* means a pilgrim or religious acolyte and has more of a Buddhistic overtone. This, added to the belief that to Mana-deva goes the credit for "heralding" Vajrayana (the Buddhist path of the Thunderbolt), a cult particularly popular in Nepal and the

Photo by Yeti Photos Centre

Photo by Yeti Photos Centre

Photo by Gyanendra Das, Das Colour Lab

Himalayas, and K.C.'s assertion that "Bharavi made his Dvaipayana introduce the principles and practices of *Agama* to the court of king Yudhisthira", leads us to wonder if Bharavi was also a follower of Buddhism, besides being a great poet--and 'certainly' a Nepali !

Bhojpuri Ramayana:A Triangle of Love ?

The story of the *Ramayana* is too well-known to deserve repetition here. But some folklore connected with it provide interesting and curious sidelights.

Bhojpuri is a dialect widely spoken in southern Nepal bordering India, from Kapilvastu district in the south-west to the river Bagmati in the mid-east, besides, of course, the adjacent territories of north Bihar and Uttar Pradesh. Unlike its sister dialects, Awadhi and Maithili, it does not boast a literature worth the name, but the Bhojpuri treasure-house of folkore is both rich and varied. Given here are some portions of the Rama story gleaned from these folklore.

The story of Sita-- that she had been found by king Janaka while he was ploughing a field--isn't the whole truth, if we are to go by the Bhojpuri version. For it says that she was found in a wooden basket that came floating down a river. One day, king Janaka, in the course of his daily visit to the river for his ablutions, saw the floating basket and had his boatmen pull it ashore. When they opened it, to their utter surprise they saw a beautiful new baby-girl inside. King Janaka immediately decided to adopt her and gave her the name Sita.

Also, the usual story is that Kaikeyi, Rama's stepmother, had helped king Dasaratha in the field of battle and in return obtained the king's promise to grant her two wishes. When it was time for Rama's coronation, Kaikeyi came up to king Dasaratha and asked him to fulfil his promise. Her first demand was that Rama be banished to the forest and, the second, that her own son, Bharata, be crowned instead. King Dasaratha had no option but to yield to her wishes.

No, says the Bhojpuri version. In fact, according to it 'the tussle between Kaushalya, Rama's mother, and Kaikeyi had started the very day Rama was born. It says that Kaikeyi went to see the new-born babe, but was denied access to him. Infuriated at this insult, Kaikeyi swore that she would have Rama banished to the forest as soon as he attained twelve years of age.

King Dasaratha was disconsolate at this quarrel between his two wives and consulted his court *pandit* and astrologers as to how he could prevent Rama's banishment. But the astrologers were helpless against what the stars had in store for Rama: he was foredoomed to a life of exile, they told him!

The *Ramayana* story goes that Ravana assumed the form of a golden deer to divert Rama's attention, and when the latter went in chase after the deer, Sita, left alone in the hut, was abducted by Ravana. But this episode is put differently in the Bhojpuri version. It says, instead, that it was Rama's brother, Lakshmana, who ran after the deer and killed it.

Ravana was defeated in the battle and Rama rescued Sita. On their arrival back home, Rama decided that Sita should undergo the "fire trial" in order to prove her fidelity. But it was not merely a fire trial, says the Bhojpuri folklore, and lists four different trials that Sita was required to undergo. No sooner, for instance, did she hold a glowing ember in her hands, than it died down. Next she was asked to hold a *Tulsi* (Basil) plant in her hands, but it also immediately wilted. And so on...

But the real reason why Rama abandoned his wife, Sita, was not limited to these tests, the Bhojpuri stories tell us. They go further and mention that Sita was somehow enamoured of Ravana and, in her private moments, used to draw his portrait ! One day, Rama's younger sister (who, curiously enough, does not figure anywhere in most *Ramayana* texts), caught Sita in the act and reported the matter to Rama. An infuriated Rama immediately decided to banish Sita !

Curiously enough, the stories also say that Sita used to draw such portraits of Ravana out of sheer jealousy of her co-wives ! That Rama had more than one wife is thus indicated and is yet another revelation not mentioned in almost all versions of the *Ramayana* epic !

Sita, in the course of her banishment, gives birth to Lava and Kusha. As soon as Rama heard this, he proceeds to the forest where his wife was then living. He visited the place thrice at different intervals, so relate the Bhojpuri stories, but on all these three occasions Sita refused even to see his face ! He then sent a number of messengers to bring her back, but Sita refused to oblige any of them, saying' "It is impossible for me to return. Why did Rama banish me in the first place ? Let the gods never again unify us".

Sita, thus, is presented not only as a woman of self-respect and dignity, but also of a vengeful nature. The stories also seek to portray her as being innocent and as one who was wrongly punished. What's more, she detested Rama so much that she didn't even reveal to her sons that Rama was their father ! In fact, the stories have it that once, when Rama did come across his sons and asked them who their mother and father were, the young kids replied, "Sita is our mother; but who our father is, we do not know" ! (Could they be Ravana's progeny, after all?)

Lastly, the usual *Ramayana* story that sage Vasistha ultimately succeeded in persuading Sita to visit Ayodhya at a time when Rama was holding an *Ashwamedha* sacrifice is also contradicted by the Bhojpuri stories. They put it that

Sita could not disobey her preceptor, Vasistha, but did not visit Ayodhya either. She simply proceeded five steps in the direction of Ayodhya, and then returned to her hut !

In other words, the Rama story of the Bhojpuri folkore not only differs from the more popular versions in many respects, but also emerges as a remarkable human drama that ends in a tragedy. Rama wails and weeps, threatens to destroy the entire earth, but is unable to save Sita from sinking into the womb of the earth...

Was Nepal the Craddle of the Original Man ?

Did the prehistoric man originate in Asia ? More precisely, can Nepal claim the credit for giving birth to the world's first man ?

A passage in "*The Origin of Family, Private Property and the State*" by the well-known socialist and paleontologist, Freder ickEngels reads :

"Many hundreds of thousands of years ago, during an epoch not yet definitely determinable......(during) that period of the earth's history which geologists call the Tertiary, and most likely towards the end of it, a particularly highly-developed species of anthropoid apes lived somewhere in the Tropical zone--probably on a great continent that has now sunk into the bottom of the Indian Ocean."

Engel's statement finds further corroboration in the discovery of fossil remains of *Ramapithecus* or the Rama Ape belonging to the Upper Miocene and Lower Pliocene periods in this part of the world. What's more, the fossil remains of yet another creature, whom we can liken to Man and which belongs to the lower Pliestocene period, have been discovered in parts of Asia as well. And, *Ramapithecus* or the Rama Ape is not only a rare species of Hominidae, but also the direct ancestor of modern man, adds Janak Lal Sharma, a Nepali scholar.

Another site in Asia where fossil remains similar to those of the Rama Ape were found was in Kaiyuan in the People's Republic of China; between 1957 and 1958. But as the basic features of these creatures also matched those of the ape discovered by Lewis earlier, they were also designated by the generic name of *Ramapithecus punjabicus*. Again, in 1978, some other fossil remains bearing more or less similar characteristics were discovered in Lufeng, also in the People's Republic of China, besides those found in Pakistan.

Coming nearer home, Dr. J.H. Hutchison was credited with the discovery of yet another fossil in Nepal's south-western Butawal area as late as in December 1980. A news item appearing in 'The Rising Nepal' daily dated Friday, March 27, 1981, confirmed this discovery. Summarised, the news-item read :

"A Nepalese-American joint scientific team has discovered a left upper tooth belonging to the jaw of *Ramapithecus*. The discovery was made in December 1980 on a hillside a few miles away from Butawal, on the banks of the Tinau river."

While the fossil remains of the Rama Ape discovered in Kenya are said to have been at least fourteen million (14,000,000) years old, those of the Butawal *Ramapithecus* have been estimated as being some thirty lakh (or 3 million) years younger. But, as similar discoveries in India and Pakistan have been considered to be of a much later date, the Butawal Rama Ape should be consid ered earliest in order of time.

Though, even today, scholars are engaged in taxonomical classification of the various Rama Ape fossil discoveries, there is a general consensus amongst them that the *Ramapithecus* is, by all available indications, Man's first real ancestor, and it comes closest to the *Homo sapiens* in all its basic physical characteristics.

The *Ramapithecus*, scholars presume, must have been a semi-erect creature. It vanished from the face of the earth some 7 million years ago. This simian ancestor of Man is regarded to be more manlike than most other similar anthropoid apes, or, in other words, it is this ape that crossed the Anthropoid threshold and advanced one step ahead towards the development of the Hominidae.

On the basis of the above indications, and, as most of the fossil remains of the *Ramapithecus* were discovered in various parts of Asia, it will not be too far off the mark to presume that Asia was one of the homes of the original Man. And, since fossil discoveries in Nepal antedate all other Asian discoveries of a similar nature so far, it isn't difficult to conclude, too, that Nepal could well have been the first cradle of Man in Asia !

Folk Tales

CHAPTER NINE

The Price of Silence !

There once lived a nobleman in Kathmandu, who believed that too much talk brought in its trail many an evil repercussion in one's life. As such he decided to observe the ancient motto : "silence is golden".

His parents and relatives, however, believing that he had lost his power of speech, offered a large reward to the person who would restore it to him. But nothing worked.

One day the young nobleman went with his father's friend for a hunt. As both of them were resting under the shade of a *Pipal* tree, a crow came and started making a lot of noise overhead. Greatly annoyed at this, his companion drew an arrow from his sheaf, and shot the poor crow dead.

The kind-hearted nobleman was shocked to see this, and he asked the crow in great remorse: "Why did you speak? If you had observed silence like myself, you would not have been dead today."

His father's friend could scarcely believe his ears. Had the young nobleman really spoken? Or was he dreaming? He rushed back to the town and narrated the incident but no one believed him. Because, when the boy's father went to the forest to verify the truth of his friend's story, he found that the young man was as dumb as ever!

Thinking that his friend had played a dirty joke on him, he took out his sword and thrust it into the former's heart, killing the poor man on the spot. "Why did you speak, oh foolish man?" Asked the son again. "If you had kept your mouth shut like myself, you would not have been lying dead here today". His father was amazement and remorse personified at the same time. Gathering his composure after a while, he accosted his son, saying: "It is not due to his having spoken that he lies dead here, but to your foolish obsti nacy in keeping your mouth shut. If you had spoken and explained everything in time, I would not have lost my temper and killed him. There is a time when silence is golden, but not always. The tongue given to you by your wise Creator is meant to be used, you duffer."

The more the nobleman pondered over his father's words of wisdom, the more he felt that he had been in the wrong by not putting a god's gift to its proper use. So thereafter he gave up assuming the airs of a complete dumb, and spoke a few words whenever it was necessary, thereby bringing back the longlost happiness to all the members of his family.

MORAL : Do not carry anything to the extreme.

Shall Be Gone Tomorrow !

Once upon a time a young man visiting the kingdom of Patan was very much surprised to see that an old man, Raghu, was harnessed to an oil-crushing wheel and was going round and round it instead of the usual bullock or buffalo.

"How long can you pull on like this" asked the visitor. The man replied, "Do not worry young man, all this shall be gone tomorrow."

Some years later, when the young man visited the place again, he was in for another surprise. He found the very Raghu who had been harnessed to the mill as a buffalo, was now master of the mill himself! As he congratulated the new owner, the latter (Raghu) replied, "Thank you. But all this shall also be gone tomorrow."

Next time the young man came back to the village, he was further flabbergasted. For, Raghu had already become the king of Patan! "How come, my dear friend?" asked he. Raghu told him that the old king had died recently, and according to their custom a new king was to be chosen by the state elephant by garlanding whomsoever it liked. As everybody made a beeline for the vast open space where the royal elephant was to choose the king, the animal came straight to the place where the earlier oil-mill owner was standing, threw the garland over his head and turned back!

"Oh I'm so happy to hear this exciting story, my dear friend Raghu," said the young man.

The king embraced his old friend but said, "As always, I feel that all this will be nowhere there tomorrow."

Sometime later, when the young man happened to pass through the same village, all he found was a heap of rubble, overturned earth and boulders only. There was no trace either of the palace, or the town, or the king!

Shocked to the extreme, he made enquiries, only to learn that an earthquake had demolished everything in the citystate.

Then only dawned on him the truth of Raghu's repeated words, "Shall be gone tomorrow."

MORAL : Nothing is forever.

A Foolish King

Once upon a time, a certain man was to be hanged in the market-place of Doti, in western Nepal. The Dotial king, a sadistic person, had even declared a holiday on the occasion so that the public execution was witnessed by all his subjects. A traveller who had arrived at the city that day felt sorry for the poor man.

On reaching the spot where the scaffold had been built, he found that a poor frail skeleton of a man was already on the verge of being hanged. But each time the hangman tried to tighten the noose round his neck it slipped out and the execution could not be carried out.

"Sir, it is impossible to hang this man, for his neck is too thin for the noose," complained the hangman to the king.

"But I have already declared a public holiday and people have gathered to see the exciting event. I cannot disappoint them", said the king. "Find another man whose neck will fit into the noose and hang him instead!"

The traveller, who had been within ear-shot, was shocked to hear the king's order. He decided to play a trick on the foolish king so as to save an innocent man from being hanged for no fault of his.

He entered a friend's house, smeared his whole body with ashes, donned the saffron robe of a Sadhu and quickly returned to the scene.

"Stop, Mr. Hangman", he shouted, "I know why the noose has been slipping off that condemned man's neck. Last night, during meditation, I had a vision. Lord Vishnu appeared to me and ordered me to get myself hanged here today, so that I could ascend to the paradise to rule there and to serve him. Thus have I come here. Please hang me instead."

Everybody was stunned to hear the Sadhu. "If this man of god means what he says," pondered the king's minister,

"I have to sacrifice my life today. For I am already a minister, and so I am capable of ruling the heavenly kingdom much better than the Sadhu."

The court Pandit who was there felt likewise. So did many other courtiers. Soon there was a widespread scramble for the scaffold, to prove as to who was more worthy to mount it and go to Heaven. The hangman was non-plussed and confused. When the king learnt everything about the Sadhu's vision, he became furious against his ministers and courtiers.

"How dare any of you go against my wishes ?" cried he. "As I am the ruling monarch, it is my privilege to face the noose and obey the divine order and become the ruler of the Celestial Kingdom. Clear the way for me."

All the people heard the king in stunned awe and silence, but none dared challenge him. Excitement rose as they watched him wear a brave exterior, climb the scaffold and put the hangman's noose round his own neck !

The traveller was happy to have saved the life of an innocent man, otherwise doomed to death the same day. And then he disappeared into the vast multitude, never to be seen again...

A Barber Outwitted

A prince loved his barber. Every morning, he looked forward to the pleasure of spending a couple of hours in the barber's company.

Now, if the barber hated anybody, it was the court *pundit* (priest) whom everybody else looked upon with great reverence.

When the barber could not endure the *pundit's* presence any longer, he hit upon a plan to get-rid of him.

The next day he went as usual to his master's chamber, but wouldn't talk. "What ails thee today ? Hast thou lost a wife?" the prince asked. "No, Sir", the cunning barber replied. "Last night I had a dream. I was in paradise where I came across your late noble father and stately mother. Both of them were plunged in deep grief."

"And what did he say?" asked the prince. 'The court *pundit* still enjoys his life on earth, and we do not have anyone here to look after our spiritual needs', they complained and suggested that you despatch him to paradise forthwith".

"But how?"

"That should not be too difficult", replied the barber. "He has only to be put into a coffin and then into a grave. He will soon awake in paradise!"

The priest was duly informed of all that had passed, and being a shrewd man, he made a request that he be given a month's time to prepare himself properly for his heavenward journey.

He chose a suitable spot in his garden for his grave, and employed a dozen faithful men to dig an underground tunnel from there, right up to his house. Then he had it concealed by wooden planks, strewn with grasses and weeds.

When the great day arrived, the priest was laid down in a coffin and the coffin lowered into the grave, which he opened by means of a secret device, and escaped into his house through the tunnel.

Three long years passed. And during this time he had allowed his hair, his beard and nails to grow as long as they could. One day he presented himself before the court in that disguise, to the utter shock and surprise of everybody present. When they asked who he was, he replied that he was the court priest just returned from pradise.

"But why are you wearing such long hair, and nails, and beard?" asked the prince.

"That is exactly why I am here today", said the priest. "For who would be so foolish as to leave the pleasures of paradise and return to this miserable earth, if it were not for a special reason ? Till about a year ago, your revered father had an excellent barber who was for some reason sent away for good from paradise. Finding nobody to replace him, your honoured father told me to return to you, and to request you to despatch your own barber post-haste so as to help him meet his toilet requirements."

As expected, his master ordered the barber to depart the very next day to paradise !

The barber was so suprised at the turn of events, that he was speechless for a long while. But he had no other alternative but to please his master. So, the very next day, the poor fellow was laid into a coffin and buried alive !

MORAL: As you sow, so will you reap !

The Love of A People

Once upon a time the adjoining kingdoms of Kathmandu and Kirtipur had a different ruler each.

The Kirtipur king was arrogant and a hard-hearted ruler who cared little for his subjects. But the Kathmandu king was not only gentle and kind, but was loved and revered by all his subjects.

As days went by, the people of the selfish king decided to do away with him, but as they couldn't muster enough courage, sent a group of elders to the Kathmandu king, to inform him of their plight, eek his help and ask for advice.

The king, grieved to learn about their hardship, resolved to teach his neighbour a lesson. So he told the citizens to return to their country and tell their king that a wonderful and unique fruit, named the 'Fruit of Immortality', had been found in the Kathmandu kingdom.

"Oh, is it ?" said the Kirtipur king, "What are its special qualities ?"

"Whoever eats that fruit, Your Majesty, will become immortal," was the reply.

"In that case I must have it with me as soon as possible," said the king and decided to send his best soldiers to fetch the same.

But when they reached Kathmandu, they were taken into custody and were told that they would be released only when the mound of earth outside their prison-window had completely disappeared. They must pray day and night for this miracle if they valued their liberty.

Thus all the prisoners started praying night and day, till, after about a month, a great cyclone swept over the city and, to their pleasant surprise, the huge mound of earth had completely gone ! Released from their confinement, they were soon on their way to Kirtipur. As they were leaving, the king of Kathmandu asked them to carry a message to their king. "Tell your king," said he, "that the only fruit that makes a king immortal is the love of the people. The prayers of my people will keep me alive as long as they want me. Your king can also have this fruit, if he earns the love of his subjects."

When their king heard this message, he was furious. "I will teach that impudent man a good lesson," he shouted, and ordered his army to prepare for an attack.

But just as he was about to mount the assault, a messenger came running and informed him that his only son had fallen from his horse and was badly injured.

He postponed his departure and hastened to his son's bedside. All priests and medicine-men tried their best to cure him, but the son's condition grew from bad to worse.

At last an old man in the court made bold to tell the king: "Sire, if anything can save his life, it may be your prayers alone".

The grief-stricken king had panicked at the thought of losing his only son. So, instead of getting angry, he went down in prayers for the first time in his life.

His prayers seemed to have been answered, as it were, and from that day onwards, the prince gradually recovered.

This incident was a great eye-opener for him and helped him turn over a new leaf in life. He grew devoted to his people, and earned their blessings for an eternal life.

Ghantaakarna's* Gold Jar

A Kathmandu farmer was crossing the Tundikhel meadow one evening. As he reached near a solitary Casuarina tree known as the "Tree of Ghantaakarna", he heard a voice call him. "Would you care to accept a jar of gold ?" asked the voice.

Surprised, the farmer looked around, but saw no one. It was obviously the tree that spoke, he thought, because he had often heard stories about the demon-tree talking to people. "When merciful Ghantaakarna takes pity on a poor man like me, who am I to refuse its gift ?" thought he and asked, "Where can I find the jar?"

"It will reach your home soon enough," the voice rang out in the wilderness once again.

The farmer hurried home and was greatly elated to find the prom ised jar already there ! He opened its lid but found it half- empty, that is, only half filled with gold *asharfi* coins.

---

* *Ghantaa* = bell, *Karna* = Ears. It is the popular name of a demon, who, it is said, is buried under a tree at the Tundikhel parade ground near Bhadrakali.

Since that day on, he was gripped with a feverish urge--an urge that drove him virtually crazy. "I must somehow fill up this jar with coins," thought he and even started selling his belongings in order to procure them. But try as much as he may, the vessel remained partially empty all the time, and this distressed him.

In his consuming passion for more gold, he began to economize on his food and clothes and everything; he denied himself and his family every pleasure in order to save. And all his savings were thrown into the jar.

One day an elderly and kindly neighbour, who had been watching the farmer's plight for sometime, said, "What has hap pened to you? You do not look as happy and contended as you used to. The harvest was better this time than previous years and your earnings have gone up too. But in spite of your increased income you look all the poorer. Haven't you, by any chance, become the owner of a haunted gold jar?"

The farmer was amazement personified. "How do you know?", he asked. "Have you been keeping an eye on my movements?"

"Nothing of the kind" said the neighbour. "But I have grown up in age and have seen that whoever has accepted the offer of the jars of Ghantaakarna's gold has become like you -- reduced to abject misery."

The farmer fell on the elder's feet and sought a way out. "It is simple," came the neighbour's advice. "Just take back your jar of gold and deliver it to the tree at dead of night."

He didn't carry the jar to Tundikhel but went there that very night with a view to plead with Ghantaakarna to withdraw the jar.

When he returned home, he found, to his utter relief, that the jar had gone, leaving only the few coins painfully collected by him. He felt greatly relieved, and thereafter lived happily as ever, rid of the greed that had been lurking in his heart for all these days.

MORAL: Be contented, be happy!

The Winning of Disciples

Siddhartha Gautama, the great son of Nepal, was once passing through a forest on his way to the stream where he took his daily bath. His heart was filled with joy to hear the birds singing overhead and the sunbeams dance over the greenery everywhere.

Suddenly, there was a piercing cry from among the trees and a bird dropped heavily a few yards away. It fluttered in a fruit less effort to rise, then lay still with an arrow pierced through its heart.

The compassionate Gautama hurried to where the bird lay, picked it up gently, and, removing the arrow which had ended its life, broke it in two and cast it away, as he pressed the still warm body to his breast and stroked the feathers, musing to himself:"Who could have so wantonly destroyed a beautiful crea ture like this ?" As he was looking for a safe place to bury the bird, he heard footsteps behind him. Three hunters came out of the forest.

Buddha's eyes were wet with tears. But the hunters, not knowing who he was, were greatly taken aback to see him weeping over the loss of a mere bird. "Who are you", they asked, "and why are you crying so?"

"My friends", replied the Buddha, "the Lord has granted us human beings a greater power and a superior intelligence than he has given to these poor creatures. These innocent lesser creatures are at our mercy and we lower ourselves to the level of the wild beasts of the forest by not doplaying the kindness expected of us. Don't you agree ?"

The hunters were amazed to hear this and in a fit of remorse, they surrendered their weapons at the feet of the

Buddha. "We are indeed grateful to you, whoever you are", said they. "We urge you to kindly guide and help us in changing this vile occupation of ours".

The Englightened One gladly agreed to this, and from that day onward the hunters became his disciples.

The Right Place

Once upon a time a merchant in Biratnagar purchased a mango grove. He had a trusted servant, Manay, who took immense pains for its proper upkeep. He always weeded the grove, tended every tree and drove away the birds when the fruits were ripe.

One day, in the course of a chit-chat with his assistant gardener, he said, "I am always wondering why god hangs so light a fruit as a mango on so tall and solid a tree, while He allows a big pumpkin to grow on a delicate creeper ? If I had a power to change this scheme of things, I would make pumpkins grow on the mango trees."

"There must be a good reason for it, "answered the assistant, "but why do you want to do that?"

"Look at all the trouble I have in chasing away the birds that keep pecking at the ripe mango fruits day in and day out. Had there been pumpkins in place of mangoes, would these birds pester me so? Besides, I have to climb up the tree everytime to pluck the mangoes, at such a great risk to my life."

Many days later, as the gardener Manay was working under the same mango tree, a ripe fruit dropped upon his head with a thud.

"Oh, my goodness", shouted Manay. "It may have broken my head...Help, help!"

Hearing him cry out thus, his assistant came running and poured some water over his head. Manay hadn't been hurt badly, however, and he recovered soon enough. His assistant was greatly amused as he recalled their earlier discussion and asked Manay : "Do you still think the mango tree was the proper place for the pumpkin ? What if a nice big pumpkin had fallen on your head instead of this tiny mango?"

"Yes, thank god it was only a mango," said Manay. "Otherwise my head would have cracked into smithereens if a heavy pumpkin had fallen on me from such a tall tree!"

MORAL: We shouldn't try to change everything on earth.

The Story of Kaukuti*

At the feet of the beautiful Himalaya mountains, there once lived a rich businessman. But he was also a cruel man, and anyone who caused him the slightest loss was heavily punished.

His wife, however, was quite the opposite in nature, and grieved deeply to see poor people suffer at the hands of her greedy husband.

At last, when she could bear it no longer, she decided to leave him, and slipped away one night into a nearby forest.

After trudging a long distance, she came to a glade where she saw an old woman sitting in front of her hut. "What brings you here, fair lady?" asked the old woman. The visitor related her tale of woe, whereupon the old woman said, "Be of good cheer and return to your home. I promise that hereafter your husband will never be as cruel as he now is, nor will he punish anybody unjustly. Just take my friend *Kaukuti* to live with you, and you shall see how everything changes."

---

*Kaukuti - Tickle.

The lady could scarcely believe this story, but decided at last to return to her home along with *Kaukuti*.

A few days later, a poor beggar was accused of theft by his servants and brought before the businessman.

"How dare you enter my house to steal?" thundered he.

"Sir," said the poor beggar timidly, "I have not stolen anything." But he could not even finish his sentence when the businessman ordered that he be flogged in public.

As a burly servant raised his whip high in the air, and was about to bring it down with all his force on the back of the poor beggar,s the whip seemed to fly away from his hand, and he com menced to dance, first on one foot, and then on the other. "Ha ha", he laughed, unable to hold himself !

Everyone present was thunderstruck at this performance and at first they did not realise what was happening. Soon one man after another commenced to laugh, till the whole court was filled with such a merriment that the beggar was entirely forgot ten. Surprised, the businessman took the fallen whip into his own hands and tried to lash the beggar with it. But once more the whip flew away out of his hands, and he commenced to act exactly like his servant !

"Ho-ho-ho-ho"! laughed the businessman as he rolled on the floor. "But who is tickling my sides thus?" asked he.

The attendants were asked to find out what caused the tickling, but everyone failed. So everybody went home laughing, unable to understand the cause of it.

At last his wife fetched a soothing drink which would help the businessman to calm down and go to sleep. After several hours of a refreshing sleep, when her husband at last awoke, he forgot all about the beggar and his punishment. The tickling sensation had also stopped by then.

Each time he thought of punishing somebody, the sensa tion used to return, however. So, much against his wishes, he was compelled to shake off his cruel disposition, and gradually he learnt to be kind and just. He and his wife, as also others in the household, lived happily ever after.

Evolution in Reverse !

Near the mythical *Shleshmaantak* forest, the site in which the monkey-infested Pashupatinath and Guhyeshwari temples are located today, a skinny couple lived in the days of pre-history. There never was a more skinny old man--and his wife was no better. But the monkey tribe, believed by science to be the predecessors of humankind, was not yet even born on earth !

The emaciated man and woman stole into a nearby village one day and made a quick job of any booty they could lay their hands on. The villagers, coming to know of the thieves, chased them out of the village and deep into the *Shleshmaantak* forest. At last, in sheer desperation, the couple climbed up a tall tree.

"Return the money you have stolen", shouted the villagers who had gathered at the foot of the tree," or we shall not let you come down."

Not only that. The villagers took turns in keeping up the vigil and, in order not to let the 'thief-couple' come down from the tree, even built huts at its bottom and camped there.

Time went by. The skinny old couple found plenty of fruits in the tree and faced no problem of food. Once they ran out of the fruits, they lived on succulent new leaves and sprouts. After that, they turned to the bark, but weren't too happy eating it.

As it is, they were extremely scrawny. Living on bitter and tough bark left them no more than bones and skin. They couldn't sleep because of hunger, and their eyeballs receded deeper into their sockets. At the same time, with all that chewing and biting the bark, their teeth protruded out and grew longer, more pointed. The longer they stayed out in the open, fighting against the elements of nature, their skin got tougher and their nails grew long and claw-like. Their bodies shrank further too !

As the cold weather set in, the old man even saw his wife getting covered with thicker and ever thicker hair. The same was the case with himself, but only it was his wife who noticed it first -- longish black hairs were growing all over their skinny bodies !

"Why, I even get a queer feeling that something is growing out from the bottom of my spine", said the husband, in utter sur prise.

"I have a tingling sensation *there*, too", replied the wife. And before long they witnessed the curious spectacle of tails sticking out from between their haunches !

No longer able to bear the shock of such a transformation, they started shouting and screaming. But their voices had changed too, and, not words, but mere squeaks were coming instead ! To the utter astonishment of themselves as also the villagers down below, what escaped their mouths was not understandable at all !

They recovered from the shock soon enough, however, and were seen jumping from one branch to another with the help of their long nails and claw, -- and tails. Swinging from one tree to another, they soon went out of sight of the villagers, dropping the money bag in the process. The villagers, contented at last at their long vigil having come to an end, collected the money and pro ceeded homewards.

In the meanwhile, the lantern-faced shrunken couple made the trees their home and even started begetting children. In no time, the forest was filled with creatures of their kind, all swinging and jumping on the trees, chattering and squeaking like monkeys.

Like monkeys, I say ? No, they had turned into monkeys, actual four-footeds ! The skinny couple did recall, however, that one time they too had been human beings, living in huts on the ground. And, often enough, they used to come down from the trees to the ground, mix with the people, steal the offerings brought to the temples, and, when chased by people, scamper off to their tree-safe hide-outs !

It is thus that the monkeys were born out of human beings. Never, therefore, make a mistake, dear readers, and be beguiled by the gibberish that Darwin or whoever may have told you. No,12 Ape was not the forefather of Man. It was *vice-versa* !

Legends

CHAPTER TEN

Hallowed Lumbini Gardens

"Your Majesty, this is the sanctified spot where Lord Gautama was born", said Upagupta, Ashoka's counsellor, to the emperor. "We ought to do something in order to retain its memory for posterity". That was 2200 years ago.

Emperor Ashoka agreed. And so, his visit to Lumbini in the Nepalese *terai* stands commemorated in the shape of a majestic stone pillar.

But the story of Lord Buddha's birth has immortalized itself otherwise, particularly in terms of numerous traditions, written or verbal, and is solidly entrenched in the minds of the monastics, if not also of the laity, in this part of the world. And so it goes:

Mahamaya, wife of king Suddhodhana of Kapilavastu, was bathing in a pond in the Lumbini gardens of yore when the pangs of labour gripped her. She cut her ablutions short, approached a nearby tree, faced east, and grabbed a dropping branch for support. There was the prince Gautama born.

A slightly varying version has it that queen Mahamaya was on her way to the neighbouring principality of Koliya where her father ruled. On arrival at Lumbini enroute, she gave premature birth to prince Gautama.

Versions and stories may vary. But Lumbini's claim as the birth place of Lord Buddha has nowhere been effectively chal lenged to date.

Interestingly, some legends have this spice to add: as soon as baby Gautama tottered on his young legs, *Indra*, the Hindu rain-god, lifted the child from the ground. Meanwhile, as a sur prised Prajapati Gautami, Mahamaya's sister, and others watched, Gautama crawled seven steps forward and was helped in his ablu tions by two *naga* - kings who had arrived there as if from nowhere.

Turning to history, we have on the authority of the noted traveller-historian, Fa-hien, that the Lumbini gardens were situated at a distance of 50 *Li* (about 9 miles) to the east of Kapilavastu.

Yuan-Chuang, another Chinese traveller, corrroborated this and added that the pond at Lumbini was constructed by the Sakyas, the then ruling clan of Kapilavastu. This latter scholar also testi fied to the existence of two stupas at the site where Gautama reputedly had his first ablution. And nearby stood a huge pillar too, presumably the one Ashoka had built.

When Dr. Feuhrer, the noted archaeologist, discovered the Lumbini site in 1866, there was no stupa around. But he did discover the pillar which, upon excavation, turned out to be 22.4 feet tall with the circumference, at the base, measuring 8.3 feet.

"In the twentieth year of his imperial reigon", reads the pillar inscription "Priyadasi Ashoka revisited this place and worshipped here...and had a stone pillar erected...to commemorate that... (Gautama Buddha) was born here."

Much of it is there at Lumbini for all of us to see. The legendary Lumbini lake, approximately 50 feet square, conjures up before us the vision of Mahamaya and her entourage who bathed there. Flowing nearby is the Tilar river, its water as oily and slimey as the traveller historians of yore must have found it. As well, some scattered remains of ancient structures and some mounds presumably with the glories of a bygone era entombed underneath, all go to add to the hallowed memories of the historic Lumbini. One almost fears stepping inadvertently over the foot-prints of a hoary history as one looks around to re-live the stories of the *naga*-kings helping in the ablutions of a newly-born Gautama, of Lord Indra holding the baby aloft in his arms, of bangles of courtesans jingling and of the entourage merry-making in celebration of such a gala occasion...

A 'Perspiring' Idol

The ultimate tragedy that befell the Rana regime in its century old family rule in Nepal was the popular insurrection in 1950 that sounded its deathknell.

If the Ranas had any premonition of the impending doom, a stone idol enshrined in a small village town of Dolakha in mideastern Nepal, it is said, had its contribution. For it had profusly "perspired" some time prior to the revolution.

Now, extremely rare as such an oracle is, the local elders say, it also traditionally forebodes castastrophe. As such, they advised the temple priest to wipe the sweat off the idol, in keeping with another time-honoured practice, with a piece of cotton-wool and despatched the same post-haste to capital Kathmandu, ostensibly as a sound of alarm. Whether the then powers-that-be heeded the warning and sent ritual offerings, as another tradition demands on such occasions, to the Dolakha deity, is not known, but nothing helped them to forestall that calamity.

This Dolakha shrine is dedicated to the mythological strong man Bhimsen who is mentioned in the "Vanaparva" of the *Mahabhara ta* epic as having trekked to the Himalayas in search of a flower on the request of

Draupadee. A side-story not found in the original epic but nevertheless popular amongst the populace in this part of the Himalayas has it that Bhimsen strayed away one day from where the five Pandava brothers had been camping and reached the vicinity of Dolakha. A farmer in the nearby village of Sunkhani was salvaging what little had remained of his farm land in the aftermath of a landslide but was finding the task beyond his single handed, unaided efforts. Bhimsen came to his rescue and the manmountain that he was, did the Herculean job of eight men! Immensely amazed and grateful beyonds words, the farmer went to his home nearby in order to fetch some food for this seemingly god-sent helping hand, but when he returned with the food, Bhimsen had gone!

Puzzled again, the farmer looked for the missing Bhimsen all over the place, but nowhere was he to be found. Utimately Bhimsen was located near the present marketplace. But lo and behold, as soon as the farmer accosted Bhimsen, the latter, before the further flabbergasted eyes of the farmer, instantly froze into a stone ! The farmer and his kinsmen enshrined the same stone in a hurriedly improvised temple.

The local people have also made a custom of offering oranges and oranges, alone, at this shrine on a certain day of the year and thereby hangs another tale. A local orchard-owner is once said to have boasted that he would completely cover the image with his offerings of oranges. But vainly did he try, for, dump as many oranges as he may, the stone-image apparently refused to be covered, and many basketfuls of oranges later, its head stuck out as ever! Utterly dumbfounded, people that had gathered there on the occasion decided to set one day in the orange season apart for ceremonially offering oranges in a bid to commemorate the event.

A house in the Nepalese countryside without a dhikee*
may well be out of the ordinary, except, however in Dolakha, where such grindmills are taboo. For, Bhimeshwar or Bhimsen, it is said, disapproves of offerings of rice beaten out of paddy with the help of a dhikee, and lest they offend the sensibili ties of their deity, the Dolakhans would rather go without a dhikee in their houses !

The mythological name of this small hill-town was Ahhayapur. And it was here, as referred to above, that the Pandava brothers lived for a while during their twelve-year - long exile from their kingdom in ancient Hastinapur. The Newars, who form a dominant strain in 'urban' Dolakha, use a dialect that differs from Kathmandu Newari in the sense that it has a fair sprinkling of seemingly foreign words and phrases. Some would have us believe that this foreign 'interpolation' represents of a code language used by the Pandava princes in order completely to disguise their identity during their years of exile!

An Oriental Helen

If Helen's was the fair face that launched a thousand ships and burned the towers of Ilium, Nepal had an eternal feminine flower not born to blush unseen in what today is an obscure little town, Janak pur. Sita...her beauty made a dim world bright but made herself an unenviable central figure in a tragedy of epic dimen sions.

The story of the *Ramayana* does not bear repitition here. But in Nepal, where the Princess of Mithila symbolises a lotus rather than a Venus – a daughter of the soil whose exemplary womanhood conjures up visions of a Great Age in the country's own pre-history, many a folk-song or a bard-song has come down count less generations as a legacy of the past extolling the virtues of king

---

*A longish log-contraption for rice-pounding. It is laid athwart about a foot above the ground level with a foot-long pestle denting vertically down-wards at one end. The mortar is laid at the ground level.

Janaka as also of Sita, but which in no way feature in the famous Epic.

If there is any possibility of ascertaining the age of origin of the Kathmandu valley following the draining out of a lake, we may, perhaps by cross-reference, also establish the era during which the great legendary foster-father of Sita ruled an empire with its capital in the vicinity of today's Janakpur Dham in south- eastern Nepal.

As the stories go, following the founding of civilisation by Manjushree in the Nepal valley, Dharmakara, one of the savant's disciples, became the king of Kathmandu. This king had no issues, however, and was succeeded by one Dharmpala, a contemporary of Krakuchhanda Buddha.

That Rama, the Prince of Ayodhya, had to enter into a traditional feat of archery in order to win the hands of Sita is well known. What is little known, however, is that Dharmapala's descendant and successor to the throne of Kathmandu, Sudhanwa, had also set forth for Janaka's capital with a view to matching his talents in archery with all the other princes gathered there to compete for the coveted hand of Sita. But somehow, a battle ensued between king Janaka and Sudhanwa in which the latter was killed. If we set this against the historical belief, held by some, that the story of the Ramayana dates roughly back to the 7th century B.C., the Kathmanduites may have some food for thought about the timing of their own legendary civilisation indeed.

Now for the other part of the story. So intimately woven is Sita's name into the local legendary fabric that, given credence, many a Nepalese tribe, like the Maithilis, would be found with her own blood running in their veins!

Even an obscure little community, the Chepangs, claim to be the direct descendants of Sita. While living in exile at sage Valmiki's hermitage on the banks of the river

Gandaki, so goes their legend, Sita had given birth to a son, Lohari by name. One day Sita took the wailing Lohari to the river to bathe. Returning to the hermitage in the meanwhile, Valmiki saw-Lohari's cradle empty and thought the baby must have fallen a prey either to some wild animals or to baby-lifters. Apprehensive that Sita would create a scene upon her discovery of the loss, Valmiki hurriedly created a living likeness of Lohari out of the holy *Kusa* grass and left it in the cradle. Upon her return with Lohari, Sita was spell-bound to see another child playing in her son's cradle and it was not until Valmiki explained the whole thing that her doubts were set at rest. Valmiki also advised her to bring up both as twins and named the second one Kushari (born out of *Kusha* grass). Chepangs hold fast to the belief that they are thus the direct descendants of Lohari whereas Kushari's descendants are the Kusundas, a food-gathering and hunting tribe living today in forested areas west of the Chepang country.

The First Martyrs

The Magars, as a community, are known for their simplicity. Hardly do we come across a Magar who dabbles in diplomacy or even *chiplomacy,* if we may be permitted to coin such an expres sion. It is this very rusticity and straight- forwardness in their dealings that perhaps make the Magars the most disciplined armymen ever, here as well as elsewhere.

Yet, we come across, once in a long while, certain exemplary exceptions. And the career of one Lakhan Thapa Magar, otherwise a simple villager hailing from the remote backwaters of the Gorkha district, is one such example that shines across the firmament of Nepalese religio-politics, giving rise not only to diverse leg ends, but also leading many of his community folk to regard him as a virtual divinity. *Lakhaney Deota* deity is said to have been the appellation given to him and to the shrine built by him.

But this Lakhan Thapa is not to be confused with his namesake - another legendary figure and contemporary of king Ram Shah. As such, we might even term him Lakhan Thapa II. Also, unlike Lakhan Thapa I, he was a political mobiliser of sorts and his movement was said to have been directed against the then premier Janga Bahadur Rana. Not less than seven of his followers, including Ajakh Shingh Chumi and Achhaami Magar, faced death as 'rebels' against Janga Bahadur a full 62 years before Shukra Raj Shastri, Gangalall and others attained martyrdom in 1942, on charges of sedition.

This legend of a man, Lakhan, was born in the Manakamana area of Gorkha district. It is said that, for a while, he had been in some sort of government service in Kathmandu, but returned to Gorkha with another colleague, Ajakh Singh, to settle in Bhugot Kaule Bhangar village till his death in the year 1934 B.S. (1877A.D.)

From the little that we have come to know about him, he appears to have been a fervent devotee of goddess Manakamana, whose temple, till this day, is one of the most sought-after pilgrimages in Nepal. According to others, he was a *Siddha* of the Josmani cult and his reportedly divine propensities had attracted not only people from his own community but also from amongst Brahmans, Chhetris and others, precisely because the Josmanis are basically caste-defiant. It is also said of him that he would forecast the possiblility of his seizing the reins of power from Janga Bahadur, and, if ever he succeeded, he would share the spoils of power among his followers. It could be the lure of possible pelf and power that many of the village idlers to his side.

Among his Brahman followers was one Kalu Lamsal. But, even as seven other members of Lakhan's coterie were allegedly hanged on the orders of Janga Bahadur, Lamsal is said to have escaped the ultimate punishment simply by virtue of his being a Brahman, as killing a *Baahun* was against the tenets of Hinduism.

Lakhan Thapa is said to have built for himself a palatial building at Kaul Bhangar, complete with a shrine of Manakamana. People from many surrounding areas thronged to the place to pay obeisance to the goddess and listen to Lakhan's religious dis courses, in the process of which, it is said, he also used to mobilise popular opinion against the powers that be in Kathmandu.

Lakhan Thapa's 'supernatural' propensities are also believed to have included the drinking of fresh blood gushing out of birds and animals that used to be sacrificed at his Mahakamana altar evey day ! It is understandable that, in a relatively backward and superstition-ridden society, attributes such as this lent him an instant halo of spiritual 'prowess' as an accomplished Tan trik. "Nothing is impossible for him", his followers are believed to have felt, and, as a result, hundreds of people also used to visit him for succour, physical or otherwise.

This widespread popularity and influence of his could easily have given an extra edge to his political appetites too, and, in order, perhaps, to give a concrete shape to his dreams, he is believed to have set up a 'rebel government' of sorts in Gorkha with himself as the *Mukhtiyaar* (premier) and Ajakh Singh as a 'General'. A remarkable marksman, Singh was reputed to be able to easily shoot down a little bird perched on the hump of a bull without the animal receiving even a scratch !

The central government in Kathmandu had hardly any office in the vicinity of Gorkha at the time, thus making it immensely easier for Lakhan to run his show without much resistance. But this didn't mean Kathmandu was completely unaware of the goings-on in Lakhan's palace. Sarbajit Thapa, who had been entrusted by Janga Bahadur

Photo by *Gyanendra Das, Das Colour Lab*

Photo by *Gyanendra Das, Das Colour Lab*

Photo by Yeti Photos Centre

Photo by *Gyanendra Das, Das Colour Lab*

to supervise state affairs in the area, kept the latter constantly fed with all information, usually spiced to suit Kathmandu's palate. That Lakhan had declared himself as goddess Manakamana's representative on earth, that he had been instigat ing people to rebel against the central authority and that he had appropriated large tracts of land for himself and his followers, were said to form the major refrain of Sarbajit's repetitious reports.

Alarmed at all this, premier Janga Bahadur sent word that Lakhan Thapa and his coterie be physically eliminated and his palace razed to the ground. Hours later, however, Jang Bahadur sent another message instructing the concerned persons to defer La khan's assassination.

Lal Bahadur Singh, a Newar shopkeeper at Bimkot Deorali, whose establishment also functioned as an exchange post-office in his capacity of *Dwaare*, had the first of the two messages des patched to the addressee posthaste, but retained the second one, for reasons best known to himself.

On hearing the sentence of death passed by Janga Bahadur against him, Lakhan Thapa is said to have told his would-be executors to spare the trouble and volunteered to hang himself by the nearest tree !

But, before he did so, he is believed to have prophesied Jral's death in the prsence of a large number of his followers gathered there in the following words:

"I am not going to die. However, if I am to turn into a corpse, Janga's Bahadur will immediately follow suit in the tradition of a **Sati**"!

Call it a coincidence if you will, but Janga Bahadur, who had been on a hunting expedition to Pattharghatta at the time of Lakhan's execution, is said to have died the same day under mysterious circumstances. (Some would have us believe that he died at the hands of a jilted husband, who, incidentally, was also a Magar; others hold that he was a victim of a court conspiracy; still others believe that he was mauled to death by a 'white' tiger !)

The 'palace' of Lakhan Thapa is reduced to a shambles today. But the shrine of *Lakhaney Deota* remains, though it has seemingly been removed from there to a nearby locale. If Lakhan Thapa and seven of his followers had, in fact, been hanged at Manakamana on the orders of premier Janga Bahadur, they should rightly be entitled to don the mantle of 'The First Martyrs' to the cause of the country's liberation from the Rana rule-- a process that culminated in the latter's ultimate downfall in 1950.

Ram Krishna Kunwar

Ram Krishna Kunwar was one of king Prithvi Narayan Shah's able military commanders, known for his outstanding exploits in the course of the Gorkha king's eastward expansion. In the heroic battle of Sindhuli, for instance, he was instrumental in driving away the invading British hordes of the East India Company and dealt an equally brilliant blow on another intruder-- this time the invading army of Moghuls led by Gurgin Khan.

Expectedly enough, a highly pleased and grateful king Prithvi Narayan Shah decided that it was time for him to adequately reward the architects of these superb victories that had taken the Gorkhas one more step ahead in fulfilling their dream of Nepal's unification. Many were the heroes, both dead and alive, who were honoured or suitably rewarded amidst a glittering function organised on the 21st day of *Paush*, 1826 B.S. (towards the first week of January, 1769). Present on this historic gathering of leading war luminaries was the outstanding soldier above mentioned, Ram Krishna Kunwar, son of Ahiram Kunwar of Kaski, and the eldest brother of another unforgettable war-hero, Amar Singh, who had predeceased him in the battle of Timal, some seven years earlier.

When the turn came for *Sardar* Ram Krishna to receive the once-in-a lifetime Royal reward, he was found temporarily 'missing' However, people sent to search for him did locate him si lently brooding beside a palace-window and presented him before the monarch, who asked him: "What can I do for you, Ram Krishna ? Ask and you will have it."

His head hung low, his palms joined together in supplication, Ram Krishna made no reply.

Several times the king repeated his question, but somehow Ram Krishna's lips appeared to be sealed. When he did ultimately speak up, his reply further astounded almost everyone present.

"The public road linking the temples of Pashupati and Guheshwari," said he, "is virtually in a shambles. Devotees visiting these holy precincts are facing perennial problems as a result. May I be permitted to rebuild it, if it pleases Your Majesty."

"Alright" replied the king,"Go ahead and rebuild it; I will ask the Royal treasurer to provide you funds for the purpose."

But even that offer was unacceptable to Ram krishna. For his reply was: "May it please Your Majesty to let me undertake the job out of my own resources !"

Ram Krishna's spirit of selfless public service highly Pleased king Prithvi Narayan. He readily granted his permission, but added

"Wouldn't you like to ask anything for yourself ?"

"I have already had the honour and satisfaction of serving Your Majesty. What else can I ask ? May I be permitted to serve Your Majesty to the best of my ability, as long as I live?"

Ram Krishna Kunwar not only had the road rebuilt, but he also constructed a *Shivalaya* and a rest house for pilgrims, be sides apportioning funds for setting up a Guthi (religious trust) for their maintenance and upkeep.

But even then king Prithvi Narayan felt that he must do something for this brave and loyal soldier as a reward for the excellent services rendered by him in the past. As a result, some three years later, while Ram Krishna was leading a successful expedition to incorporate areas to the east of Kathmandu in to the expanding Gorkha kingdom, king Prithvi Naryan Shah, in a letter addressed to him, made a land-grant of the Simbu and Dhulikhel areas to be enjoyed by this loyal and faithful soldier and his posterity. But, what's more interesting, the donor wasn't him self satisfied with the gift so made !

"For all your bravery and other excellent qualities of head and heart, it wouldn't be enough of a reward, were I to gift away, to you, even half of my entire kingdom," wrote the magnanimous king.

The 'Mahiravan Badh'[*]

One of Nepal's first historic documents, a piece of dramatic literature from Patan, makes immensely absorbing reading. This is known as the 'Mahiravan Badh', is credited to one poet Jayant, and is dated 1394 B.S. (1337 A.D.).

The Rama-Sita legend is too well-known to deserve repetition here. But the same story, as depicted by the aforesaid play, *Mahiravan Badh*, presents a curious departure from the generally accepted versions.

One is that there figures, in this story, not merely one Ravan. There also other Ravans, and at least two of them figuring in the play were known as Mahi Ravan and Ahi Ravan. They have, at places, been described as the

---

[*] 'The Slaying of Mahiravan'

'principal' Ravan's allies (or *mits*) and, at others, as his preceptors or seniors. One is thus led to surmise that the appellation 'Ravan' did not, as in the case of the Janakas of Mithila (also of the Ramayan epic fame), refer to just one character but to a community or tribe to which they belonged.

More interestingly, whereas the 'regular' Ramayans tell us the story of the abduction of Sita, Ram's wife, at the hands of the ten-headed and twenty-armed Ravan, here we come across an episode that revolves round the kidnapping of Ram and Lakshman themselves!

No less amusing is the pride of place accorded to Hanuman as the virtual 'hero' of the play. Unlike the relatively less signifi cant errand-boy or messenger role played by this so-called 'monkey- god' in most Ramayan stories, here he emerges as the principal figure, who ultimately saves Rama, otherwise the epic-hero! Also Hanuman was not a mere monkey, but a full-fledged human being. He may have, for reasons of a dramatic disguise or by virtue of a tradition peculiar to his tribe, donned the mask of a monkey. Why, Mahiravan even eulogises Hanuman as an eminent gram marian and, also perhaps, as an author of the Ramayan epic itself!

However, coming now to the 'Mahiravan' story proper, as is said to appear in the 11th canto of Ananda Ramayan, it briefly unfolds in the play thus :

Mahiravan, the lord of the underworld, is approached by a messenger sent by Ravan who relates to him incidents such as the widespread damage caused to the beautiful Ashok garden, the physical elimination of Akshay Kumar, and the like, wrought by Hanuman. Mahiravan decides to come to Ravan's rescue and proceeds to the shores of the sea where Ram and Lakshman are resting under the protection of Hanu man. There Mahiravan assumes the form of Shugriva, a cousin of Hanuman, and before the latter realises what is happening, grabs both Ram and Lakshman, and vanishes from the scene !

Next we see Ram and Lakshman being dragged to the temple of a goddess as prisoners, their hands and feet tied with the legend ary *Nagpas*. As Mahiravan is preparing to behead the two brothers as sacrifice at the altar of goddess Durga, the helpless prisoners are seen praying to Hanuman to spare their lives. When Mahiravan advises them to bow before the goddess, however, Ram's reply is: "We haven't learnt to do such a thing."

As if in answer to the prayer of the two brother-prisoners, Hanuman dramatically enters the scene and is immediately involved in a fisticuff with Mahiravan. At the end of a long drawn-out fight, Mahiravan succumbs to Hanuman's blows.

Hanuman then turns his attention towards Ram and Lakshman. He tries his best to disentangle them from the *Nagpas* (a noose made of serpents) but finds himself unsuccessful. Meanwhile, the man-bird *Garud*--traditionally the vehicle of lord Vishnu, whose human incarnation Ram is believed to be -- ar rives there and rescues them from the serpents with a violent flapping of his wings.

The story ends with a scene of a happy reunion between Ram, Lakshman and Hanuman on the one hand and the waiting Shugriv, Bibhishan, etc. on the other.

From the story recounted above, the "Mahiravan Badh" appears to be a play within a play--that is, it highlights and dramatises just one sequence taken out of the Ramayan epic-story. But, even as a separate play, it is complete in itself and nowhere does it appear as being detached from the main context.

A few points may, however, be noted here. One is the fact, referred to above, of Hanuman being regarded by Mahiravan as an eminent grammarian and an erudite scholar, Which only goes to support the surmise that Hanuman was a human being and not a monkey.

Secondly, the story revolves round some further exploits of Hanuman, often missing in most other versions of the Ramayan epic.

The third point of note is Ram's refusal to pay obeisance at the altar of goddess Durga ("as he didn't know such a thing") who, on the other hand, is apparently a patron deity of Mahiravan or the *Rakshasas*. It implies, in other words, that Durga-wor ship, which forms such an important and integral part of today's Hinduism, particularly of the variety practised in Nepal, was perhaps unknown at the time the "Mahiravan Badh" was written in the early part of the 14th century.

Of the Mahabharata Legends

A mythological story has it that the famous Aryan sage, Kaushika Vishwamitra, once went to Ayodhya and fetched Rama and Lakshmana with a view to fight against the *Rakshasas* (demons) who had for long been pestering him in his *Ashram*. The two princes were successful in curbing the demons and after escorting them up to Janakpur, where Rama was later to be wedded to Sita, the sage proceeded northwards towards the Himalayan foot-hills. On being asked why he wanted to retire to the mountain fastnesses, sage Kaushika is said to have replied : "Thanks to the love and affection bestowed on me by kaushiki, my *didi* (elder sister), I find myself always at home in the laps of the Himalayas."

The above anecdote featuring in the well-known Sanskrit treatise, the Valmiki Ramayan (Bala Kanda, 3/-33), goes to indicate that the present-day Koshi region in eastern Nepal has had its associations with ancient sages like Vishwamitra-personages, in other words, as old as the story of the Ramayan epic itself. Also, that the term Koshi, denoting a river and applied to many rivers to the east of Kathmandu such as the Sun Koshi, Tama Koshi, Dudh Koshi, etc., isn't a new nomenclature but has come down to us almost as a prehistoric legacy.

Coincidentally as it were, the word Kushi or Khushi also means a river in Newari, as is evidenced in terms like Bhacha Khushi, Sama Khushi, etc. but the same is not always true in the case of rivers to the west of the Kathmandu valley in general. What's more, as the ancient Kirats were said to have been the first historic rulers of the entire Nepal Himalayas, and, as it is the Kirat people who are still predominant in the hill areas extend ing right up to Nepal's eastern borders, a school of thought holds that terms like Koshi and Kushi are not only synonymous but also derivatives from a common stock–most probably a Kirati one, rather than Sanskrit.

Vijayapur, the capital of the medieval Sen Kings lying in the vicinity of Dharan--and still a popular pilgrimage center--finds frequent references as a beautiful hilltop city in many earlier texts such as *Rudrakhsharanya Mahatmya*. While it isn't immediately clear as to how ancient this text is, it may be mentioned, in passing, that the famous shrine of Budaa Subba, which makes the area so popular, features certain unique traits. It is said, for instance, that a huge bamboo grove that almost forms a canopy over the shrine, is "topless" in the sense that every single tree in it has a mysteriously "truncated" top ! Also, unlike most other temples throughout Hindu Nepal, the priest here belongs not to the Brahmin, but to the Magar stock. And, thirdly, it is said that neither crows nor dewdrops are ever seen in the area, whatever the time of the year !

Local traditions seek also to establish links between the foundation of Vijayapur and the Mahabharata epic, much as is the case with the Koshi region as a whole. It is said, for instance, that the entire Vijayapur hillock was, in fact, a huge sacrificial *Mandap* erected by, among others, the

Hercules of the Orient, Bhimsen--the second of the Pandava brothers. It was also he who is said to have driven away all crows and jackals from the area lest they contaminate his noly *mandap*--and, ever since, these birds and animals have never ventured to return there--so goes the local belief!

Other place-names which not only lay equal claim to antiquity but would also have us believe that the Pandava brothers lived in this very area during their long exile include the present-day settlement of Kicchakbadh on the banks of the Mechi river said to have been named after Kichchak, a local chieftain. The story goes that Bhimsen, the he-man among Pandavas, killed Kichchak on seeing him make erotic overtures towards Draupadi, the common wife of himself and his four brothers.

Likewise, Biratnagar in eastern Nepal is another notable place to find mention in the Mahabharata epic. It is said that it was the capital of king Birat who ruled over the then Matsyadesh or "The Fish Country". Noted historians like Todd, Cunningham and HC.Roy Chowdhury have ruled out the possibility of this Biratnagar having anything whatever to do with the one mentioned in the Mahabharata--and for good reasons too. For one thing, the great physical distance separating Hastinapur, the capital of the Pandava kingdom in the present day Punjab, from our own Biratnagar, negates the possibility of the Pandavas' travel to this place. But then, some other historians like Hunter and Buchanan do offer a counter opinion. "The river Kartoya separated the *Matsyadesh* with Kamrupa" (present-day Assam), Buchanan is quoted as writing, and Kartoya has been identified with the present-day river Teesta in north Bengal, thereby lending support to the belief that the present Koshi and Mechi zone *terai* areas of Nepal may, in fact, have formed a part of the mythological *Matsyadesh*.

Supporters of the present-day Biratnagar connection with the Pandavas would add, for extra effect, that the Koches, a tribe presently inhabiting parts of south-eastern Nepal and adjacent areas in India, did in fact derive their clan name from Kichchak, and are, therefore, king Birat's descendants !

Susamayagarh, in the Jhapa district, it is also said, was the capital city of Susharma, king of ancient Trigarta (Tirhut). Also, the Satashi Dham in Jhapa, Sanguri Dandaa in between Dharan and Dhankuta, Birat Pokhar near Anarmani, etc., are also said to have been connected with the Pandavas one way or the other, which means, in other words, that not only the name Koshi, but also many other areas in the vicinity can lay claim to no less an antiquity than that of the Ramayana and Mahabharata stories themselves !

A King's Test

It is well known that the great king, Janaka, ruled in Mithila near the present Janakpur. Sage Yajnavalkya, who was as much noted for his piety as the king, also lived there.

Every morning, Yajnavalkya bathed himself in the cool waters of the nearby river and then commenced his famous discourses for the benefit of his disciples.

One morning while he was preaching as usual, his disciples noticed that their *Guru* was constantly looking at the door, as if he were expecting somebody. And, true enough, Janaka arrived there shortly after to listen to the discourses.

Some disciples became jealous of this special attention given to Janaka, for, they thought, all disciples should be equal in the eyes of a spiritual man. At last, they decided to ask their *Guru*.

"Master," said one of them, "why should you, a man of God, favour anybody in particular. And why do you have a greater regard for Janaka ?"

"My brothers," replied the sage, "you are greatly mistaken if you think that I prefer Janaka to any of you. But Janaka is not only a king in the earthly sense of the word, but a *Siddha Puru sha* (a perfected man) above many mortals like us."

At another time while the great Yogi was once more preaching to his disciples in the presence of king Janaka, a greatly distressed royal guard came running into the hut and shouted that the king's palace was on fire.

The whole place was thrown into utter confusion on hearing this. Almost everybody got up and started to rush towards the palace. Some said that they had relatives working there, while others feared for the safety of their homesteads and fields, which lay adjoining the palace grounds. But Janaka alone sat undisturbed, waiting for the confusion to subside.

Meanwhile, the guard who had brought the news, thought that the king had not heard him right. As such, he repeated the news again in a much louder voice.

" I have heard you," replied Janaka, "But I do not think earthly wealth is more valuable than the golden words of wisdom I hear from my Master's lips. What's more, if the palace is on fire, such indeed must be the will of our lord. Also, I have many people charged with its protection, who will do their best. What will be the use if I ran like mad ?"

Hearing these words, even Yajnavalkya was surprised, and pleased. Some hours later, the disciples returned one by one, and they recalled the earlier words of the sage. Never again did they doubt the wisdom of Janaka. Is it any wonder, then, that Janaka has always been remembered as one of the greatest personages in our history ?

The Rama Story in Tibet

The Tung Haang, the Maar-chhong, Jay-dun-tel and Rin- Spung-pa are some of the Ramayana versions prevalent in Tibet. Since most versions, basically, do not differ from the all-too- common Ramayana story in most details, it would perhaps suffice here to limit ourselves to the variations and the diversions. Another point worth mentioning is that, as one of these versions is referred to in a biography of Atisha who had been to Tibet in or around 1040 A.D., the Rama story was not unknown in Tibet in the 10th century A.D. or even earlier.

Both the *Maar-chhong* and the older *Tung Haang* versions reveal interesting differences. While the *Maar-chhong* version refers to Bhimsen as the third brother of 'Raman' and Lakumaa, the name of Bharat is nowhere mentioned in either version. And, unlike in the *Tung Haang*, 'Ma rutse' does not convert himself into a golden deer, but appears only as a mirage created by Dasagri va, Yaksokovi or Tisay Giri (i.e., Ravana).

Rama has been described as having come to the assistance of Sugriva in his fist-fight with Baali. While the Tung version has it that a piece of mirror was tied to Sugriva's tail in order to help Raman identify him easily, the Maarchhong version shows the mirror as having been tied to Sugriva's forehead. Also, when the demons of Lanka set Hanuman's tail on fire, the Naagas of the sea are shown as coming to his rescue, according to the Maar-chhong, but not the Tung version.

The *Jay-dun-fel* version is said to have been published from Thimpu, the Bhuxanese capital, in 1976, though as part of a different treatise. An interesting difference visible in this version is that Sita is described as the daughter of Ravana hi himself, whom he had discarded at her birth and who had later been married to Rama. Ignorant that Sita was his own progeny, Ravana abducts her!

While Sita's search was on, Rama arrives at a river, which is not only muddy, but its water warm and stinking. It is so because two monkey kings are engaged in a physical bout on its banks and their perspiration has made the water stink. Two very elderly monkey-women, keeping vigil, happen to be mothers of the two kings. One of these, that is Sugriva's mother, requests Rama to help her son ascend the throne by killing his adversary ! Rama agrees and a cowrie shell is tied across Sugriva's head the next day, thus enabling *Raman* to kill the one not wearing the cowrie shell.

Now it is the monkey-king's turn to assist Rama in the search for his lost wife. The monkey-troops reach the ocean, but find it impossible to cross to the other side where, in the Lanka island, lies the capital of Dasagriva. The monkey king urges *Raman* to shoot an arrow into the air so that it drops on the shores of the island capital. A tiny monkey clings to the arrow, is tied to it, and is hurtled across the ocean as the arrow is shot !

Later, a bridge is constructed and the army of monkeys cross to the other side. But, once they confront the ten-headed Dasagriva, they lose heart: how can they possibly kill a ten - headed monster? Raman explains to them that it is a king of mirage-- a reflection in the precious stones embedded into the palace walls-- that gives an impression of a multiplicity of heads. He also asks the doubting Thomases among the monkeys to take a closer look to convince themselves. And, lo, to their pleasant surprise, only one of the heads is warm and the rest are as cold as the stones that reflect them ! Once thus conviced, the monkey- king finds its easy to vanquish Dasagriva.

Raman, is his turn, churns the ocean with his giant bow and thus kills all the demons. Indra, friend of the demons, showers hundreds of arrows from the heaven, killing all the members of the monkey army. But, later, afraid that Raman may take a serious revenge, he sprinkles nectar so as to enable the monkeys to be revived again !

The Tung Haang version also has it that Dasagriva, in the course of his meditation to appease Lord Mahadeva and obtain a boon, had one of his ten heads cut off as an offering to the Lord. Mahade va's wife, Upadey, or Upaney, would like to 'transfer' her prow ess to the remaining heads, but they would have none of a "wom an's prowess", as they derisively call it. An infuriated Upadey curses them to the effect that a woman would be the cause of their ruin and extermination !

Lord Vishnu is re-born as Raman and his son as Raman's brother Lakumaa, or Lagoan.

Around the same time, a daughter is born to Dasagriva. But as it is prophesied that she would bring about his ruin and downfall, she was put inside a copper container and cast into the river. Some farmers come to her rescue, raise her up, name her Noredmaa and get her married to Raman, who renames her Sita.

Another interesting departure is that it is not Bharata (who nowhere figures as Rama's third brother anyway !) but Lagsona who ascends the throne following Raman's exile. Also, during the years of exile, Raman comes into contact with Purpal, a sister of Dasagriva, and not with Surpanakhaa. What's more, what Raman gives Hanumanta for passing on to Sita is not a ring but a let ter. Sita also, in return, replies to Raman in writing, and hands it over to Hanumanta !

Lava and Kusa, the two sons of Raman, are not born to Sita after she had been exiled to the forest, but actually accompanied their mother to the forest ! And, when Lava was lost one day, the sages in the forest created his replica out of the *Kusha* grass!

Proverbs, Idioms and Riddles

CHAPTER ELEVEN

Proverbs

1. Spit on the sky, it falls on your face.
2. River ahead, precipice behind.
3. A branded dog gets jittery at the lightning.
4. Mr. Bellyfull would like to have his food on the other side of the hill, Mr. Empty-belly wants to have it on this side !
5. An earlier porter can select his resting place, later ones can't.
6. Bitterness in the beginning (will mean) sweetness at the end.
7. Thinking ahead means happiness, thinking afterwards means the reverse.
8. God brings the food to the python's mouth.
9. Face an assembly after eating ginger, retire to the forest after eating a radish !
10. Close your eyes in the country of the blind, show your limp in the country of the lame.

11. Slave for others and ever remain hungry.
12. Don't climb the rooftop on seeing others ride an elephant.
13. Advice and medicine never taste sweet.
14. Doesn't want saltless food, doesn't want to break the rock salt.
15. Lazy in the legs, gourmet in the tongue.
16. One-eyed to look at, 'Beautiful-Eyed' by name.
17. Open your mouth and you betray yourself.
18. A hair can't grow before the bold.
19. A tiger doesn't touch the brave.
20. Mango if I win, pebbles (stick) if I lose.
21. Don't count the stars when the house is on fire.
22. Fire relieves a fire-burn.
23. Warm yourself in log-fire, listen to an old man.
24. Start digging a pond when the house is on fire.
25. Died today, medicine the next day.
26. Deal worth half a dime, feast worth a full dime.
27. A dog barks when the master is beside (behind).
28. Half a water jug makes noise, not a full one.
29. Work is complete if you do it yourself, half complete if your assign it to others.
30. Himself an ascetic, dies after food.
31. Himself a beggar, wants his son to wed.
32. I aim at the log, the axe aims at my knee.

33. Paradise is visible only when you yourself die.
34. Be good yourself and the world will be good towards you.
35. He who digs a grave, falls in it himself.
36. Himself a witch, himself a doctor.
37. Hitting your own leg with an axe
38. One who doesn't see a buffalo on one's own back, sees a louse on that of others.
39. Fasten your purse tight, don't blame others (for theft).
40. Going for the father's knee after sucking the mother's breast.
41. Neither an uncle on the mother's side, nor one on the father's.
42. The parents hanker after the children, the children after the pebbles.
43. More meetings more attachment, less meetings less.
44. Eat potatoes, brag about *pedas* (sweetmeat).
45. Hope, but don't depend.
46. Honour is a million, wealth is a cipher.
47. Fish and meat for the diligent, tears for the lazybone.
48. Too sprightly a cow, a tiger's food.
49. Fern-flowering, boulder-sprouting.
50. The fish that escapes is big.
51. Himself a thief, chastises the constable.

52. One ear, two ears and the wide field (world).
53. Hear with one ear, let go through another.
54. A spit dries up, a million spits make a river.
55. Two jobs at one go.
56. Winter isn't over in just one month (of Maagh).
57. It needs two hands to clap.
58. One-sided baking doesn't make a bread.
59. Even a Brihaspati (sage) is a liar if he is alone.
60. Once the hand is inside the mortar, why fear the pestle?
61. Even a calf chases a deer going downhill.
62. A dew-drop doesn't quench the thirst.
63. Stand on a finger and you'll stand on a leg.
64. Give him a finger and he swallows an arm.
65. The dose of a half-baked doctor ensures a journey to hell.
66. Sometimes the mother-in-law's turn, sometimes the daughter-in-law's.
67. The crow goes on cawing, grains go on drying.
68. The crow is neither happy nor unhappy at the ripening of the *Bael* fruit.
69. Smearing salt and vinegar on a raw wound.
70. Animal wealth (is like) a wooden leg.
71. A silken saddle-cover for a wooden horse.
72. Lend your ears, not your tongue.
73. What is a new moon or a full moon to a blind bull?

74. Work should elicit juice, talk should elicit gaity.
75. Kalu put in the labour, bhalu (bear) eats up the maize.
76. Utensil while it's useful, junk after the work is over.
77. Work endears, not talk.
78. Break a diamond if need be, but not even a pebble otherwise.
79. Keep work pending and it falls to your lot, save food and it goes to the others.
80. Black letters look like buffaloes.
81. Either the bold or the bluffer prospers.
82. Why does a black-pepper look shrunk? Because of its own bitterness.
83. Either you learn through books or through experience.
84. Worms spoil even a diamond.
85. A dog's tail cannot be straight even after it is kept for twelve years inside a pipe.
86. Dogs keep on barking, the elephant keeps on its journey.
87. Like lending meat to the dog.
88. Water differs from pond to pond, intelligence (opinion) differs from head to head.
89. Conversation and canals go whichever direction you choose to take them.
90. Dirt deserving to be swept away, was blown by the wind.

91. What is a blind man after? Eyes, of course!
92. Wisdom deserts at an ill-starred moment.
93. Constant digging brings down even a mountain.
94. Ramay eats and drinks, Chamay gets the thrashing.
95. Foods and dress are life's essences, but once you die it's all the same.
96. Once reduced to ashes, how long can you stop it from being blown away?
97. A moustache doesn't stand in the way of a glutton.
98. Stream crossed, pole (crutches) forgotten.
99. Roaring tigers don't bite.
100. Thundering cloud brings no rain.
101. Lose the bucks and be laughed-at too.
102. The plough, which brings luck, gets its head drilled and pierced.
103. Teacher remains bagasse, student becomes sugar.
104. Tiger at home, cat outside.
105. Swallow a bone according to your throat.
106. Where did the *ghee* spill over? On to the food (lentil).
107. Go round and round, only to reach Rumjatar (once again).
108. Scholarship for the studious, rich harvest for the labourious.
109. It's a horse-rider who falls.
110. The *Champa* blossoms at one place, the fragrance is every where.

111. A beak is the bird's only asset.
112. The leopard roared, the goat vanished.
113. Sweet tongue (has a) sour mind.
114. Log in the fire (is like an) old man in the corner.
115. The flea jumps away, the louse is caught.
116. You have balls (coins), everyone is around; no balls, no one around.
117. Beat the daughter, scare the daughter-in-law.
118. Every *jogi* (yogi) has a slit ear.
119. As the night falls, the wife warms up.
120. It's the thirsty who runs after the stream.
121. The thirsty chases the stream, not the other way round.
122. Eat coal, emit coal.
123. Whoever taps the beehive, licks the fingers.
124. Where the fruit ripens, the birds throng.
125. Wood is wood's enemy.
126. One firefly doesn't brighten the skies.
127. Eat off the plate and spit at the same.
128. He who raises a row falls into the trap.
129. It's the short-statured who is poked with the club.
130. The curse of a fly doesn't kill an ox.
131. You pull at a creeper and the mountain rumbles.
132. Pain in the head, ointment at the navel.

133. The bigger bird falls into a snare, the smaller one dies of shock.
134. Taking shelter under a large tree protects at least from one shower.
135. A boat doesn't ply on the road, nor does a cart sail on the river.
136. Verify a bluffer's invitation by attending it.
137. A boulder is supported by the earth, earth by the boulder.
138. Search for a stone, find a God.
139. Don't enter from a window when there's a door.
140. A tiger that devours you, devours me.
141. Tiwari at one opportunity and a Gotame at the next.
142. Swallow hot, die of burns.
143. The pan hasn't warmed, the handle has.
144. *Titra's*[*] enemy is it's own (chirping) beak.
145. A *Khukri* worth three *sukaas*, a handle worth nine.
146. You're a queen, so am I; who will fetch water from the pond?
147. Shall I eat the plate or the rice?
148. A decrepit house is the rodents' heaven.
149. Many a drop fills up the jar.
150. A husband with two wives has to shed tears in a corner.

---

[*] A Bird

151. Boiling milk falls into the fire, buoyant daughter fails into a ditch.
152. A cat is no witness to milk.
153. One should tolerate the kick of a milch cow.
154. Soft to the eyes, hard to the teeth.
155. Dress as the natives do.
156. Riches have wings.
157. Red is the face of money.
158. Mahadev has three eyes when it comes to money.
159. Even nectar is poisonous when it's too much.
160. A *Dhobi's* dog is neither welcome in the house nor in the *ghaat*.
161. Why use an axe when the knife is enough?
162. Don't ask the way when you aren't going to that village.
163. An underestimated river can wash you away.
164. Drops come large from a cloud without rain.
165. No bamboo, no flute.
166. A one-eyed uncle is better than none.
167. The naked dances in a thousand ways.
168. Scaring an elephant with the beating of a *nanglo*.
169. A bad dancer blames the courtyard.
170. The shit is bigger than the baby.
171. To see Tibet while staying in Nepal.
172. Comes last, wants to sleep in the middle.

173. Selling fishes while visiting the Pasupati (temple).
174. Five fingers aren't equal.
175. Gossip is more watery than water.
176. Enmity with a croc while staying in water.
177. Sin shouts from the housetop.
178. Calves are crushed as the bulls fight.
179. Worms are crushed along with the flour.
180. The mother-in-law died last year, tears are shed today.
181. A tree is known from the fruit it bears.
182. Darkness under the lamp.
183. A monkey's tail is neither a stick nor a weapon.
184. A coconut in the hands of a monkey.
185. An old tiger picks up the grasshopper.
186. An old tiger and a young fox (never are a match).
187. Walking along the road will help avoid thorns.
188. Mother for the young ones, wife for the elderly.
189. Squeezing the sand doesn't yield oil.
190. Twelve sons and thirteen grandsons, the old man's burden remains on his own shoulders.
191. Even a river shifts its course in twelve years.
192. My husband returned after twelve years, and I the bitch had a fever.
193. A spoilt man (has a) wrecked house.
194. In a common cold hides a long ailment, in a joke the seeds of a fight.

195. Youth lends burliness (rosiness) even to a fox.
196. Good turns kill ingratitude.
197. A gourd in a goat's mouth.
198. If grains could be threshed by goats, where is the need for bulls?
199. Speak out and you can sell even grain-dust, do not and you can't sell even rice.
200. Ruined country, wayward ways.
201. Even fools exploit a broken household.
202. A cook's error spolis a dish, a farmer's spoils a whole year's harvest.
203. A barking dog seldom bites.
204. A flea can be fatal to an elephant.
205. Sheep go in for sheep's company, goats go in for goats'.
206. Wait at the graveyard, a corpse will eventually turn up.
207. Thrusting a hand where there is fish, removing it where there is snake.
208. Seven villages can be flooded as the boatmen deliberate.
209. The race of a Miyan[*] ends at the mosque.
210. Open your fist and the bird is off.
211. Opportunity comes but doesn't wait, a flowing river doesn't return.
212. Disturb the shit, you only get a stink.

---

[*] A Muslim

213. Only a jeweller can give a jewel its due respect.
214. Shout the whole night and come a cropper.
215. Even a teakwood may sprout overnight.
216. Be not afraid of debts, be afraid of bad days.
217. Get angry yourself and make others wise.
218. Count the rupees a hundred times, but know a man in one deal.
219. By a goat, recognize the man.
220. Bragging without money (is like) a meat-dish without spices.
221. Even a duffer is a hero in a land of dumb-mutes.
222. The dullard falls down once, smarty falls down thrice.
223. What a daring swain accomplishes in a year, a daring woman accomplishes in a moment.
224. Conjugal quarrel (is like) a fire in the haystack.
225. A bird is happy only in the bush.
226. Whether a real tiger eats one up or not, the mental one does.
227. Everyone sees a forest-fire, who sees a fire in one's heart ?
228. As a snake without poison is useless, so is a man without an ambition.
229. A head adorns the body, fortitude adorns the great.
230. A jar can't be filled with dewdrops.
231. For a hundred persons a mere stick each, for one a full load.
232. A serpent can see the feet of another.

233. Let the snake be killed but let not the stick snap.
234. Cheap food (brings) death with dysentery.
235. The interest is higher than the principal.
236. There's greenery all around for a bull gone blind in a monsoon.
237. While there's life, there's hope.
238. You can hide your face, but can't hide your troubles.
239. The goldsmith's hundred strikes, the ironsmith's one.
240. You can't block the sun with your palm.
241. *Ghee** cannot be pulled out with a straight finger.
242. Go fox-hunting, carry tiger-weapons.
243. The elephant has two kinds of teeth--one for display, the other for food.
244. The elephant passed through, the tail got stuck.
245. Ask a goat from one who promises you an elephant.
246. Smooth leaves mean a plant with promise, rough ones mean otherwise.
247. When you are lucky, even a bull bears a calf.
248. Save your skin in a melee, save your seed in a famine.
249. Not seen a tiger? Look at a cat!
250. Not seen an enemy? Look at your brother.

---

* Clarified butter.

Common Idioms
I. About the eye
1. To open one's eyes: to be cautions: to remove misunderstanding
2. Dirt in the eye: object of dislike
3. Doll of one's eyes: object of great love and affection
4. To kill poison of the eye: to go to sleep
5. To devour the eyes: to dazzle the eyes
6. To entomb (bury) the eye: to cast covetous eyes
7. To beguile one's eyes: to play a trick
8. Duel of the eyes: exchanging amorous glances
9. Wink of the eye: a sly hint
10. To make the eyes big: to get angry
11. To close one's eyes: (a) to breathe one's last; (b) to ignore someone's lapse
12. To cast dust in (other's) eyes: to beguile; to cheat; to deceive
13. To sit on one's eyes: to be loved, respected
14. Not to hurt (someone's) eyes: to be a gentleman; mild mannered, courteous

II. About the Ear
15. To eat one's ears: to get mad at a noise or sound
16. To raise one's ears: to listen carefully; to eavesdrop
17. To warm one's ears: to be very angry
18. To blow at (someone's) ears: to spread gossip; to backbite

19. To pour oil in (one's) ears: to refuse to listen; to ignore
20. To catch (one's) ears: to repent; to promise to mend one's ways

III. About the Nose
21. To dismember one's nose : to bring oneself to shame
22. To crumple one's nose: to despise; to be unhappy (about someone or something)
23. The going of one's nose: losing one's face; being humiliated
24. To put a ring in (someone's) nose: to curb; to subdue
25. Snuffing (someone's) nose: to punish; to reprimand
26. Rubbing one's nose (against something): seeking to appease
27. Keeping one's nose: Saving one's honour

IV. About the Mouth
28. Saving one's mouth: not being unpleasant (to others)
29. To shut or block (someone's) mouth: to render (him/her) speechless
30. Hurting one's mouth: chattering too long
31. Showing one's mouth (face): making a brief appearance or visit
32. Turning one's mouth (face) away: getting angry
33. A blown-up mouth: an angry face
34. To break-open (one's) mouth: to be forced to speak out

35. Opening (one's) mouth wide: to be more avaricious
36. Fencing the mouth : controlling one's diet
37. To twitch one's mouth (face): not to enjoy eating
38. Stuffing one's mouth: keeping quiet, speechless
39. To hide one's mouth: to feel ashamed
40. To correct one's mouth: to mind one's language
41. Sewing-up (one's) mouth: maintaining absolute silence
42. To see the mouth (face) before making allottments: to discriminate

(Note : The terms 'mouth' and 'face' are often used synonymously in Nepali)

V. About the Hand

43. To lengthen one's hand: to steal
44. Cutting one's hand: relinquishing one's right
45. Scum of the hand: useless, insignificant
46. Hand-itching: feeling like bashing-up someone !
47. Withdrawing (one's) hand: backing out of (work or venture)
48. To let go of (one's) hand: to strike (someone)
49. To wash (one's) hand: to withdraw; to be disappointed
50. Stretching a hand: begging
51. Hand-gripping: snatching (from others)
52. Hand-binding (crossing): remaining inactive; ceasing work

53. To be hand-broken: to miss (someone or something) badly
54. Getting an upper hand: placing oneself in an advantageous position
55. To join hand with mouth: to eke out a living
56. To take in (one's) hand: to bring (others) to one's side, to win-over

Verbal Idioms

I. To Cut
1. To 'cut' a guess: to make an assumption
2. To 'cut' a conversation: to but-in
3. To cut one's pigtail: to become a *Sanyaasi*; to 'renounce' the world
4. To 'cut' a hill: to make one's escape; to get lost
5. To 'cut' a day: to while away one's time
6. To cut (one's) nose: to invite a stigma
7. To cut (one's) path: to cover the distance
8. To 'cut' one's hand: to sacrifice despite one's own discomfort

II. To Eat
9. To 'eat' one's head: to cause a headache, annoyance
10. To 'eat' one's ear: to be disturbed by the noise or din
11. To 'eat' (someone's) words: to listen (favourably) to someone
12. To 'eat' the field: to submerge or chunk - away (especially by a river)

13. To 'eat' the salt: to be in someone's payroll
14. To 'eat' the earth: to die
15. To 'eat' the air:

    (a) to be out on a stroll;

    (b) to lose or be unsuccessful

III. To Kill
16. To kill one's body: to put oneself to undue physical hardship
17. To kill (one's) belly-worms; to indulge in satirical gossip at someone else's cost
18. To kill the mind: to lose heart
19. To kill the dead: to exploit even the helpless
20. To kill affection: to cease loving ; to forget (someone)

IV. To See
21. To see the fun: (a) to remain indifferent (in the face of troubles); (b) to be a silent spectator
22. To see the book: to read
23. To see the man: to judge one's nature ; to test
24. To see the house: to keep guard
25. To see the world: to be wary, cautious

3. Miscellaneous

1. Fruit in the sky: an impossibility
2. Fifteenth of the month of *Ashaar*: a hectic and busy time
3. Already three leaves while sprouting: precocious

4. Moon on an *Aunshi*: an impossibility
5. Relationship based on the sale of a bull: an insignificant relationship
6. Double-mouthed (or tongued): an unreliable person; double-talker
7. Like the finger and nail: very intimate
8. *Phariyaa* (skirt)-link: accomplishment obtained through one's wife; intimacy developed through family females
9. Fire and water: great enmity
10. Each beating his/her own drum: blowing one's own trumpet
11. To catch a flying bird: to be oversmart
12. To raise a finger: to caution; to warn
13. To become a doll: to play second fiddle
14. To stretch one's legs: to breath one's last
15. To swallow a bone according to one's throat: to cut a coat according to one's cloth
16. The Moon on one's right: favourable circumstances
17. To feel cold in (one's) heart: to be suspicious
18. To die alive: to feel helpless (as if one is dead)
19. To uproot (someone's) moustache: to subdue another
20. To sprout from the top: to get an undeserved jump in life
21. To get (one's) head: stepped on to pamper (someone) unduly

22. To make one's neck erect: to drink (booze)
23. To raise one's tail erect: to take to the heels
24. To see mustard flowers: (a) to get blind with rage; (b) to suffer a severe pain (due to an accident)
25. To draw sweat from the teeth: to be extremely stingy
26. To step onto two boats: to attempt two disparate works at a time; to hesitate
27. To be like a salt-eaten chicken: to be listless, exhausted
28. Perfume on top of gold: doubly beneficial/beautiful
29. Showing a lamp to the sun : advising one's superiors
30. To keep life on (one's) palm: to be recklessly bold

"Village Eating" Stories!

This is a term used to describe riddles, popular through the Nepalese world, particularly as a rural children's pastime of fun. Why they have come to be known as *Gaaun Khaaney Kathaa* (village-eating stories) can be better explained by describing the procedure followed in playing this game, which goes somewhat like this:

A :"Let's tell village-eating stories."
B : "Okey, go ahead."
A : "He who brings, doesn't wear. He who wears, doesn't bring it?"
Kay ho (what is it) ?

(This "What's it ?" is a common refrain that follows every riddle. Needless to add, readers of the riddles that follow are expected to presume that this expression comes at the end of each 'story', but has been deleted to avoid repitition). The game continues thus:

B : "I give up. You yourself tell me its meaning."
A : "Not unless you give me a village."
B : "Okay, I give you our own village."

A : "In that case, whatever is good in this village, including its wealth, are mine. But whatever is bad, like its filth, I leave as your share."

B : "Agreed. Now come out with the answer to the riddle."

A : "A Shroud."

(Then it is B's turn to accost A with another riddle. So on it goes.)

Now that you know how our riddles got their name, how about some more examples? Here they are:

1. Beard below the chin, beard above the head, for the rural folk, he is an alarm-clock, (what's it?)
   Rooster

2. Fiery to the touch, tasteful to eat.
   Nettle

3. Flowers are silver, fruit is gold
   Berry 'Aiselu'

4. Stars from heaven alighted on earth, to the utmost pleasure of the bees.
   Mustard blossom

5. Red as it advances, black as it recedes
   Forest fire

6. Brightness and light we owe a tiny dot.
   Even the days are dark without this tiny dot.
   Pupil of the eye

7. Both lips had a row of teeth
   As a train passes, the two often meet.
   Fastener

8. Not a bird, but it has a beak
   that leaves, when at work, a fine streak.
   Pen

9. It has no feet, but it often walks,
   Nor has it hands but it slaps as it walks.
   A pair of slippers

10. Fruits of the skies, white and round
    Water is all that they leave behind.
    Hail stones

11. It looks beautiful as it breaks.
    Silk Cotton

12. Out of its house, out of its life.
    Fish

13. In the ocean while it lives,
    On the altar once it dies.
    Conch shell

14. With a swollen tummy I lie most of the time,
    Place your head on me and have a good time.
    Pillow

15. I must come with you if you go shopping,
    You return with what you buy, but I'm not coming.
    Money

16. Of the two look-alike twins,
    One is headless, the other eyeless.
    Needle and Pin

17. It spread brightness all around as its vertical pigtail dances and jumps,

Unable to bear the burning pain, to the ground it
ultimately slumps.
Candle

18. I have often taken it,
    But never have I tasted it.
    Oath

19. Either you draw me or I carry you,
    Don't annoy me, or I'll kick you.
    Horse

20. Coil at its behind, a bump on its back,
    Press on the bump and it's no more dark.
    Flashlight

21. A toothless old wench it may be,
    chews hard bones with utmost glee.
    Logs in a oven

22. A tiny mouth, but shouts out aloud.
    Pistol

23. Hair outside, bony beside,
    Fleshy next, water inside.
    Coconut

24. All the ten brothers got beheaded,
    But not a drop of blood was shed.
    Pairing of nails

25. With hands on my ears, perching on my nose
    A proud glance all round it throws.
    Specs

26. May not be bird but flies allright,
    If it tastes blood, sucks with all its might.
    Mosquito

27. Silvery vessel concealed in green.
    Cauliflower

28. Stab it and it springs to life.
    Lock

29. Not a lamp, but it sparkles and beams.
    Firefly

30. Feed it with air, tighten its mouth,
    Lo and behold, it flies north and south.
    Balloon

31. It steals, but a burglar it isn't.
    Rodent

32. The more you slap on both its cheeks,
    With further joy it shouts and shrieks.
    Maadal drum

33. Watery dome, that's my home,
    Kiths eat me, while I eat some.
    Fish

34. Fluid-filled tummy, cap on my head,
    Empty the fluid, and I'm as good as dead.
    Fountain Pen

35. Papery me, I look like a picture,
    I often slip away, even if I'm your treasure
    Currency Note

36. It has horns, but no tail,
    Nor has it legs, but it walks well.
    Snail

37. I walk, I play but speak I can't,

    Once it is dark, hold you I can't.
    Shadow

38. Progress may mean going uphill,
    But I prefer stumbling downhill.
    Water

39. Sound of conch-shell in front, a flag waves behind.
    Dog-bark

40. Looks like a fan, as also an eye, but it is neither.
    Peacock-feather

41. Queen of the skies landed on earth,

    Quickly she vanishes on seeing the sun.
    Dewdrops

42. Fire on top, water at the bottom, suck the pipe and it rumbles like a tomtom or drum
    Hubble-bubble

43. A mere paper, but can do wonders.
    Currency Note

44. The daughter left after hanging the mother
    Lock & Key

45. Mother gives, daughter drinks.

    Water pouring from a jug to a mug

46. Mother resembles a witch, daughter a nectar.
    Respberry

47. It flies but isn't a bird, it has a tail but is no animal either.
    Kite

48. Hums like a bee which it isn't,
    Wears a holy thread, but a priest it isn't.
    Spinning Wheel

49. It whistles, but can't be seen,
    Enters everywhere, even the house within.
    Wind

50. It can run, but can't walk.
    Stream

51. Slash the eye and it dies,
    Slash the throat and it revives.
    Sugarcane

52. Not a temple despite its dome, nor a creature despite its ribs.
    Umbrella

53. Stretch and it hurts, cut and it doesn't.
    Hair

54. Four-footed but lifeless,
    has a body, no bone and flesh
    Chair

55. How does it hear without ears?
    But dance it does, as if it hears!
    Snake

56. Can't look or see with its 'eye',
    Only it serves to please the fly.
    'Eye' of a sore

57. Water-filled but it's no jug,
    Perches on the tree, tho it's no bird
    Coconut

58. Neither dead nor alive
    Egg

59. A dead ox breathes and also walks.
    Bellows; Shoes

60. Once the vessel breaks, the contents are known.
    Egg

61. Pond inside, tap outside.
    Teapot

62. Silver within, gold without.
    Banana

63. Gold within, silver without.
    Egg

64. Works like a donkey, makes noise like one,
    but only when you pull it by its single horn.
    Mill stone

65. The goat stays put, the leash goes in search of food.
    Pumpkin and its plant

66. Footless and wingless, but climbs hilltops and pours cream.
    Cloud

67. Bark outside, hollow inside.
    Football

68. Father is not seen anywhere, son is already at house top.
    Smoke

69. Fruit is seen by one, another goes to steal it, the third picks it up and is eaten by the fourth.
    Eyes, Legs, Hands, Mouth

70. Cut at the base, it dies; cut the top, it grows elsewhere.
    Sugarcane

71. Press on the tail, it gets up abruptly,
    let go of it and it strikes with the beak.
    Pounding log

72. The pond dried up, the her on died.
    Wocler-lamp

73. Leaves are nil, branches are galore.
    Cactus

74. Five brothers enter into the same cave.
    Shoes

75. Five brothers eat off one plate.
    Palm

76. It can't be cooked, nor can it be boiled, but it is instantly burnt.
    Hair

77. It doesn't demand any food or drink, but it guards the house all the same.
    Padlock

78. It's my first kill after a whole day, I feel I must eat it; but it resembles my paternal uncle, so how can I eat it ?
    Momkey

79. The child strikes, the mother weeps.
    Church bell

80. Fruit atop a tree, tree atop a fruit.
    Pineapple

81. Parents on either side, children in the middle.
    Staircase

82. A door opens, five brothers roam about, yet another pulls (it) in and all enter into the cave
    Eating

83. Lies low the whole day, stands up the whole night.
    The door-bolt(Wooden)

84. Whole day the brothers live apart, after nightfall one is with the other.
    Door-flanks

85. The thing is your very own but others use it for you.
    One's name

86. I look at him, he looks at me, he makes way for me as I go, but never follows me.
    Door

87. Three brothers, a common turban.
    Tripod

88. My name is a three-letter word, you need me for opening your eyes.
    Pen

89. People suck you and yet spit you out.
    Sugarcane

90. Pull at the moustaches and he smiles.
    Purse

91. It can go, it can't return.
    River

92. The more you draw, the more it goes.
    Breath

93. The more you cut, the bigger it grows
    Pit

94. If you cut me it's painful, if I cut you it's not.
    Nail

95. It has neither hands nor feet, but measures cubits like an expert.
    Leech

96. It has hands but not feet, has body but no eyes, has a neck but no head.
    Shirt

97. Branches are nil, leaves are countless.
    Banana tree

98. A pearl-studded bird, wrapped in a shawl, is standing yonder.
    Corneob

99. A staircase going to the heaven, fire for its heart, water for its bones.
    Rainbow

100. Black buffaloes in a white forest.
Letters(in a book)

101. A white *Theki*,* a green lid.
Radish

102. Sleep sleep, oh wife mine, I would like to slip-in
Shoes

103. A tiny pond, intolerant even of a dust.
Eyes

104. A tiny tree which can't be climbed, but gives you chillblanes if it were touched.
Nettle

105. A tiny mouth shouts with great noise.
Gun

106. Wears a wrap-around when a child, throws its wrap-around when it's grown.
Bamboo

107. Gives food when young, gives house when old.
Bamboo

108. A sleek white baby, shrieks loud when kissed.
Conch

109. A tiny child, its belly split.
Wheat

110. Always one step ahead of its master.
Stick

111. A small and bright baby, fond of sucking oil or *ghee*.
Wickerlamp

112. Stairs on this side, stairs on the other, look at the middle, it's but your daddy's rickety ribs !
Suspension Bridge

---

* A wooden jar

113. Gold on the outside, inside,
     Sweet is the juice yielded by the silver inside,
     Orange

114. Looks like a huge elephant, on earth as it lies,
     Once it rises, it reaches right upto the skies.
     Cloud

115. You sow gold, out comes a grass.
     Paddy

116. A single cave where five brothers enter,
     But each one has a room for his own shelter.
     Gloves

117. He who brings doesn't see.
     Shroud

118. An umbrella over my head, I grow out of the earth
     whichever uses me for food is a happy hearth.
     Mushroom

119. Once it escapes, it cannot be caught,
     Nor can it be seen or brought back.
     Words

120. Timber as its garment, its colour is white,
     Once it emerges, people tremble with fright.
     The Khukris word

121. Food while it's a child,
     Outgrows the housetop when it's wild.
     Bamboo

122. It's years since the tree has died,
     But the leaves are still to be wilted or dried.
     Peacock feather

123. A single pumpkin has holes seven.
     Human head

124. I am underground, my fruits are above,
     We both make a curry that you'll love.
     Squash

125. Flowers without fruits, fruits without flowers.
     Hemp

126. It looks like a boat and loves to swing,
     Specially when it carries a sweet young thing.
     Craddle

127. A tormenting witch is the mother
     Lovely and sweet is her daughter.
     Rose

128. The groom is dark and leads the procession
     Green and yellow friends follow in succession.
     Banana plant

129. Depressed and silent when it has no food
     Dances in circles the moment it has food.
     Kol (Oil press)

130. A sister on this side, a sister on the other, never the twain shall meet.
     Eyes

131. Jury all around, judge in the center.
     Teeth and tongu

132. I was born in the forest, which is my home,
     Have been rotting in water for years, can I ever hope to go home?
     Boat

133. When on my way to the woods it looks towards the house, when I'm on way back home, looks towards the woods.
     Axe

134. Takes you towards the sky but is made neither of stones nor of mud.
     Woodens taircase

135. Tendril-like mother, flower-like elder sister, skull-like younger brother.
    Gourd

136. Tasty food yielded by a long creeper.
    Fish

137. I am coming to fetch you, but why did you come? Leave me alone and go, I want to fetch you!
    Rain while going to the river for water

138. Lives on the tree, but a bird it isn't
    Has long hairs and whiskerss, but *yogi* it isn't.
    Coconut

139. A red purse full of coins.
    Chilly

140. His house is flooded day and night
    But it calls for help only at night.
    Frog

141. A red cow became black when she quenched her thirst.
    Log-fire

142. Sleeps during the bright day, wakes up in the dark.
    Lamp

143. Its body is mere mud, but serves like a stone.
    Brick

144. When you start eating one, it becomes two or three.
    Peanut

145. Chirps like chicken, but breaks walls like an ox.
    The rat

146. It can be seen, but can't be caught
    Shadow

147. Two when looked at, one when not looked at.
Mirror

148. It sparkles but it isn't a diamond,
It obstructs but it isn't a wall.
Glass

149. A dark forest above the Himalayas
Hair

150. Fire atop a mountain, rumbling at its base.
Hubble-bubble

151. Paints the ground as it walks
The snail

152. Wipes out its footprints as it advances.
Boat

153. The elephant passed through, the tail got stuck.
Needle & thread

154. Spread with your hands, pik-up with your eyes.
Letters

155. As my hands are raised high, I drink with my feet
Tree

156. Drenches the elephant, drenches the horse,
But it doesn't fill even a pitcher.
Dew

Photo by *Gyanendra Das, Das Colour Lab*

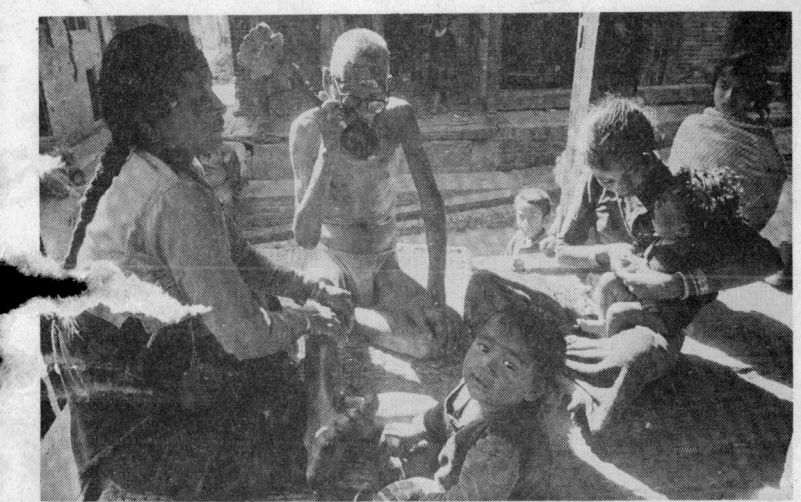

Photo by *Gyanendra Das, Das Colour Lab*

Photo by Yeti Photos Centre

Photo by Yeti Photos Centre